SCHOOL ADMINISTRATOR'S FACULTY SUPERVISION HANDBOOK

Ronald T. Hyman
Professor of Education
Graduate School of Education
Rutgers University

Prentice-Hall
Englewood Cliffs, N.J.

Prentice-Hall International, Inc., *London*
Prentice-Hall of Australia, Pty. Ltd., *Sydney*
Prentice-Hall Canada, Inc., *Toronto*
Prentice-Hall of India Private Ltd., *New Delhi*
Prentice-Hall of Japan, Inc., *Tokyo*
Prentice-Hall of Southeast Asia Pte. Ltd., *Singapore*
Whitehall Books, Ltd., Wellington, New Zealand
Editora Prentice-Hall do Brasil Ltda., *Rio de Janeiro*
Prentice Hall Hispanoamericana, S.A., *Mexico*

Third Printing . . . . . October 1987

Dedicated, once again,

to

Suzanne, Jonathan, Elana,

and Rachel

Library of Congress Cataloging-in-Publication Data

Hyman, Ronald T.
    School administrator's faculty supervision handbook.

    Includes index.
    1. School supervision—United States.   2. Teachers—
In-service training—United States.   3. Teachers—
United States—Rating of.   4. Observation (Educational
method)   I. Title.
LB2822.2.H96 1986   371.1'44   85-28249

ISBN 0-13-792409-7 NBZI

ABOUT THE AUTHOR

Ronald T. Hyman, Ed.D. (Columbia University, New York), M.A.T. (Vanderbilt University, Nashville), has been involved with education for over thirty years.

During that time, he has been a public school teacher and chairperson, research assistant, graduate school department chairperson, and college professor. In addition, Dr. Hyman has written and co-authored over twenty books, including *School Administrator's Handbook of Teacher Supervision and Evaluation Methods* (Prentice-Hall, Inc., 1975), and over fifty-five articles and reviews for such professional publications as *Educational Leadership, Journal of Teacher Education,* and *Educational Administration Quarterly.*

Dr. Hyman is presently a professor of education in the Graduate School of Education at Rutgers University (New Brunswick, New Jersey).

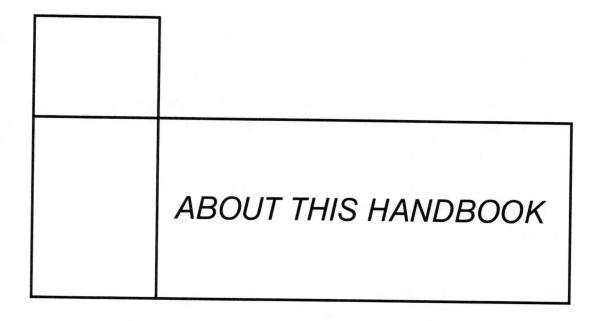

ABOUT THIS HANDBOOK

The *School Administrator's Faculty Supervision Handbook* is for K–12 supervising school administrators who wish to help their staffs grow professionally. It clarifies and expands skills you, as supervisors, need to use in observing, conferring, and writing reports.

Unlike most other books on supervision which deal primarily with theory, this *Handbook* is practical, providing charts, figures, and models of completed forms to demonstrate key points of supervision. Read it and you will learn new skills to put into practice in your school as you supervise your own staff.

Chapter 1 provides background information for supervising in today's schools and explains the difference between supervising and evaluating. This chapter will help you if you often ask yourself questions like these:

- What must I, as a school administrator, know about supervision?
- How do I write up my supervisory goals and intended action?
- What are my legal responsibilities and constraints as a supervisor?

Chapter 2 looks at teacher motivation, organization, and development, and guides you in helping teachers understand their job of teaching. It covers the following topics:

- What a teacher needs to be satisfied and to feel good about his or her job
- How the "Supervisor's Guide for Facilitating Teacher Change" form will help the administrator work with a teacher
- How to set up a development plan with the teacher

Chapter 3 explores the skill of observing teachers and offers a set of simple and straightforward methods for observation. The chapter covers such topics as:

- How a formal teacher observation form looks
- When to observe a teacher's or student's actions
- Teacher actions of which administrators should be aware

Chapter 4 deals with the relationship between observing and conferring. It offers guidelines for you to follow when preparing for a conference, such as:

- Why I *must* conduct a conference with the teacher I have just observed
- Whether to use concrete observation notes to show the teacher rather than merely talking to him or her
- What to do if the teacher resists observational data

Chapter 5 describes several conference skills and assessment approaches for you to use in dealing with your teachers. A sample of chapter 5's contents includes:

- How to determine if the teacher and I are both contributing to the post-observation conference
- Some of the ways to assess the conference
- How to deal with any great difference in reactions between myself and the teacher

Chapter 6 explains the various types of post-observation conferences you can conduct and the strategies and tactics you can use to help achieve your goals. Some topics discussed are:

- Whether to decide with the teacher the direction and focus the conference should take
- How to deal with teacher dissonance and conflict
- Why the "mapping" of an observation is important and useful

Chapter 7 discusses questioning from the supervisor's perspective. It looks at the role of questioning in supervision, the types of questions to ask, and techniques for asking them. This chapter highlights the following ideas and techniques:

- Preventing unintended consequences arising from questions
- Some examples of divergent questions
- Sample questioning tactics to use

Chapter 8 deals with the final written report you put together after an observation and conference. The chapter offers the reasons for writing the reports, describes the various kinds from which to choose, and suggests writing style guidelines. Chapter 8 discusses:

- The necessity of written reports in addition to teacher conferences
- The difference between an observation report and an evaluation report
- How I can develop my writing style to help strengthen my supervisory relationship with the teacher

Remember, the *Administrator's Faculty Supervision Handbook* does not attempt to be a comprehensive book on self-help or school administration. Rather, it concentrates on practical, concrete techniques you can use to integrate observation and conferencing skills into your busy schedule. Once you accomplish this, you and your faculty will reap the rewards.

All the information in this handbook will be useful every day, particularly when combined with the activities in my companion volume: *School Administrator's Staff Development Activities Manual,* also published by Prentice-Hall. The manual will offer structured activities to help with staff development once you have observed and conferred with teachers.

Ronald T. Hyman

CONTENTS

Chapter 3   OBSERVING THE TEACHING PROCESS • 65

1

SUPERVISING IN TODAY'S SCHOOLS

Supervision of teachers, like the schools in which it is conducted, is always in a state of change. Although supervision and the schools at any given moment may appear stable to an outside observer, it is possible to note changes over a long sweep of time. Especially today, when our general society is undergoing fairly rapid change, it is important to keep in mind that the schools are changing, too.

As a supervisor, it is helpful for you to recognize the state of supervision today and the possible directions it can take. Rather than merely allow the path of supervision to be directed by others, however, you can take an active position by assuming a new perspective, by answering differently the fundamental questions involved in supervision, and by changing in some way your relationship with your teachers. When you do this, you alter, however slightly, the context for supervision and influence what happens in your school.

After reading this chapter, you should be able to:

- Understand the condition of supervision today in light of some possible perspectives, trends, key questions, and the supervisor's legal responsibilities.
- Describe two negative metaphors and one positive metaphor for schools.
- Explain the difference between supervision and evaluation.
- List at least five trends in supervision today and some possible causes for them.
- Explain the purpose of supervision, emphasizing the development of teachers and students.
- List and answer at least four key questions that every school must answer about supervision.
- Describe at least four broad legal responsibilities of a supervisor stemming from the United States Constitution and other sources bearing on the school.

METAPHORICAL PERSPECTIVES OF THE SCHOOL

You may be wondering why a section on metaphors appears here. The reason is simple: It is helpful to use metaphors in explaining new ideas and in presenting new ways to think about solving old problems. The purpose, therefore, is to add a spark to one treatment of supervision, to sensitize you to the language we all use when talking about our schools, and to challenge you to think of and accept new approaches to supervision as one way of continued professional development. With this brief treatment of metaphors early in the book, it is hoped that you will be all the more receptive to the various approaches to supervision derived from different views and metaphors.

As a supervisor, you are influenced in the way you act toward your teachers and students by the concept you have of school. If you think of school as an opportunity to learn in order to be a free person in a free society, your actions will be quite different from the supervisor who views school as a process by which students are taught to take their place in a society in which the nation's welfare precludes individual choice on economic decisions, including career choice. Your concept influences your behavior, which in turn influences your concept. In any case, whether or not you are conscious of it, you act according to deep-seated beliefs.

Regardless of our economic or political views, there are prevalent views on schooling that we modify to suit our particular set of beliefs. For example, we can think about the school as a factory, prison, garden, battlefield, ladder, bazaar, supermarket, or just about anything else.

It is possible to consider avoiding altogether the use of metaphors when thinking about school and thus eliminate the need for choosing which perspective to use. The simple approach of stopping the use of metaphors, however, is impossible because it is difficult to be completely literal when talking about schooling, teaching, supervising, and learning. Much of our daily language consists of metaphorical terms and phrases to be used especially for ideas concerned with our feelings, values, and relationships.

Metaphors serve a persuasive function. By choosing an appealing metaphor, a person can persuade others to accept a particular point of view. A teacher can conceive of homework as a basketball practice game, design interesting exercises for it, and thereby hope to achieve a positive attitude toward it on the part of the students. On the other hand, if the teacher thinks that doing homework can be compared to doing the dishes after dinner, an unpleasant chore that must be done, the teacher may inadvertently persuade the students to dislike homework. It is desirable to use metaphors, because they serve in one of the main functions of language—persuasion.

Before looking at some specific metaphors, read the list of words in Figure 1-1. Mark each word in the following four ways. Do each step completely before moving to the next one.

1. Circle the number of each term that you believe you can apply to the school when talking about it.

2. In column *A,* write an F (for Factory) or P (for Prison) to indicate which you believe is the institution most closely connected with the term. You may leave a term blank or even write both F and P for any term. If you do make two markings for a term, circle the one that fits better.

3. In column *B,* write A (for Adult in Society) or S (for Student) to indicate which is the person most likely to use the term, in your opinion. Do this for all twenty-eight terms. You may leave a term blank, or even write both A and S for each term. Again, if you do make two markings for a term, circle the one that fits better.

4. In column *C,* write a plus sign (+), a minus sign (−), or an N (for Neutral) if you believe the term has a positive, or negative, or neutral meaning connected with it.

	A	B	C		A	B	C
1. achievement				15. lose			
2. alienation				16. motivation			
3. apathy				17. obedience			
4. authority				18. penalty			
5. boredom				19. powerlessness			
6. conformity				20. probation			
7. control				21. product			
8. detention				22. punishment			
9. discipline				23. rules			
10. efficiency				24. standardization			
11. freedom				25. success			
12. guard				26. warden			
13. guilt				27. wasting time			
14. loafing				28. worker			

FIGURE 1-1. Twenty-eight terms to apply to schools.

After marking the twenty-eight terms, review the list again, looking for any patterns or meanings. You can consider such things as the way adults in society view schools compared with the way students view schools. If you wish, add some new terms to the list and mark those in the same four ways.

With the foregoing section about metaphors and your markings of the twenty-eight terms in mind, let us look at the school from several well-known and prevalent metaphorical perspectives since each permits us to see the school differently. Each will sensitize us to a view we need to keep in mind as we think further about supervision in our schools.

The School as a Factory

The most pervasive, yet unnoticed, metaphor is the factory (or manufacturing) metaphor. Perhaps it is unnoticed because the factory has been with us ever since the Industrial Revolution transformed our economic lives and influenced our culture and language. When we think of factories, some of the terms we use include: production, work, efficiency, quality control, economy, division of labor, industry, mass production, job, assembly line, timeclocks, collective bargaining, supervisor, raw material, and strike. The metaphorical use of these concepts in regard to the school leads to school behavior that reflects the manufacturing mind-set and that may impede supervisors, teachers, and students from developing autonomy and creativity.

The factory metaphor fosters the fragmentation of knowledge and learning processes into small segments, causing teachers and students to lose sight of the larger subject matter context and the interpersonal context—of what and who is involved in teaching in the school. In a school, an assembly-line mentality emerges that leads to student dissatisfaction, boredom, and a narrow outlook. Metaphorically, the auto factory workers see doors, engines, wheels, or steering wheels, but seldom get the satisfaction that comes from viewing the entire automobile. The effect of the factory metaphor occurs even when we are unaware of it. This is the point that Alvin Toffler makes in his now classic book, *Future Shock,* when treating the relationship between schooling and industrialism:

> —the whole idea of assembling masses of students (raw material) to be processed by teachers (workers) in a centrally located school (factory) was a stroke of industrial genius. The whole administrative hierarchy of education, as it grew up, followed the model of industrial bureaucracy. The very organization of knowledge into permanent disciplines was grounded on industrial assumptions. Children marched from place to place and sat in assigned stations. Bells rang to announce changes of time.

The factory metaphor is a deadly one. Its pervasiveness reflects our society's emphasis on getting and spending, on producing and consuming. It is deadly because it subverts humane interaction between the people involved in school life. Behavior according to the school as factory leads the teacher to treat the students as inanimate objects, as things (not people) to be processed, stamped out, and finished on the conveyor belt assembly line instead of as developing, emerging, evolving human beings. Unfortunately, there are adult citizens today who still demand that we "build" this year's model of students to the streamlined specifications they have laid down.

The School as a Prison

Teachers and other educators seldom view the school as a prison because this metaphor is too damaging to their self-concepts and role definitions. However, students do consider the school this way. Prison is the most common metaphor used by students when talking about school. The students see themselves as prisoners in jail, the teachers as guards, and the principal as warden. The school is a prison for the students because they believe that they share with prisoners the key characteristic of being in prison—the loss of freedom. Students legally must attend school, mostly from age six to sixteen. Compulsory attendance laws, combined with family and social pressures, yield a feeling of captivity and restraint, and this feeling is maintained even by students who remain in high school beyond the permissible leaving age.

In his book *Asylums,* anthropologist Erving Goffman writes about the characteristics of total institutions. A total institution is defined "as a place of residence and work where a large number of like-situated individuals, cut off from the wider society for an appreciable period of time, together lead an enclosed, formally administered round of life."[2] One point of introducing this concept of total institution is to show that schools, by virtue of being either a bona fide total institution or in the least a partial one, have certain characteristics and effects on the people within them. In light of our concern with schools, another point to keep in mind is that Goffman in his essay on total institutions goes on to make three more significant statements:

1. "…prisons serve as a clear example" of the total institution[3] (p. xiii).
2. "What is prison-like about prisons is found in institutions whose members have broken no laws"[4] (p. xiii).
3. None of the characteristics "seems peculiar to total institutions"[5] (p. 5).

These three statements serve to guide the application of the prison metaphor to the school.

Although teachers often do not use the prison metaphor themselves, their language and concerns may be seen within the prison framework. Student control is a central problem for teachers. Teachers are most concerned with discipline and how to keep the students motivated and attentive when they would rather be somewhere else or at least doing something else. Teachers spend a good portion of their energy in an effort to control the students and to get them to comply to the rules of the school. The school socializes the teachers into a more custodial and authoritarian orientation than what they held while in college. In a research study on student control,[6] teachers were significantly more custodial after one year of teaching than a control group of prospective teachers who did not become teachers.

Students need to be disciplined and controlled by the teachers because they are alienated, bored, weak, and angry—all characteristics of prisoners. High alienation stems from the coercion that schools, as do prisons, use in forcing attendance and participation, according to sociologist Amitai Etzioni in his book, *Comparative Analysis of Complex Organizations.*[7] Students feel that they are wasting their time attending school, but they know that they must do so anyway. Due to these characteristics, learning suffers significantly. It is not a question of which came first, the teachers' attitudes and behaviors or the students' attitudes and behaviors. What is important is the realization that both sets of attitudes and behaviors by the teachers and students exist side by side in the school and are interdependent.

The School as a Sports Stadium

The two previous metaphors are negative, but popular. However, a positive metaphor guides us to think of the school as a sports stadium.

Although sports is an important element in school life and has been since the time of the ancient Greeks, the school as sports stadium is not a common metaphor. Sports, or athletics, constitute the main part of that required subject in American schools officially called *physical education*. Nevertheless, teachers and students do not often see themselves as players in a game. Nor do principals and other supervisory staff consider themselves as being in a sports stadium either as coaches, players, referees, score-keepers, or spectators. In spite of the infrequency of using the stadium metaphor by the school participants themselves, it is worthwhile to examine.

There are many concepts that go along with sports stadium, such as game, players, rules, and competition, which apply to the school. In school, there are games, literal and figurative, being played at all times. Most schools have full-time teachers certified for sports education who devote their time and energy to teaching students how to play such games as baseball, football, basketball, tennis, field hockey, volleyball, and kickball as well as nongames such as swimming, wrestling, and gymnastics.

Indeed, the attitudes of sports are present in the school in part because of the respect and time given to athletics. The first and foremost evidence of this is the fact that sports are required of all students. Second, much money is devoted to sports, both interscholastic and intrascholastic. Third, schools even cancel or shorten academic classes in order to conduct pep rallies in which uniformed, specially chosen and trained cheerleaders help the student body achieve the proper spirit and enthusiasm for the games being played in their stadium. Fourth is the respect given to the athletes, who occupy the highest prestige level of the students in the school and are secure in that position.

There are other "games" going on in the school with their rules and penalties for infraction. Many students compete with each other to be the best student or the one who erases the chalkboard, or the most popular one with the opposite sex, or whatever. Some students in the higher grades even compete with the teachers to demonstrate who knows the subject matter better, seeing the teacher as an opponent rather than as their coach or scorekeeper. Other students play the learning game so that they just pass the course with the minimum amount of effort needed to "win." Other students play the game of "getting away with it" by competing with other students to see how much disruption they can cause without being penalized by the teacher.

The academic interaction in the classroom between teacher and student also follows the pattern of a game in that there are certain explicit as well as implicit rules that govern the discourse. It is for this reason that the philosopher Wittgenstein spoke of everyday conversation as being a language game and that educational researchers have investigated the "language game of the classroom."[8]

Academic learning in the classroom as the official game of the school has one major limitation, however. It offers the students as players little opportunity to become heroes or earn glory for their school. To improve the lot of the academic stars and to raise the image of academic achievement in a way that channels adolescent "energies into directions of learning," Coleman, the well-known sociologist and educational researcher, turns to the sports stadium metaphor for his solution. He suggests that schools conduct "scholastic fairs" where students can compete in interscholastic academic games and exhibits. Such a venture, claims Coleman, might "have a profound effect on the education climate in the participating schools."[9] Perhaps the subsequent interscholastic contests established in the 1960s and 1970s in mathematics stem from Coleman's suggestion. Perhaps not, but the interesting point is that the math teams consisting of "mathletes," as they are called, have succeeded in becoming a way for the all-stars of the academic program to improve school spirit.

Making the classroom into a playing field is desirable. The research bears out this effect. A report in the *Review of Educational Research*[10] shows that students participating in the teams-games-tournament strategy of teaching learn more than students in regular classrooms.

Despite the problem of competition that comes with using the stadium metaphor, it is preferable to the factory or prison. There is simply no way to overturn the negativism arising with the factory and prison metaphors, but there are ways to deal with the element of competition in the stadium metaphor:

- First, agree at the outset that teaching is a noncompetitive game. Teaching may be likened to rowing a boat. The crew of a large rowboat must pull their oars together. When they do, they succeed in moving the boat forward smoothly and quickly. When they do not, the boat moves chaotically and jerkily.

- Second, redirect feelings of competition that may exist between teacher and students. Redirection of competition does not mean elimination or reduction with a possible corresponding decrease in motivation to learn. Competition must be redirected to be internal rather than external. In the teaching game, the teacher as dominant player must help the students redirect their feelings of competition inwardly so that each student competes with him- or herself. This is similar to what the athlete does who competes with him- or herself to perform at the highest level possible rather than with the opponent.

- Third, define "win" within the teaching game. In sports, to win means to defeat the other player, to score more points, to be victor. In teaching, to win should be understood as the experience of doing one's best given the capabilities of the players. Winning becomes a concept associated with positive self-competition, rather than with an effort against someone else to cause that person's loss.

The sports stadium metaphor is not perfect, however; it has flaws. But it is basically positive and has potential for helping us in supervision.

A Case in Point

Thomas J. Peters and Robert H. Waterman, Jr. have written an account of the theory and practice of selected successful corporations. Their book, *In Search of Excellence: Lessons from America's Best-Run Companies,* has been a hardcover best-seller for several years. The message of the book is appealing and clear. What also is clear is the use of metaphors by the authors. Not only do they use the sports metaphor continually with their terms *champions* (the company leaders), *winners* (the best-run companies), and *internal competitions,* but they use many other positive metaphors to make their points about excellence.

Several brief quotations from *In Search of Excellence,* which has been recommended as "required reading" for school leaders, illustrate the authors' characteristic use of metaphors throughout their book:

> The champion is not a blue-sky dreamer or an intellectual giant. The champion might even be an idea thief. But, above all, he's the pragmatic one who grabs onto someone else's theoretical construct if necessary and bull-headedly pushes it to fruition.[11]

> Champions are pioneers and pioneers get shot at...[the best-run] companies have rich support networks so their champions will flourish....No support systems, no champions. No champions, no innovations.[12]

> Leaders unleash excitement.[13]

You may well claim that Peters and Waterman succeed because their message about excellence is timely in American life. However, you also may claim that in large measure the success of the book is due to the fluid and conversational writing style that relies on a large dose of positive metaphors to convey the sophisticated ideas and convictions of the authors. Their words mirror the winning hoopla that they attribute to champions. They are champions of metaphor.

SOME CURRENT TRENDS IN SUPERVISION AND THEIR CAUSES

Although the data are somewhat murky, it is possible to discern some trends in supervision that reflect the general events occurring in our society at large.

The Trends

The following seven trends are interrelated:

1. Supervision of teachers is becoming more and more legalistic. Faculty and supervisors are much more concerned today than in the boom years of the 1950s with the strict adherence to the rules established by contract and tradition. (Perhaps this is due to the pressure that society is putting on the schools to perform excellently.) Grievances based on procedural abuses are increasing. The process of supervision is legalistic, and the dissatisfied faculty are quite ready to go through some school district grievance process or to go to civil court, if necessary. Thus, teachers reflect our litigious society as well as help make it so. In short, the trend is for faculty to be both legalistic in their approach to supervision and litigious in their reactions to it.

2. Teachers, through their professional organizations, are taking a growing share of responsibility for developing and implementing supervision procedures. Teachers are working along with school supervisors to improve and refine the supervision procedures of their school districts. The day of the 100 percent supervisor-imposed set of procedures has passed in most districts and is quickly fading in the remainder.

3. The emphasis is on staff development, especially in established school districts where there is a settled and stable faculty. Faculty stability arises because of the lack of job mobility, partly due to the overall change in student enrollment.

4. "Hard data" are being emphasized over subjective, broad opinions about a teacher's performance, especially classroom performance. "Old boy double-talk" has declined in favor of objectivity and measurement in one form or another.

5. Teachers and supervisors are striving to clarify the criteria used in supervision when evaluative judgments are made. They also are clarifying the weights given to each component of the teacher's job (for example, the weight of classroom performance and the weight of performance in school activities) and the supervisory instruments used to gather data about the teacher's performance.

6. There is an emphasis on formative supervision with a consequent decline in *summative* supervision. The trend (even where the law is silent) is to observe and confer several times during the academic year and during a teacher's career in order to help a teacher redirect professional efforts when necessary. Supervisors are not relying solely or even mainly on year-end supervisory conferences to speak with their teachers about professional development.

7. There is a growing recognition that supervision takes place within a complex web of conditions and that supervisor and teacher must understand the contexts these conditions create. Therefore, two teachers, for example, may teach in the same district or even the same school but may have different contexts from one another; hence, different instruments and approaches to supervision are required as the supervisor works within a different context. For example, a high school teacher of honors and advanced placement mathematics courses for graduating college prep seniors has a different context from the teacher of commercial mathematics at the freshman level in a trades program.

The Causes

The causes for these trends are many and complex. No one can point to a single event or condition as the cause of what is occurring in the educational scene. Our lives are too complex for a single event or condition to account for the trends previously listed. Some causes are:

- advances in the field of observation and measurement of human behavior
- the squeezed job market and the lack of teacher mobility
- the increased availability of legal services to teachers
- advances in the field of school supervision and administration
- the bureaucratization of our schools which leads to the acceptance of an industrial perspective on the relationship between teachers and supervisors ·
- the diversity of the teachers and supervisors in terms of economic position and security
- acceptance of the fact that the supervision of others has always been complex and of deep concern as evidenced by numerous references in ancient times to the need for care when judging another person
- acceptance of the obligation of educational leaders to improve the status quo rather than to be complacent with it, in light of our country's rapidly changing social-political-technological-economic conditions

THE RELATIONSHIP OF SUPERVISION TO EVALUATION

One of the perennial questions that educational writers and professors pose is, "What is the relationship of supervision to evaluation?" The point of the question is to call attention to evaluation in its relation to other activities such as observing, conferring, and writing reports. The question prods the respondent to think of the relation of evaluation to the entire task of the supervisor, because all too often evaluation appears isolated and as an end in itself. This is not the case with other supervisory activities.

We can think of evaluating as being one aspect of the more general activity called supervising. In supervising, the supervisor performs many specific tasks such as observing, conferring, planning, scheduling, and evaluating. This relationship between supervision and evaluation is in accord with the definition of teacher supervision offered in the *Dictionary of Education* edited by Good. Teacher supervision is "all efforts of designated school officials directed toward providing leadership to teachers in the improvement of instruction; involves the stimulation of professional growth and development of teachers, the selection and revision of educational objectives, materials of instruction, and methods of teaching, and the evaluation of instruction."[14]

In another view, supervision and evaluation are seen as parallel activities. There are many major activities a superintendent, principal, or chairperson does, such as supervising teachers, administering the school program, meeting with parents and community members, and evaluating programs and teachers. Here, evaluation is separated from supervision and given equal generality.

The second view, which is conceptually in error, suggests that evaluation can be done meaningfully without being an integral part of the school's efforts toward providing for continued development of the staff and school program. It also suggests that evaluation is not within the overall context of supervision. It further suggests that it is possible to evaluate without doing supervising provided that someone else performs

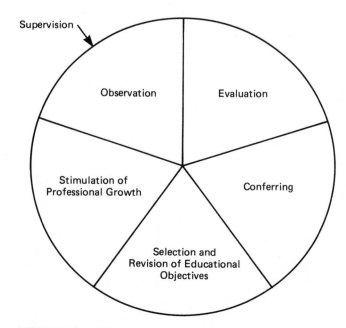

FIGURE 1-2. The components of supervision.

what is then called supervision. This error arises because evaluation of teachers is seen as the "bottom line" or the purpose of supervision.

The purpose of supervision is not to create the conditions for evaluating teachers. *The purpose of supervision is to create continued efforts toward providing a high-quality educational program in which students can learn well.* Evaluation of teachers is but one aspect of a supervisory program, and it derives its purpose from being an important part of supervision. Indeed, evaluation, precisely because it is a part of supervision, shares the ultimate purpose of supervision.

Notice the similarity between the purpose of evaluation, as stated in the administrative code of New Jersey, which recently established the annual evaluation of tenured teachers, and the definition of supervision offered above in the *Dictionary of Education.*

> The purpose of the annual evaluation shall be to:
>   1. Promote professional excellence and improve the skills of teaching staff members;
>   2. Improve student learning and growth;
>   3. Provide a basis for the review of performance of tenured teaching staff members.[15]

The key words, as well as the intention of this mandated purpose of evaluation, are similar to the purpose of supervision as built into the definition of supervision offered by the *Dictionary of Education.* The purpose is development of the people involved—the development of the teachers in their skills and the development of the students in their learning. The ultimate purpose of evaluation as a subsumed activity is the provision of an excellent educational program for our developing students. It is on this basis that we can and shall speak of *developmental supervision.* (See Figure 1-3 for one school district's statement on evaluation as a developmental process.)

QUESTIONS EVERY SCHOOL MUST ANSWER ABOUT SUPERVISION

There are seven major questions every school must answer as it engages in supervision. There is no prescribed order that everyone must follow, and, whatever the order, the earlier answers help determine the answers given to the later questions. The answers to these major questions provide the structural framework for the supervisory system that the school provides for its staff.

What Is the Purpose of Supervision?

The purpose of supervision was previously stated as the provision of an excellent program for developing students. Ultimately, the purpose must be congruent with the purpose of schooling. Supervision aims to create continued efforts toward improving the quality of the educational program the school provides its students through the teachers, the curriculum, and the facilities. The purpose of supervision is the development of the people involved—the teachers and the students.

Stating the purpose as developmental provides a basic approach to supervision that can guide our actions. This answer obviously influences the answers to the next six questions, so it is discussed first. The determination of purpose is basic. If teachers and supervisors disagree on the purpose, there is potential for conflict in their mutual endeavors. If there is tension regarding the purpose of supervision in general (or of

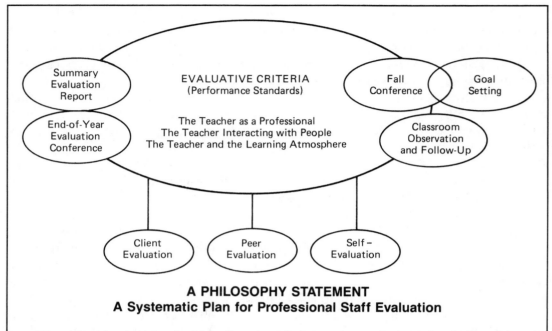

A PHILOSOPHY STATEMENT
A Systematic Plan for Professional Staff Evaluation

The purpose of professional staff evaluation for the Metropolitan School District of Washington Township is to improve the quality of students' learning experiences. This purpose reflects a correlating concern for staff members' growth and development in the profession. Administrative support is an integral part of evaluation.

Evaluative data should be collected from multiple sources on multiple occasions. These data can provide the basis for improving the quality of instruction by determining staff strengths and needs. These data can also provide a supportive, *documented* source for considering changes in contractual agreements, such as different assignments, dismissal, increases in professional responsibilities, transfers within the school system or between grade levels, or promotions.

Evaluation consists of a clearly defined set of procedures wherein the individual being evaluated and the ones responsible for evaluation cooperate to achieve specified goals. It is a process which is done *with* people, not to them. Furthermore, *all* certified staff members should be evaluated—teachers, professional service personnel, counselors, heads of departments and units, school administrators, and central office administrators.

Reprinted with permission of the Metropolitan School District of Washington Township, Indianapolis, Indiana.

FIGURE 1-3. A systematic plan for professional staff evaluation.

evaluation in particular), such tension will permeate all the subsequent issues. For this reason, it is important for the school system and the individual supervisor to accept the developmental purpose of supervision and to clarify it with their teachers.

INTENTIONAL SIDE OF SUPERVISION

Supervision, at levels from kindergarten through grade 12, is generally intended to foster the improvement of education. When supervision functions as it should, the school system can make informed personnel decisions. Supervisors will know whom to rehire, promote, reward with merit pay, and grant tenure; they will know whom to dismiss, lay off, or not rehire among the probationary teachers. Supervision also has the purpose of identifying strengths and weaknesses of faculty so as to permit maintenance of the strengths and correction of the deficiencies.

UNINTENTIONAL SIDE OF SUPERVISION

The other side of supervision recognizes that the procedures used in a supervisory system often create tension, anxiety, and even some fear among teachers. Teachers being supervised quite often do not enjoy the process and often suffer emotional distress and feelings of powerlessness. These unintended outcomes often are not discussed in school or in texts, but they exist.

Some people try to avoid the controversy about the negative outcomes by using the term *hidden agenda*. However, this term doesn't succeed at all because the negative affective outcomes of supervision are not at all hidden nor are they on any agenda of successful supervisors. Anyone who talks with teachers, especially probationary ones, will note the presence of these negative outcomes. In any case, supervisors generally do not *enjoy* their power over teachers or even desire to use it to evoke anxiety or anger in order to keep teachers in line and on their toes. The concept of "unintended consequences" helps explain the presence of the negative outcomes which occur in large measure when supervisors are not as skilled as they should be. For this reason, we shall speak of negative outcomes as unintended and seek ways to prevent them rather than consider them as being on the agenda (that is, intended) but hidden.

The chief way to deemphasize the unintentional consequences is to tailor the involvement of the teachers with their supervisors according to needs and professional maturity. Some teachers, especially beginning teachers, need much direction from their supervisors, who assume a high degree of responsibility for determining the alternative practices to be tried by these teachers. Most teachers, in fact, need to discuss alternatives closely with their supervisors so that they can combine their own professional preferences with contributions to the overall well-being of the school. In this way, there is mutuality and reciprocity between teachers and their supervisors as they collaborate on determining alternative practices. Some few teachers, because of their professional excellence and maturity, need little discussion with or direction from their supervisors. They willingly assume a high degree of personal responsibility for their own professional development. These teachers seem to do best when given a great deal of leeway by their supervisors. Almost on their own they determine and implement their own alternative practices.

With all three of these types of teachers, there is some collaboration with the supervisors. It is not all or nothing. It is a sliding process along a continuum from high to low direction. Glickman[16] has labeled these three approaches directive, collaborative, and nondirective, respectively. Yet all of them involve direction, collaboration, and nondirection in one form or another simply because supervision by its nature involves a teacher working with a supervisor. Similarly, Glatthorn[17] suggests four different options to be offered to teachers, ranging from cooperative professional development (teacher collegial cooperation) to administrative monitoring. Again, simply because no two teachers are alike, there must be differentiated supervision in some form. All in all, it seems best just to use the term *personalized collaboration* when speaking about supervision, because without collaboration tailored to the individual teacher, there can be no supervision at all.

ECLECTIC AND PERSONAL SUPERVISION

In short, no one pure approach works well with all teachers or with any given teacher all the time. It is necessary for supervision to be eclectic and personal. For example, at times with teacher Bob Smith, you will choose to be basically directive, telling him what is necessary to be done for the interests of the school. At other times, you will barely nudge Smith, allowing him to direct himself essentially. Most of the time, you will talk things over closely with Smith to find ways that both of you can satisfy your individual needs which stem from your respective viewpoints. At all times, you will be collaborating with Smith in performing your obligation as prescribed by law and local policy—to supervise your teachers with the purpose of providing an excellent educational program. What you do with Smith will be different from what you do with other teachers because Smith is Smith and not Jones. Notice in Figure 1-4 how one principal stated her goal and intended action regarding individualized collaborative supervision for growth.

Who Will Supervise the Teachers?

In elementary and high schools, specially certified and designated staff officially supervise the teachers. However, within the certified group of available supervisors there is still room for selecting those specific people who will observe, confer, and write reports about the teachers. The principal of a school is always an official supervisor, but that does not mean that the principal is the only supervisor. The department chairperson and the assistant principal also may supervise teachers.

Furthermore, the question is not only who is officially designated as supervisor but who in reality observes, confers, and writes reports. While the superintendent of a school district is the head of the official supervisors, the superintendent may not do much, if any, observing and conferring with teachers. Will anyone from the central office administration such as the district's science coordinator, personnel director, or assistant superintendent for curriculum supervise teachers officially? Will anyone from the county or regional office of education, or even state department of education, supervise teachers officially? In short, each school system must decide who will supervise its teachers officially and in reality.

Once the school system decides on who will perform the function of supervising, the next questions focus on the degree of participation and the weight of that participation. For example, in a medium-size school the chairperson of the Science Department may supervise teachers and file reports with the principal, even discussing

MEMO FROM THE PRINCIPAL

TO: Faculty
FROM: Mildred Ness
RE: Teacher evaluations

In an issue of *Impact on Instructional Improvement,* the journal of NYS ASCD, Dr. George Rentsch, Professor of Education at SUNY Brockport and former Assistant Superintendent of Instruction with the City School District, stated:

> "The thesis of this journal is that it is the specific behaviors of teachers which make the most significant difference as far as student learning is concerned. Further, supervisors are most accountable for insuring that teachers utilize the most effective behaviors."

There are important implications for us in this statement and if you believe the thesis to be valid, as I do, there are steps you and I can take to improve instruction of all of our students.

We are assisted in addressing the problem by Dr. Donald Medley, Professor of Research Methodology in the School of Education at the University of Virginia, who, in this same issue, develops a case for PROCESS EVALUATION—"based on the assumption that teacher evaluation is not to find out who is the best teacher in the school and who is the worst; the purpose is to improve instruction and thereby make the schools more effective."

PROCESS EVALUATION is described by Dr. Medley as having the following characteristics:

1. It is based on assessment of change, growth or improvement in teacher competence, not on status at any point in time.

2. The change must be an improvement; teachers must be encouraged to change in ways likely, if not certain, to improve their effectiveness.

3. It is *personalized.* Not all teachers need improvement in the same areas; therefore, not all teachers can be assessed on the same criteria.

4. Goals are mutually determined; the criteria are generally agreed upon beforehand by evaluator and evaluatee. The teacher must have a voice in defining the criterion or criteria on which to be evaluated.

Although in Dr. Medley's estimation, *process* evaluation is far superior to *product* evaluation, it should tend to improve the product of teaching because the changes are designed to enhance a teacher's effectiveness in facilitating pupil learning.

During the next school year, I should like to implement PROCESS EVALUATION by following these steps:

1. Arrange an individual conference with each teacher to review mutual goals. The set of competencies articulated in our City School District evaluation form will be the basis for review although not necessarily the only criteria. Teacher and supervisor should jointly select an area or areas for desired teacher growth and improvement.

FIGURE 1-4. A principal's stated goal and intended action.

2. Identify those teacher behaviors which we believe (or know) are likely to bring about improved student learning. A means of measuring those behaviors should be discussed and agreed upon.

3. Assist teachers in utilizing more appropriate methods to achieve the desired improvement.

4. Plan one or more observations to measure growth in area chosen.

5. Complete and share a written evaluation based on the above steps.

Ralph Forgione, our Vice-Principal, will share the supervisory role with me and work with some teachers in this process.

By contract, written evaluations are to be completed by January 27. But teachers and administrators have the option of extending this period by mutual agreement. Please let me know if you wish to defer your evaluation until the second semester, but no later than March.

Reprinted with permission of Mildred G. Ness, Principal, James P. B. Duffy School #12, Rochester, New York.

FIGURE 1-4. (continued)

the reports with the principal when filing them. The principal then may observe, confer, and write a report based on the chairperson's previous work. However, only the principal's report may be filed in the personnel office of the school district. Thus, while the Science chairperson may observe teachers more frequently, official weight may be given only to the principal's work. This does not deny the influence of the Science chairperson on the principal (and the teacher). Nevertheless, members of the board of education might not read the chairperson's independent reports to determine and consider any differences of opinion in their capacity as the ultimate deciders.

In short, there may be some conflict or disagreement, for example, between the principal and a department chairperson or between the principal and a curriculum coordinator from the district's central office personnel. In such cases, there must be some weight assigned to each official supervisory viewpoint so as to determine how to resolve the differences of opinion.

The question of who will supervise raises another important distinction that supervisors must be sensitive to. This distinction refers to two concepts—merit and worth. When we determine *merit,* we look at the value of a teacher in terms of intrinsic ability to perform professional duties as a teacher. When we determine *worth,* we look at the overall value of a teacher to the school or school system as a whole. For example, if the Science Department chairperson supervises a teacher and evaluates the value of that teacher, the emphasis will probably be on merit—that is, the chairperson will concentrate on improving the teacher's ability to teach in the classroom and laboratory.

When the superintendent evaluates that teacher, the emphasis is more likely to be on *worth*—that is, the superintendent will concentrate on the broad needs of the school district and the entire school involved. It is possible that a probationary teacher may have merit but not great worth to a school system in which there is a rapid decline in enrollment in the offing and many tenured teachers with seniority. In such a case, the direction of the supervision, especially the recommendation to the board of education concerning the granting of tenure, will differ depending on the emphasis on *merit or worth,* and this emphasis may be a factor of who is the supervisor writing the recommendation. It is hoped that the teacher will know that a distinction is being made between merit and worth. Supervisors, if they are to function sensibly, must be aware of that distinction at all times.

What Will Be Observed, Conferred About, Evaluated, and Reported?

In elementary and high schools, there is little disagreement that classroom performance is the main activity of the teacher. Nevertheless, there is still a general question about a teacher's responsibilities outside of classroom teaching. For example, will you supervise and give much weight to the teacher's participation in P.T.A. meetings, in faculty meetings, in student clubs and activities, in the local teacher's organization? What if the teacher is a superb classroom teacher but a poor hall monitor during the three-minute passing time between periods? There is no implication that institutional activities are unimportant. It is a matter of establishing relative weights for the various areas of a teacher's responsibilities.

Even after the distinction between institutional and pedagogical spheres is made, there is still the need to specify what aspects of classroom teaching will be observed, conferred about, evaluated, and reported. It is possible to concentrate supervision on the cognitive aspects of the classroom almost to the exclusion of the affective aspects. For example, a supervisor may be virtually unconcerned with the tone of the classroom as long as students are occupied doing "school work" at all times. The students may hate the teacher, the school, and the subject matter precisely because they are spending 80 percent or better of their time doing drill worksheets silently at their desks.

In some cases, the answer to this question of "what" will be determined by the answer to the previous question of "who" will supervise. Therefore, it is necessary and important that the teacher and supervisor talk about this question so that it is clear to both what will be the focus of the observations in the classroom. This does not suggest a static condition regarding the answer to "what." It does suggest that for supervision to be sensible both teacher and supervisor need to be clear about this issue. This leads to the fourth question.

What Will Be the Sources of the Information Needed in Supervision?

The concern with sources of information is evident in the literature on the supervision of teachers. There has been and still is lively interest, experimentation, and research about sources of information since this topic covers the subtopic of data instruments. While some educators discuss the broad topic of supervision, others confine their discussions to instrumentation because they can avoid abstract generalities and get right to the "nitty gritty." Indeed, once a school system decides on the instruments, it automatically provides an answer to "what will be observed" and in large measure also answers the question of "who will observe." There may even be a strong implication as to the purpose of supervision, too.

The school system and supervisor must decide what sources of information will be used. For example, in regard to the classroom teaching of a group of sixteen-year-old students in an art class, will the supervisor rely strictly on firsthand, personal observation? Will the students submit answers to a questionnaire? Will the supervisor gather data about the teacher by speaking directly with the students, the students' parents, and the art teacher's colleagues? Will the supervisor view videotape recordings of the classroom as provided by the art teacher?

As with other questions, the answer to one question influences other answers. The determination of sources of information influences what type of data will be obtained and in turn what will be observed, conferred about, evaluated, and reported. Furthermore, since administratively there cannot be a multitude of instruments used, the choice of a particular instrument or small set of instruments has the effect of excluding and including certain information. By using instruments A and B, the school decides to forget about or deemphasize aspects L, M, N, O, and P of the teacher's responsibilities. The instruments as sources of information lead the school in a particular direction and may even lock it into combination that may be narrowing. Yet, the use of a particular instrument is an explicit, concrete, and effective way to decide what source of information will be used in supervision.

What Criteria Will Be Used in Supervising Teachers?

This question concerns the standards that will be used in determining the merit and worth of a teacher. Though it appears as a simple and straightforward question, it seldom elicits simple and straightforward answers. First, there is confusion regarding the meaning of the term *criteria*. For example, let's suppose that Rockland Elementary School decides that it will rate each teacher as Outstanding, Average, or Below Average with regard to Classroom Teaching, Service to School and School District, Personal Characteristics, and Professional Involvement. Some people at Rockland may believe that once they have determined that they will rate these four areas, they have indicated their criteria. However, they are wrong because they are confusing criteria with *areas* of a teacher's responsibilities. The four areas do not indicate to the supervisor and teacher of Rockland Elementary School what level of ability and performance will constitute Outstanding Service or Average Service.

ABSENCE OF CRITERIA

The result of the confusion of criteria with areas of responsibility is an evaluation without known criteria. The absence of criteria then creates a sense of insecurity and uneasiness because of the lack of direction. The teacher has no fair way to do self-assessment in order to be prepared for working with the supervisor. The supervisor also has no way of assuring fairness to the teacher and consistency over time. The possibility and probability of arbitrariness are high, and this is unacceptable. Negative unintended consequences will no doubt appear readily.

The absence of criteria creates the possibility that the teacher and supervisor are not communicating effectively when they speak about the meaning of the data gathered from the various sources. Without interpretation, the data themselves are of limited use. Information alone concerning a teacher is not helpful unless you know what it indicates. Both information *and* criteria are necessary in order to evaluate a teacher in a reasonable way. Both are needed to make fair evaluations in a sound supervisory system. Unfortunately, many schools do not set forth both explicitly to their supervisors and teachers.

In research conducted at Stanford University, the data show that teachers reported knowing less about criteria than principals believed the teachers knew. According to that research, "about half of the teachers reported that they did not know the criteria they were being evaluated on or the information used to evaluate them. By contrast, nearly all the principals believed that teachers knew more about the criteria used and the information collected than teachers reported knowing."[18] It is to avoid such data and to ensure fairness that supervisors must make sure that once reasonable criteria are established, the criteria are made known to their teachers explicitly.

SET OF EVALUATIVE CRITERIA

Figure 1-5 shows a set of evaluative criteria developed in Indianapolis.

Several key points are noteworthy: (1) the criteria were developed jointly by teachers and supervisors; (2) there is no explicit statement that each item is to be striven for and achieved; yet, because of the context and the positive language in which they are phrased, these three sets of items serve as specific criteria for the three broad areas designated to be evaluated; in short, each item implies an answer of "yes," and each set serves to explicate the area being evaluated; (3) the criteria are combined with a simple checklist to provide some type of continuum of achievement; and (4) there is provision for adding criteria in order to personalize the evaluation procedure.

What Is the Overall Context for Faculty Supervison?

The supervision of teachers take place within the context of the school, and each school's context is unique. Nevertheless, it is possible to identify some common points concerning the contexts of schools.

THE SOCIAL-POLITICAL ASPECT

This deals with the social and political factors influencing supervision. For example, in today's world we are pulling back in our high schools in such fields as social problems courses while expanding in computer literacy courses and basic writing courses. The demand for teachers for computer programming courses is high, yet the supply lags. The overall job market influences who is entering the teaching profession, and the job market is a reflection of the political, social, and economic status of the country.

After the expansionary period of the 1960s and early 1970s came a neoconservative period in our country that demanded a return to traditional societal values. This overall societal mood inevitably influences the supervisory policies of a school. The supervisors of teacher Bob Smith in the mid-1980s bring with them a different mind-set from the people who supervised teacher Sue Jones during the expansionist era of the mid-1960s.

THE LEGAL ASPECT

This aspect deals with the rules and regulations pertaining to supervision in a school. A school operating under a collective bargaining agreement between a strong teacher organization and the school district's board of education will be subject to a set of legal guidelines quite different from the set in effect when there is no collective

These evaluative criteria were jointly developed by teachers and administrators to represent desirable and effective teacher behaviors and are basic to the overall evaluation process.

These criteria may be used for the following purposes: as a guide for teacher self-evaluation or peer-evaluation; as a source of ideas for goal writing; as a resource for the year-end evaluation conference and summary evaluation report.

These criteria should serve to guide the thinking of the evaluator and the person being evaluated. Use of these criteria for teacher self-evaluation purposes is optional. Those criteria which are of special interest or concern to either party should be discussed and analyzed in terms of their impact on the instructional process: particular attention should be given to Significant Strengths and Professional Growth Needs.

Significant Strengths | Professional Growth Needs |

I. THE TEACHER AS A PROFESSIONAL

The Teacher:

_____ _____ 1. Interprets and complies with the policies of the school and school system.

_____ _____ 2. Accepts responsibilities for cooperating with requests made by the administration.

_____ _____ 3. Maintains complete and accurate records as required by law, school policy, and administrative regulation.

_____ _____ 4. Demonstrates responsibility for the care of materials.

_____ _____ 5. Is cooperative with certificated members and other employees.

_____ _____ 6. Is punctual and regular in attendance to class, required meetings, assignments.

_____ _____ 7. Establishes and seriously attempts to achieve professional goals.

_____ _____ 8. Assumes responsibility for professional growth (e.g., in-service, workshops, graduate study, professional conferences, etc.)

_____ _____ 9. Is knowledgeable and current in subject content and learning processes.

_____ _____ 10. Is willing to seek and implement promising new ideas; shares ideas and techniques with others.

_____ _____ 11. Reflects poise and confidence in meeting emotional and crisis situations.

_____ _____ 12. Reflects admirable traits of appropriate personal conduct.

_____ _____ 13. Evidences good health through regular attendance and vitality.

_____ _____ 14. Other:

II. THE TEACHER INTERACTING WITH PEOPLE

The Teacher:

_____ _____ 1. Respects the worth and dignity of all individuals.

_____ _____ 2. Is sensitive to others (i.e., listens, looks for and acknowledges strengths of others).

_____ _____ 3. Is empathetic to the problems of others.

FIGURE 1-5. Teacher evaluative criteria.

—— —— 4. Communicates so others understand.
—— —— 5. Has a sense of humor.
—— —— 6. Is tolerant and fair.
—— —— 7. Is self-confident.
—— —— 8. Is tactful.
—— —— 9. Is reasonable and realistic in self-evaluation.
—— —— 10. Other:

III. THE TEACHER AND THE LEARNING ATMOSPHERE

The Teacher:

—— —— 1. Creates a stimulating, nonthreatening learning atmosphere.
—— —— 2. Creates a feeling of trust and openness with students.
—— —— 3. Encourages student involvement in decisions related to their learning and conduct.
—— —— 4. Plans learning experiences to meet individual needs based on prior diagnosis.
—— —— 5. Uses various approaches to meet variant needs of students.
—— —— 6. Maintains a balance between freedom and control.
—— —— 7. Encourages excellence, commitment, and seriousness of purpose.
—— —— 8. Creates a sense of unity and cohesiveness.
—— —— 9. Disciplines in a dignified, fair, and positive manner, striving toward student self-control.
—— —— 10. Controls physical aspects as far as possible (i.e., lights, ventilation, heat, etc.)
—— —— 11. Creatively arranges physical equipment to encourage interest and involvement (i.e., seating, interest centers, exhibits, etc.)
—— —— 12. Uses a variety of materials, media, and resources.
—— —— 13. Is a good listener and utilizes student responses and feedback to facilitate learning.
—— —— 14. Uses a variety of teaching techniques (i.e., lecture, demonstration, dialogue, simulation, discovery, problem solving), and matches the technique to the situation.
—— —— 15. Draws upon student experiences to enrich and give meaning to content.
—— —— 16. Utilizes outside resources and helps students use the resources which are available from the schools and the community.
—— —— 17. Uses varied and appropriate evaluative techniques for student appraisal.
—— —— 18. Makes evaluation a continual part of the learning process and relates it directly to the instructional goals.
—— —— 19. Encourages responses above recall and memory.
—— —— 20. Provides experience which helps students to become responsible, self-directed learners.
—— —— 21. Other:

Reprinted with permission of the Metropolitan School District of Washington Township, Indianapolis, Indiana.

FIGURE 1-5. (continued)

agreement and no teacher union. Also, the interpretation of educational law and general law as it applies to education is in a constant state of flux, and the changing interpretation influences supervision. For example, until recently, a school could decide not to rehire a teacher at the end of three years without giving reasons to the teacher. Today, a school generally must give reasons to a teacher who requests them according to court decisions interpreting the laws.

Although educational laws are state laws, there are enough federal acts relating to education and enough United States Supreme Court decisions that all schools must be aware of the legal context on the national level. Supervisors must be aware of federal laws and court decisions concerning racial discrimination, sex discrimination, and due process as they work with individual teachers within their specific school district.

THE EDUCATIONAL ASPECT

This deals with such matters as the physical facilities available for the teacher's use, the characteristics of the teacher's students in terms of ability, interests, and background, the courses taught by the teacher, and human support services available to aid the teacher for effective teaching. Although two teachers may be colleagues in the same school, the educational context may be quite different due in large measure to their subject fields, the levels of their courses, and the ability of their students.

Though no one item may be significant, the cumulative effect of differences on many educational aspects will yield a context for one teacher which varies significantly from that applicable to another teacher. The effect of the data from the various sources of information will be different and in this way there will be a noticeable effect on the way supervisor and teacher interact during a conference following an observation visit to the classroom. Supervisory expectations and goals will vary as the educational context changes.

THE ORGANIZATIONAL ASPECT

This deals with the structural relationships and the informal relationships that exist among people in the school. This context deals with the bureaucracy of the school and its hierarchies that establish the patterns of decision making and power. A school district's and school's organizational framework, explicit and implicit, influences supervision by establishing a chain of command and the comparative weights of the various viewpoints on a given issue and teacher.

The main element in the organizational context for our purposes concerns the approach to supervision used by a supervisor for a particular teacher. In many cases, supervisors do not vary their approach, with the result that there is little individualization in supervision. Many supervisors simply treat all their teachers alike even though they may expect their teachers to treat the students differently. The supervisory approach deals with the nature of the relationship between supervisor and teacher.

What Is Special About This School?

Every school system is different in some way from every other school system. Likewise, every school is different from every other school, and the difference makes each school unique. The main difference may be the influence of the makeup of the students, or the economic conditions of the community, or the characteristics of the faculty, or whatever. Or, the difference may be due to a combination of small variations on several levels. No matter how it occurs, each school is somehow special.

It is necessary that the school leadership try to identify the qualities which make the school special. These qualities make it impossible for a school to borrow another school's supervisory system in total, and rightly so. Although all schools share some concepts, criteria, procedures, instruments, and problems regarding supervision, there are elements that need to fit a particular school uniquely. The school can begin to identify the elements of its supervisory system that need to be tailor-made only when it begins to recognize what it is that makes it special. Outsiders may think that one school is the same as the next. Insiders, however, know that their school is special in some way.

When the supervisors and faculty recognize the special qualities of the school, they then need to examine their ongoing supervisory system to be sure that there is a good fit. They need to ask if the system takes into account the special qualities of the school. What needs to be adjusted so as to create a proper match between the qualities of the school and the supervisory system? What needs to be added and what needs to be subtracted from the current supervisory system? How have schools with somewhat similar qualities tailor-made their system?

With answers to such questions, the staff can begin. However, since the answers are always changing because the school is a dynamic, rather than static, institution, the staff must be aware that its task of making adjustments is neverending. There is no such thing as the forever-perfect supervisory system. The staff must continually alter procedures, criteria, and instruments for gathering information in light of the ongoing changes characteristic of a dynamic set of human interrelationships. Although the changes may appear to be occurring slowly, they are nevertheless present, and they demand the staff's attention if supervision is to be meaningful, helpful, and fair.

LEGAL RESPONSIBILITIES OF THE SUPERVISOR

Your legal responsibilities as a supervisor are most important because they directly affect the jobs of teachers, the education of the students, and your job. They are complex because they stem from several sources simultaneously—the United States Constitution; your state constitution; federal, state, and local laws; court cases; your board of education's policies; and the contract between your board of education and the teacher's organization. Even though education law is complex and sometimes confusing, it is not too difficult to set forth and know the law regarding supervision in broad strokes. You must know the law because our society presumes that people know the law; ignorance of the law by school leaders is not an acceptable defense in a court case where your adversary seeks to win.

Note two points in the preceding paragraph. First, the best we can do in this book is to speak of the law in broad outline. There is no single set of education laws pertaining to *all* schools, except for some federal statutory laws such as the Civil Rights Act of 1964 as they apply to educational matters and except for the laws stemming from decisions made by U.S. Supreme Court justices as they interpret the Constitution and the states' laws. Since education in America is a state matter and not a federal matter, there is no set of federal laws to govern education as there is in regard to imports and exports, for example. Education laws essentially are made by each of the fifty states for their own schools. Naturally, these laws vary from state to state as do the regulations established by the local boards of education and the contracts signed by them with their teachers' organizations.

Furthermore, education law is always in a state of flux. Law-making bodies, such as the Congress, state legislatures, and boards of education, are constantly passing new laws that affect supervision. Also, the Supreme Court, the only court whose decisions are binding on the entire country, is always handing down new decisions and thus altering in some way your legal responsibilities as a supervisor. The result of all of this is that there is no way today to specify what the law will be tomorrow in regard to a particular issue. The only course open to us is to talk about education law in broad strokes.

Second, notice that this section does not intend to offer a comprehensive treatment of the topic of laws pertaining to supervision, citing statutes and court case decisions. Nor is there an intent to offer comprehensive legal advice because such an attempt would be both foolish and illegal. If you wish the citation of statutes and all pertinent court cases for support of the following points, consult your local pertinent statutes directly and any of the excellent education law books that devote themselves exclusively to the massive amount of material in this area.

Constitutional Civil Rights Influencing Supervision

Teachers have personal civil rights that they do not give up once they begin teaching. These civil rights are well known: the right to freedom of expression, freedom of association, procedural due process to protect liberty and property interests, privacy, freedom of religion, and equal protection. Statutory laws cannot infringe on these constitutional rights unless there is a compelling state interest, a very strong governmental interest rather than only a rational connection between the law and school needs.

The Court recognizes that there may arise a conflict of interest between the school (that is, the State) and the individual teacher (that is, the citizen). The first task of the Court, then, is to determine if the speech of a teacher is constitutionally protected expression. If there is protected speech, the task entails arriving "at a balance between the interests of the teacher, as a citizen, in commenting upon matters of public concern and the interest of the State, as employer, in promoting the efficiency of the public services it performs through its employees," wrote the Supreme Court in *Pickering*[19] when it decided in favor of Marvin Pickering, a teacher in Illinois, who claimed that he lost his job because his letter published in a local newspaper criticized his board of education. The Court has protected teachers' rights fiercely.

In cases subsequent to *Pickering*, the Supreme Court has strengthened and classified its position regarding protected public speech by teachers. School boards and supervisors must also show by a "preponderance of evidence" that the termination of the teacher's employment would have occurred even if the issue of protected free speech, as claimed by the teachers, were not considered. If protected speech is shown to be a "substantial" factor in the termination of the teacher, the teacher may be reinstated for violation of constitutional rights.

The Court has also ruled in *Givhan*[20] that a teacher's private criticism of a principal in his office is protected and cannot be the main reason for termination of employment. A teacher does not give up freedom of speech even in the supervisor's office. Moreover, it does not matter whether the teacher is a tenured or probationary teacher when the First

Amendment right to free speech is an issue. As the Court said in its *Mt. Healthy*[21] decision, a teacher may "establish a claim to reinstatement if the decision not to rehire him was made by reason of his exercise of constitutionally protected First Amendment freedoms."

Although there are some variations from state to state as specified in statutes, it is possible to list the following requirements prior to terminating a teacher's employment:

1. Give the teacher a clear and timely notice of pending termination.
2. Give reasons for termination in sufficient detail to enable the teacher to prepare a defense.
3. Give the names of the people who have made charges against the teacher and the specific nature of and facts behind those charges.
4. Give the teacher a reasonable time after the notice in order to present contrary evidence.
5. Give the teacher an opportunity to be heard meaningfully before an impartial tribunal where defense witnesses can appear and adverse witnesses can be cross-examined. (The Supreme Court has ruled in *Hortonville*[22] that the school board may be the proper hearing tribunal.) The tribunal must decide based on the evidence and findings of the hearing.
6. Follow the requirements specified in your state's laws, your school board's regulations, and the teacher's contract.
7. Provide a record of the hearing.
8. The teacher has the right to legal counsel.
9. The teacher has the right to avoid self-incrimination.
10. The teacher has the right to appeal an adverse decision to a higher tribunal.

If these procedures are not followed by the supervisor and the school board, the teacher may be reinstated as well as receive money damages. You, as supervisor, are responsible because it is from you that the school board, as legal employer, receives its information.

You should follow these procedures when working with all teachers, tenured or nontenured, even though nontenured teachers in general do not have a constitutional right to due process because of a property claim. To be fair and to be sure—since a probationary teacher can claim a property interest by implied tenure or by contract—you should give notice and specific reasons for your recommendations to all teachers. You should also give reasons because they may be required by state law, local school board policy, teacher contract, or court precedent.

The ethical, professionally sound reason for giving reasons is supported by the New Jersey Supreme Court in its *Donaldson*[23] decision, which said, "It appears evident to us that on balance the arguments supporting the teacher's request for a statement of reasons overwhelm any arguments to the contrary. The teacher is a professional who has spent years in the course of attaining the necessary education and training. When he is engaged as a teacher, he is fully aware that he is serving a probationary period and may or may not ultimately attain tenure. If he is not reengaged and tenure is thus precluded, he is surely interested in knowing why and every consideration along with all thoughts of elemental fairness and justice suggest that, when he asks, he be told why."

You cannot go wrong by having adequate documentation for what you recommend to the teacher and school board to do. Make sure that your documents give evidence that is substantial; is relevant to the teacher's primary responsibilities; is factual in regard to time, place, date, and any witnesses; and is relevant to the charges being made against the teacher. Be sure that you do not make public statements damaging to the teacher's character or good name so as to prevent him from getting another job. Obviously, you should notify your teachers early on in your relationship about what your supervisory policies and procedures are and how your supervision is related to continued employment. Although all of this may seem difficult and burdensome, it is your responsibility to act according to the law. It is your ethical responsibility to act toward your teachers as you would expect to be treated under a similar circumstance in which your employment was being terminated.

The requirement of due process in no way means that it is not correct or not possible to terminate a teacher's job whether that teacher is tenured, under contract, or probationary. Indeed, there is a long list of causes for termination such as incompetency, insubordination, neglect of duty, moral misconduct, and offensive language. Indeed, with a tenured teacher you must overcome the presumption of competence if you seek dismissal. In any case, the requirement of due process only means that where fairness and rights are involved you must proceed carefully, ethically, and legally. Due process is a fundamental right under our Constitution and the courts have enforced it over and over again in favor of teacher who proved that violations existed. It is appropriate here to recall the words of Supreme Court Justice Felix Frankfurter in *McNabb*,[24] "The history of liberty has largely been the history of observance of procedural safeguards."

In addition to the right of freedom of speech and of due process the Constitution also gives the teacher the rights of freedom of religion, press, assembly, protection from self-incrimination, privacy, and equal protection of the laws. It is your legal responsibility not to infringe on these rights. On the other hand, you, as supervisor, have the responsibility to work for the improvement of the school, and the Constitution does not prohibit you from taking action. For example, the school upon your recommendation can require a teacher to participate in a program of continued professional development with the purpose of improving student learning. Such a requirement is not unconstitutional, according to *Harrah*.[25]

A Bill of Rights for Teacher Supervision

It is with the Constitution and Supreme Court decisions in mind that Professors Strike and Bull[26] draw up a Bill of Rights related to the legal and moral issues in teacher evaluation. With slight modification, prepared with the permission and approval of Professor Strike, so as to apply in general to supervision and not only to evaluation in particular, their "Bill of Rights" appears in Figure 1-6. Notice that both the school and the teacher have rights that are to be protected. Also notice that under this bill educators should try to settle their differences through mediation geared to conflict resolution rather than formal litigation in some form of court.

Statutory Civil Rights Influencing Supervision

The single most influential law affecting supervision of teachers today is the Civil Rights Act of 1964 with its various updating amendments. The specific section relevant to employment is Title VII which prohibits employment discrimination based on "race, color, religion, sex, or national origin." In decisions starting in 1971 with a landmark case

Rights of Educational Institutions:

1. Educational institutions have the right to exercise supervision and to make personnel decisions intended to improve the quality of the education they provide.
2. Educational institutions have the right to collect information relevant to their supervisory roles.
3. Educational institutions have the right to act on such relevant information in the best interest of the students whom they seek to educate.
4. Educational institutions have the right to the cooperation of the teaching staff in implementing and executing a fair and effective system of supervision.

Rights of Teachers:

1. Professional rights
   a. Teachers have a right to reasonable job security.
   b. Teachers have a right to a reasonable degree of professional discretion in the performance of the jobs.
   c. Teachers have a right to reasonable participation in decisions concerning both professional and employment-related aspects of their jobs.

2. Evidential rights
   a. Teachers have the right to have decisions made on the basis of evidence.
   b. Teachers have a right to be evaluated on relevant criteria.
   c. Teachers have the right not to be evaluated on the basis of hearsay, rumor, or unchecked complaints.

3. Procedural rights
   a. Teachers have the right to be evaluated according to general, public, and comprehensible standards.
   b. Teachers have the right to notice concerning when they will be evaluated.
   c. Teachers have the right to know the results of their supervision.
   d. Teachers have the right to express a reaction to the process and results of their supervision in a meaningful way.
   e. Teachers have the right to a statement of the reasons for any action taken in their cases.
   f. Teachers have the right to appeal adverse decisions and to have their views considered by a competent and unbiased authority.
   g. Teachers have the right to orderly and timely supervision.

4. Other humanitarian and civil rights
   a. Teachers have a right to humane supervision procedures.
   b. Teachers have the right to have their supervision kept private and confidential.
   c. Teachers have the right to supervision procedures that are not needlessly intrusive into their professional activities.
   d. Teachers have the right to have their private lives considered irrelevant to their evaluation.
   e. Teachers have the right to have supervision not be used coercively to obtain aims external to the legitimate purposes of supervision.
   f. Teachers have the right to nondiscriminatory criteria and procedures.

FIGURE 1-6. A bill of rights for teacher supervision.

g. Teachers have the right not to have supervision used to sanction the expression of unpopular views.
h. Teachers have the right to an overall assessment of their performance that is frank, honest, and consistent.

Principles of Conflict Resolution:

1. Remediation is to be preferred, where possible, to disciplinary action or termination.
2. Mediation is to be preferred, where possible, to more litigious forms of conflict resolution.
3. Informal attempts to settle disputes should precede formal ones.

Kenneth Strike and Barry Bull, "Fairness and the Legal Context of Teacher Evaluation," pp. 307-309 in *Handbook of Teacher Evaluation,* edited by Jason Millman. © 1981. Reprinted by permission of Sage Publications, Inc., and Kenneth Strike.

FIGURE 1-6. (continued)

dealing with employment in a private corporation the Supreme Court has upheld recent federal legislation aimed at strengthening the concept of equal protection of the laws. The Court has struck down discriminatory "practices that are fair in form but discriminatory in operation."

In regard to racial and gender discrimination in particular, since these two types of discrimination are the most significant at this time, the criterion used by the Court is disparate impact and not intent. That is, the Court looks to the impact of an employer's decisions rather than the intent. The employer must remove unintentional as well as intentional discrimination. Once the teacher shows a *prima facie* case of discrimination, the burden of proof shifts to the school to show that there is a legitimate non-discriminatory reason for the challenged action.

The implication of this federal civil rights legislation and the legislation on age discrimination in employment to protect people between the ages of forty and sixty-five is that as supervisor you must carefully scrutinize your own behavior. You need to be sure not only that your intents and motives are nondiscriminatory but that your behavior does not have a negative pattern. Once you can assure yourself and the school board that you are not acting discriminatorily, you need to document your actions to demonstrate that your decisions are based on legitimate reasons connected with the rational purpose of your schools. Lack of clear and adequate documentation that you have acted properly will probably result in the conclusion that you have used an illegitimate consideration such as age, gender, or race in making your supervisory decisions. As before, your legal responsibility is to abide by the civil rights laws and at the same time document your behavior as being proper.

State and Local Laws and Contract Provisions

Here, too, it is your responsibility to know and abide by the laws governing you. You should know the state laws, local laws, and contract provisions as they apply to you, for example, regarding deadlines for giving notice of termination of employment. If the law requires you to notify a teacher by April 1, a notice from you received on April 2 is unsatisfactory. Such a notice does not fulfill the requirement set by law or contract. A failure on your part in this regard may well negate your efforts in terminating the teacher's employment. You should know what in your school constitutes inefficiency (incompetency), insubordination, and moral misconduct, for example, for they are prime issues in your supervisory relationship with your teachers.

While it is true that you must give clear and timely notice to a teacher about pending termination, there is a requirement that often precedes the giving of notice. This is the requirement of helping teachers improve, and it appears in many state and local regulations. For example, if you have a teacher deficient in the manner of preparing tests, you are required to help that teacher correct that deficiency. If not, the teacher can legally, as well as ethically, respond that you did not help him develop his skill in preparing tests. If you have not performed your legal responsibility in helping the teacher change, you are likely to lose a challenge by the teacher instituted after receiving notification about termination of employment.

Not only must you know your local laws and abide by them, you also must inform your teachers explicitly of the policies and regulations established for your school. You cannot expect the teacher to act properly if there is no or poor promulgation of the changing regulations. As mentioned before regarding evaluation criteria, teachers report that the communication between supervisors and them is not as good as supervisors believe. It is, after all, your responsibility to take the initiative to open the channels of communication so that everyone will know the laws and provisions under which they work.

CHAPTER 1 ENDNOTES

1. ALVIN TOFFLER, *Future Shock* (New York: Bantam Books, 1971), 400.
2. ERVING GOFFMAN, *Asylums* (Garden City, N.Y.: Anchor, 1961), xiii.
3. ERVING GOFFMAN, *ibid.,* xiii.
4. ERVING GOFFMAN, *ibid.,* xiii.
5. ERVING GOFFMAN, *ibid.,* 5.
6. WAYNE K. HOY, "The Influence of Experience on the Beginning Teacher," *School Review* (September 1968): 312–23.
7. AMITAI ETZIONI, *Comparative Analysis of Complex Organizations* (New York: The Free Press, 1975), 27.
8. LUDWIG WITTGENSTEIN, *Philosophical Investigations* (Oxford, England: Basil Blackwell, 1958).
9. JAMES S. COLEMAN, "The Adolescent Subculture and Academic Achievement," *The American Journal of Sociology,* Vol. 65, No. 4 (January 1960): 347.
10. ROBERT E. SLAVIN, "Cooperative Learning," *Review of Educational Research,* Vol. 50, No. 2 (Summer 1980): 315–42.
11. THOMAS J. PETERS AND ROBERT H. WATERMAN, JR., *In Search of Excellence: Lessons from America's Best-Run Companies* (New York: Harper and Row, 1982), 207.
12. THOMAS J. PETERS AND ROBERT H. WATERMAN, *ibid.,* 211.
13. THOMAS J. PETERS AND ROBERT H. WATERMAN, *ibid.,* 291.
14. CARTER V. GOOD, *Dictionary of Education* (New York: McGraw-Hill, 1973), 574.
15. New Jersey Administrative Code 6:3–1.21.

16. CARL D. GLICKMAN, *Developmental Supervision* (Alexandria, Va.: Association for Supervision and Curriculum Development, 1981).

17. ALLAN GLATTHORN, *Differentiated Supervision* (Alexandria, Va.: Association for Supervision and Curriculum Development, 1984).

18. JUNE E.THOMPSON, SANFORD M. DORNBUSCH, AND W. RICHARD SCOTT, "Failure of Communication in the Evaluation of Teachers by Principals," *Technical Report No. 43,* Stanford University, 1975: 20.

19. 391 U.S. 563 (1968).

20. 439 U.S. 410 (1979).

21. 429 U.S. 274 (1977).

22. 426 U.S. 482 (1976).

23. 65 N.J. 236, 320 A.2d 857 (1974).

24. 318 U.S. 332, 347 (1943).

25. 440 U.S. 194 (1979).

26. KENNETH STRIKE AND BARRY BULL, "Fairness and the Legal Context of Teacher Evaluation," *Handbook of Teacher Evaluation,* edited by Jason Millman (Beverly Hills, Calif.: Sage, 1981), 307–09.

2

MOTIVATING, ORGANIZING, AND DEVELOPING TEACHERS

Many teachers, at one time or another, lose some of the enthusiastic spark they brought with them upon entering teaching. This is normal, as no one can stay 100 percent motivated all the time. In addition, teachers need to change in some way because the complexity of their jobs demands a constant effort to look at new and different aspects of teaching. Thus, your task, as supervisor, is to help teachers understand the job of teaching, their needs and desires, and the approaches available for further development.

Chapter 2 looks at several main themes—motivation, organization, negotiation, and development. How can you motivate a teacher to change? What does a teacher need in order to be satisfied and to feel good? Is there anything we can learn from Theory Z—the theory connected with Japanese management, which its advocates claim is the successor to Theory X and Theory Y? What does a new approach to the art of negotiation offer you as a supervisor? What are the characteristics of a workable development plan for teachers?

After reading this chapter, you should be able to:

- Understand what needs motivate teachers and what steps you can take to lead your teachers in professional growth.
- Describe the basic ideas of Maslow's, Hertzberg's, and Vroom's theories of human motivation.
- List at least ten motivation rules to follow based on theory and research.
- Describe the basic ideas of Theory X, Theory Y, Contingency Theory, and Theory Z.
- Describe the basic ideas of Principled Negotiation and its four basic points.
- Apply the basic points of negotiation in using the Supervision Window and the Supervisor's Guide for Facilitating Change.
- List the essential characteristics of a teacher development plan.
- Apply the fundamental ideas of motivation, organization, and negotiation in creating a development plan with your teachers.

WHAT IS MOTIVATION?

Motivation is the desire to do well. A teacher who is motivated to teach in a way that promotes high achievement by the students within a positive classroom environment is someone who acts out of internal commitment rather than external threat. Motivation is not necessarily a conscious or logical decision by the teacher though probably the teacher who is motivated has spent time thinking about what needs to be done and how to do it. Motivation is to be clearly distinguished from motion, the mere doing of a good job. Surely, in regard to simple tasks, a person can do a job (that is, move) out of fear without having a commitment or desire (that is, motivation) to do the job. In regard to teaching, a complex job, it is virtually impossible to be an excellent teacher without being highly motivated.

Motivation, as is obvious, involves the word motive and hence relates to our values, expectations, ambitions, and self-concept. If you value helping other people to learn skills that will facilitate their functioning, then the basis for motivation to teach well exists within you. If, however, you value and are intensely concerned about, for example, money, in order to acquire a set of expensive, high-tech items like a video recorder, jet plane, Rolls-Royce sedan, room-size television, satellite dish antenna, personal computer and printer, and indoor heated swimming pool, then the motivation to be a teacher probably is lacking. That is to say, the value system which is connected with helping others learn is different from the value system connected with acquiring a host of expensive technological innovations. This is not to say that teaching and earning money are opposites and incompatible. It is a matter of degree and emphasis. People who value *helping others* do not order their values in the same way as the people who are acquisitive regarding new products and who therefore wish to earn much money in order to *possess the things* that gratify them personally.

Since motivation is integrally connected with self-concept and values, different rewards will have different effects on people. The teacher who sees himself as a potential leader of his colleagues and who values the opportunity to guide other teachers will be motivated by the possibility of becoming a district superintendent. He has the motivation to succeed as a teacher so that he can begin on the administrative road to a superintendency. On the other hand, a teacher who sees himself as a social reformer and who values the opportunity to work in community projects will be motivated by the possibility of becoming the school district's liaison with the local community council. He has the motivation to succeed as a teacher so that he can begin an outreach program. While both teachers are motivated to teach well, a different potential reward is effective for each. While both are motivated by need satisfaction in general, the particulars for these two teachers are different because their self-concepts and values are somewhat different. While you can't see the internal abstraction called "motivation," you can see it functioning, you can estimate its strength, and you can help shape it. How to do this depends on the motivational theory you accept.

MOTIVATION THEORIES

MASLOW'S THEORY OF HUMAN MOTIVATION

Perhaps the most well-known theory of motivation is that of the psychologist Abraham Maslow who, starting as early as the 1940s, published his work on human motivation and need satisfaction. According to Maslow there are five types of need by level—the physiological, safety, love, esteem, and self-actualization. (See Figure 2-1.) The first or lowest need includes those needs each person has in order to be alive and stay alive.

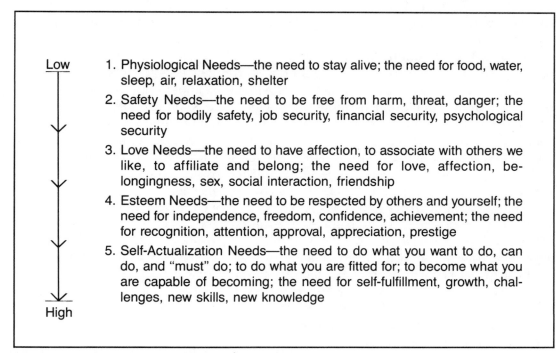

Low
1. Physiological Needs—the need to stay alive; the need for food, water, sleep, air, relaxation, shelter

2. Safety Needs—the need to be free from harm, threat, danger; the need for bodily safety, job security, financial security, psychological security

3. Love Needs—the need to have affection, to associate with others we like, to affiliate and belong; the need for love, affection, be-longingness, sex, social interaction, friendship

4. Esteem Needs—the need to be respected by others and yourself; the need for independence, freedom, confidence, achievement; the need for recognition, attention, approval, appreciation, prestige

5. Self-Actualization Needs—the need to do what you want to do, can do, and "must" do; to do what you are fitted for; to become what you are capable of becoming; the need for self-fulfillment, growth, challenges, new skills, new knowledge

High

FIGURE 2-1. Maslow's hierarchy of motivating needs.

These needs are the most powerful needs of all, according to Maslow, because until they are satisfied, at least partially, a person does not begin to be concerned with the higher needs such as respect and self-fulfillment. The higher needs are pushed into the background in this hierarchy of needs, and this hierarchy appears to hold for most human beings. New and higher needs emerge as lower needs are satisfied.

After the physiological needs are satisfied, the safety needs begin to emerge. Here, the human being—adult or child—is concerned with safety and security. This concern includes physical safety (freedom from bodily harm) as well as psychological security (freedom from emotional threat and disruption). One level higher is the set of social needs revolving around love, affection, and belongingness. Here the person expresses a need for being with others in order to receive and give love. Each person needs to love and to be loved, and also to affiliate with other people for friendship and group membership. The group to which a person belongs thus has the power to exert influence as it satisfies a basic need.

The fourth level regarding esteem deals with the need people have to be respected not only in the eyes of others but also in their own eyes. For this reason, esteem must be based firmly on achievement as opposed to illusion. People need to feel confident, adequate, and free to face the world with some sense of independence (that is, relative independence since no one is absolutely independent, and everyone is in some way dependent). Everyone needs to be respected and recognized by others, and this esteem is interrelated with self-esteem which is also needed. Self-esteem is connected to a sense of worth, importance, and confidence, while the absence of self-esteem is connected to feelings of helplessness, inadequacy, inferiority, and discouragement.

The final level deals with self-actualization, the process of becoming. Here, the human being strives to do what he or she is fitted for and wants to do. Maslow borrowed the term *self-actualization* to describe the need people have to fulfill themselves, to grow, to learn new knowledge and skills, and to create. People who are satisfying the need for self-actualization are doing what "must" be done in order to become the persons they are capable of becoming. In our society, few people are self-actualized.

According to Maslow, a person preoccupied, for example, with safety and security needs, does not think much about the higher needs of love, esteem, and self-actualization. In fact, such a person thinks that everything will be just fine, utopic, and happy once physical danger disappears. Such a narrow perspective, which screens out recognition of other future needs, will prove to be faulty when the safety need is satisfied and other needs move forward to be satisfied. Humans never fully satisfy their needs, new ones always emerging to replace those already satisfied.

Maslow's hierarchy of needs has appeal even though it clearly does not deal with several important aspects of human life. You will note the absence of values—aesthetic, ethical, and religious—in this five-step hierarchy of motivational needs. You will have to answer on your own how the need for and expression of values fits into the set of needs established by Maslow. Nevertheless, the five-step hierarchy provides a manageable and comprehensible way to view the factors that motivate a person to act. Maslow's hierarchy of needs provides a usable framework for understanding your colleagues—teachers and fellow supervisors—as you seek to provide opportunities for need satisfaction, which is another way to define motivation.

HERTZBERG'S MOTIVATORS—HYGIENES THEORY

The two-factor theory of Frederick Hertzberg is the second most well-known theory of human motivation.

Based on extensive interviews, analysis, and observation, Hertzberg conceptualizes two factors that are related to job satisfaction and dissatisfaction: motivators and hygienes. Motivators are those factors that are directly related to *job content* and are stimuli for growth in performing the job. Motivators include job achievement, performing the work itself, responsibility, advancement, and recognition. The hygiene factors are those that are related to the *job environment* and job dissatisfaction. Hygiene factors, which are contextual, include such items as company policy, supervision, working conditions, salary, status, and interpersonal relations, all of which are not directly part of job performance. They are, rather, part of the job environment. (See Figure 2-2.)

The key to understanding Hertzberg's two factors lies in the finding that certain characteristics lead to job satisfaction while other factors lead to job dissatisfaction. In this way, satisfaction and dissatisfaction are not simple opposites. For example, poor working conditions lead to job dissatisfaction, yet good working conditions do not necessarily lead to satisfaction. Therefore, improving the work conditions (that is, improving the job environment, which is related to *hygiene*) may eliminate dissatisfaction but may not bring about job satisfaction. To bring satisfaction it is necessary to make changes in the *motivators* that are connected with the actual job itself.

With the two factors—the motivators and hygienes—in mind, it is possible to examine a job or set of jobs to seek ways to motivate the workers. For Hertzberg, the key lies in how to change the motivators, for they are the most important items once some efforts are made to remove dissatisfaction through a change in hygienes. The key lies in what is called *job enrichment,* which looks at the job itself. Rather than enlarge the job, or set firm quotas, or remove unpleasant elements, job enrichment seeks to change the

Motivator factors—related to *job content*
       Work itself
       Achievement
       Recognition
       Advancement
       Possibility of Growth
       Responsibility

Hygiene factors—related to *job environment*
       Working conditions
       Status
       Job security
       Salary
       Interpersonal relations with superiors, peers, and subordinates
       Technical supervision
       Company policy and administration

Job enrichment, a continual process, consists of changing motivators so as to effect long-term *motivation.*

FIGURE 2-2. Hertzberg's two factors of motivation.

job by involving the motivators of responsibility, achievement, growth and recognition. The changes that are connected to increasing achievement while calling for responsibility are of the kind needed to enrich a job and motivate the worker.

Hertzberg's data and the data of others utilizing his theory bear out the claims made for this approach to motivation. As with Maslow's model, Hertzberg's two-factor model and the concept of job enrichment offer a usable perspective on motivation. Notice that Hertzberg's motivators are in general comparable to Maslow's esteem and self-actualization levels; the hygienes are comparable to the lower-level needs of physiology, safety, and love. With this model, you can seek long-term motivation related to job enrichment as you achieve short-term changes through changes involving the hygiene factors, which are necessary but not sufficient.

VROOM'S VALENCE-EXPECTANCY THEORY

Victor Vroom has proposed a third theory of motivation that is the least well-known, although perhaps the one that integrates empirical findings most satisfactorily. For Vroom, motivation is a process governing choices among activities. A person chooses which alternatives to take among the several that are present at all times.

A person chooses, according to Vroom, among first-level outcomes based on the perceived relationship between these outcomes and possible second-level outcomes. That is, the person chooses among level 1 outcomes A, B, and C because of their possible connections on level 2 with A_1, A_2, B_1, B_2, C_1, and C_2. Outcomes on level 1 serve as *instruments* to the outcomes on level 2, which are the desired ones. *Valence* is the strength of the desire for a particular outcome. *Expectancy* is the belief that a particular action, effort, or performance will lead to a chosen first-level outcome. For example, a teacher may *expect* that successful teaching as a high school mathematics teacher will lead to being appointed chairperson of the department. Expectancy is the relationship between efforts and outcomes.

Motivation, then, for a person to act in a certain way is the product of the valence of the level 2 outcome (reward) and the expectancy that the action will indeed lead to the reward. A teacher who seeks to become a principal (level 2 outcome), for example, will be motivated to teach well and otherwise serve the school district in a leadership capacity (level 1 outcome) to the degree that there is an expectancy that excellent teaching and peer leadership are related to appointment as a principal. That is, the teacher is motivated to perform well (level 1) as an instrument to achieving the reward (level 2) depending on the strength of the desire for the reward (valence) and the belief that high teacher performance (level 1) will lead to an administrative appointment (level 2). (See Figure 2-3.)

However, in the example given above, if there is little desire to become a principal or there is doubt that high classroom performance will lead to a principalship, then there will be very little motivation to succeed in teaching. When the valence is low or negative and/or when the expectancy is low or negative, there is little motivation to act in a given way. For example, if the teacher wants to become a principal (level 2) but believes that such an appointment results from political influence as a member of the town's dominant political party (level B_1), there will be little motivation to teach well (level A_1) as the

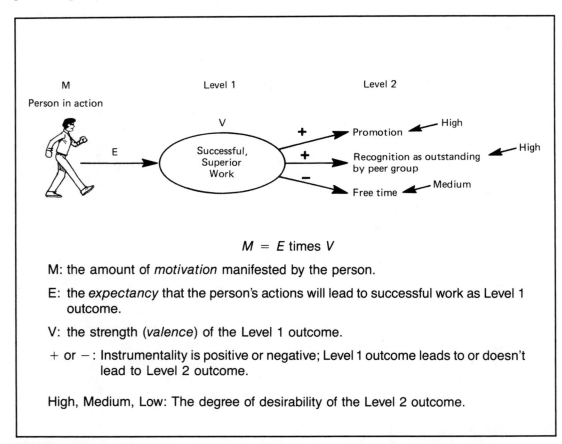

$$M = E \text{ times } V$$

M: the amount of *motivation* manifested by the person.

E: the *expectancy* that the person's actions will lead to successful work as Level 1 outcome.

V: the strength (*valence*) of the Level 1 outcome.

+ or −: Instrumentality is positive or negative; Level 1 outcome leads to or doesn't lead to Level 2 outcome.

High, Medium, Low: The degree of desirability of the Level 2 outcome.

FIGURE 2-3. An illustration of Vroom's valence-expectancy theory of motivation.

means (instrument) of being rewarded. The teacher will be motivated to become active in town politics as a member of the "right" party.

Vroom's theory of motivation has the distinct advantage of accounting for individual differences in the motivational level of people. With it, you can explain why certain teachers act as they do by inquiring into their desired outcomes, the strength of their desires, and their beliefs about the expectancy that their chosen actions will lead to first-level outcomes. You can show that teachers differ on the level 2 outcomes that they seek, on the valence of their desires for particular outcomes, and on their expectancies. You can work with teachers about all three of the foregoing possible differences. Like the Maslow and Hertzberg theories, Vroom's theory of motivation provides a useful approach to understanding why people act as they do.

IMPLICATIONS FOR SUPERVISION

Each of the foregoing three theories has its advantages over the other two. It is not critical which one you personally prefer. You probably will accept elements from each as you form your own eclectic theory of motivation. What is critical is how you apply and integrate motivational theory into your supervisory activities. In several sections, there are extensive suggestions on how to include ideas from Maslow, Hertzberg, and Vroom into supervision of your teachers. Specifically, for example, see the section on "Using the Supervision Window" and the section on "The Supervisor's Guide for Facilitating Teacher Change." However, several brief comments follow that are appropriate at this point.

As you confer with your teachers, individually or in small groups (see Chapters 5 and 6), you can integrate motivation theory through three regular actions: listening, observing, and questioning. Listen to the teachers as they talk to you and their peers; observe their actions. Surely they will give you clues about their needs (Maslow). You probably do not need to concern yourself with Maslow's two lowest levels since our teachers today are paid well enough that they don't have to focus on satisfying food, water, and safety needs. On the other hand, you may hear, for example, that a teacher is particularly concerned with personal safety and community safety because of the nuclear threat, or an asbestos problem in the school or another community building, or a water pollution problem in the town's water supply and recreation facility. Though you, as supervisor, cannot satisfy that safety need, you can understand how fundamental that need is to that particular teacher. You can understand why he or she is motivated to teach a unit on nuclear disarmament or environmental pollution, for example. You can understand why he wants to enlist teachers in the community's action program and why he leaves school promptly at 2:45 P.M. daily to work as a volunteer in your town's community center. Although you might have thought that the physiological and safety needs of your teachers were already satisfied and therefore not functioning any longer as motivations, you now realize that here is a teacher motivated at levels one and two in a special way.

If you will recognize the teacher's need, accept it, and build on it, you can facilitate that teacher's development. To speak with the teacher about his concern for water pollution and to express praise for his action on behalf of the community is to help satisfy some of the teacher's esteem need—for approval, acceptance, and recognition. You can speak about how to utilize his personal and community concern in his classroom and the school as a whole (motivators of achievement and recognition). You can ask about and then discuss how to integrate water pollution into a science, social studies, or art unit; how to develop student interest in the town's problem; and how to prepare an informative assembly program on water pollution. By accepting the teacher's concern to satisfy a legitimate, fundamental physiological/safety need, you can help satisfy other needs, including the need to succeed as a teacher. You can improve interpersonal relations (hygienes) with the teacher and *motivate the teacher* to further development.

One more example: You can observe the teacher in general and ask her what her goals are regarding teaching: "What do you desire for yourself in three or five years?" You may learn that the teacher aspires to be a county-wide supervisor in math to follow in the footsteps of her mentor and model, a former high school teacher. You can then discuss with her the valence, expectancy, and instrumentality of her preferences and actions (Vroom). Are this teacher's actions likely to bring about success as an overall leader in math education? Will success in the classroom suffice for a promotion to a county-level position? How strong is her desire for a county job as opposed to a district or state-level job? As you discuss the answers to these questions, you can find out what *motivates the teacher* and how you can help guide that motivation as a supervisor for the mutual benefit of the teacher and your school.

Figure 2-4 offers you a simple and effective way to stay alert to one significant need every theorist mentions. The form directs you to think about recognition, a higher level need, which theory and empirical findings show to be on the minds of all workers. You can use the form, "Recognition," by yourself to see where you are today as a supervisor to some people and as a subordinate to others in your system. You can also see where you are relative to others in your private life. You may also wish to use this with your teachers, asking them to complete the form as they look at you, their students, and the people in their private lives.

With some minor brainstorming you will be able to come up with several ideas on how to provide concrete expressions of recognition to your teachers. For example, you may wish to simply send notes to your teachers recognizing their achievements; commit yourself to speaking personally to each teacher regularly; contact local newspapers to print articles about special teacher feats; establish a Teacher of the Semester Award. No doubt you can think of several better and additional ideas to suit your faculty. The point here is that recognition, which is so vital to us, does not require great expense of time and money to give to others who look to us to help satisfy a basic human need.

Thirty Guiding Rules

The literature on motivation is vast, as any quick visit to a good professional library will demonstrate. To synthesize this literature Dean Spitzer[1] has formulated thirty guiding rules to help a supervisor motivate people to perform better (*Training,* March 1980). Below are his thirty rules* that synthesize the ideas of the leading writers in motivation theory.

1. Use appropriate methods of reinforcement. Appropriate reinforcement means:
    a. Rewards should always be contingent on performance.
    b. Don't give too much reinforcement; too much is almost as bad as none at all.
    c. Reinforcement is personal; what reinforces one person may not reinforce another.
    d. Dispense reinforcers as soon as possible after the desired performance occurs.

2. Eliminate unnecessary threats and punishments.
3. Make sure that accomplishment is adequately recognized.
4. Provide people with flexibility and choice.
5. Provide support when it is needed and make sure that employees don't hesitate to make use of it.
6. Provide employees with responsibility along with their accountability.

During the past three weeks have you received or given any recognition from those individuals listed below which met the following qualifications?

    . . . it was sincere
    . . . it was timely (soon after task)
    . . . it was a proper reward/recognition for task completed or performed

Check or Comment

	HAVE	HAVE NOT
I. Recognition Received		
A. Received from superiors		
B. Received from peers, colleagues		
C. Received from subordinates		
D. Received from elsewhere in the system		
E. Received from spouse, friends, relatives, neighbors		
II. Recognition Given		
A. Given to superiors		
B. Given to peers, colleagues		
C. Given to subordinates		
D. Given to someone else in the system		
E. Given to spouse, friends, relatives, neighbors		

FIGURE 2-4. Recognition.

7. Encourage employees to set their own goals.
8. Make sure that employees are aware of how their tasks relate to personal and organizational goals.
9. Clarify your expectations and make sure that employees understand them.
10. Provide an appropriate mix of extrinsic rewards and intrinsic satisfaction.
11. Design tasks and environments to be consistent with employee needs.
12. Individualize your supervision.
13. Provide immediate and relevant feedback that will help employees improve their performance in the future.
14. Recognize and help eliminate barriers to individual achievement.
15. Exhibit confidence in employees.
16. Increase the likelihood that employees will feel a sense of accomplishment.
17. Exhibit interest in and knowledge of each individual under your supervision.
18. Encourage individuals to participate in making decisions that affect them.
19. Establish a climate of trust and open communication.
20. Minimize the use of statutory powers.
21. Help individuals to see the integrity, significance, and relevance of their work in terms of organizational output.
22. Listen to and deal effectively with employee complaints.
23. Point out improvements in performance, no matter how small.
24. Demonstrate your own motivation through behavior and attitude.
25. Criticize behavior, not people.
26. Make sure that effort pays off in results.
27. Encourage employees to engage in novel and challenging activities.
28. Anxiety is fundamental to motivation, so don't eliminate it completely.
29. Don't believe that "liking" is always correlated with positive performance.
30. Be concerned with short-term and long-term motivation.

MOTIVATION AND THEORIES OF ORGANIZATION

Closely related to the topic of motivation is the topic of organization. The work of McGregor, the originator of the terms Theory X and Theory Y, is best known in this area. After we look at McGregor's work, we shall look briefly at additional theories in regard to supervision.

THEORY X

In a speech at the Massachusetts Institute of Technology in 1957 Douglas McGregor set forth the outlines of the two most well-known theories of human administration and organization (see his subsequent two books incorporating the speech, *The Human Side of Enterprise,*[2] 1960, and *Leadership and Motivation,*[3] 1966). McGregor sought to characterize what he saw as the classic, traditional type of organization and what modern social science suggested as a preferred type of organization. According to McGregor, three fundamental propositions characterize how traditional managers harness human energy to organizational needs and requirements (Theory X):

1. Management is responsible for acquiring and organizing the factors of production in order to achieve economic ends. These factors include land, people, money, materials, and equipment.

2. Management must direct the workers' efforts, motivate the workers (who do dislike work), coerce, threaten, and control them, and modify their behavior to fit the needs of the organization if objectives are to be met.

3. Management must intervene in the workers' efforts, otherwise workers would be passive, indolent, resistant to organizational objectives, and irresponsible. Workers prefer this mode of behavior by management since they wish to avoid being held responsible and have little ambition.

Several *additional* less explicit, yet widespread *assumptions* characterize traditional management.

4. People work as little as possible.
5. The average person dislikes responsibility and actually prefers to be led.
6. Workers care mainly about themselves, with little care for the needs of the organization which employs them.
7. People naturally resist change.
8. Workers are gullible, not very bright, and easily duped by unprincipled people.

Unfortunately, these propositions and assumptions do not constitute a mere foil for the modern Theory Y though they appear extreme and unacceptable to today's sensitive administrator. Many managers hold to these eight beliefs in one form or another and act on them. Indeed, the beliefs are valid in regard to some people some of the time. For example, there are times when certain people seek to avoid responsibility or seek to rest or be passive rather than work; people also are often reluctant to change. Although Theory X lacks appeal today and most educators reject it as their working theory, it is still impossible to deny its premises 100 percent in regard to organizations in general and in regard to schools in particular.

THEORY Y

For McGregor the findings of modern social science suggest a new, preferred theory of organizations. These findings suggest that for the maximization of management's efforts there is need for a new set of propositions to guide behavior. McGregor turns to Maslow's hierarchy of needs to begin his explanation of Theory Y. He accepts the five levels of need satisfaction and comments that management has now provided for the physiological and safety needs of the workers. Therefore, the burden for motivation now is at the social and esteem levels of the hierarchy, not only at home but very importantly *at work*. When management continues to focus on the two lowest levels of needs, it fails to be able to motivate workers because a need already satisfied no longer operates as a motivator.

Based on such reasoning and understanding, McGregor sets forth four basic propositions that characterize Theory Y:

1. Management is responsible for acquiring and organizing the factors of production in order to achieve economic ends. These factors include land, people, money, materials, and equipment.

2. People do *not naturally* dislike work; they are not naturally passive or resistant to the needs of the organization for which they work.

3. People have the natural capacity to accept and seek responsibility and to care for the needs of the organization. Since potential is already present, the responsibility of management is to make it possible for workers to be able to develop their natural capacities as they work toward organizational goals.

4. The essential task of management is to organize conditions, people, and things in such a way that workers can satisfy their personal needs as they direct their personal physical and mental efforts toward achieving the organization's goals.

In short, Theory Y directs management to exert leadership by organizing matters in a way that promotes self-control and self-direction on the part of the workers.

CONTINGENCY THEORY

As the field of organizational studies developed and advanced, empirical findings led to questions about the comprehensiveness of McGregor's Theory X and Theory Y. For example, some workers are not passive and some managers lack ambition. Morse and Lorsch[4] set forth their *Contingency Theory,* which goes beyond Theory Y in order to account for the new data. Contingency Theory leads managers to develop an organizational pattern so that the characteristics fit the task to be done. Four basic propositions characterize Contingency Theory:

1. Human beings, though differing in general regarding their motives and needs at a given time, are similar in that they all have a central need to be competent.

2. People satisfy their need to be competent in different ways as the competence need interacts with other powerful needs such as affiliation, independence, power, and freedom.

3. People can and will satisfy their need to be competent when there is a fit between task and organization.

4. People continue to be motivated by the need to be competent as one new and higher goal arises whenever a current goal is achieved.

With these four points in mind, the manager's task becomes one of fitting together the task, the people, and the organization so that people can satisfy their differing personal, psychological needs as well as the organizational needs. People are similar—they all have the need to be competent, which is a powerful and motivating need—and at the same time different—they differ in regard to personality, values, drives, esteem needs, and social/affiliation needs. The starting point is an analysis and understanding of the nature of the task and its demands on the people performing it. In this way, there is no one best way for all organizations and even for any particular organization since the fit changes as people and tasks change.

Contingency Theory asks, "What should the organization be like in light of the people and tasks involved?" "What is appropriate at this point so as to foster the satisfying of the competence need all people have in common?" No simple, single answer is available yet.

THEORY Z

With the growth of Japan as an advanced industrial giant during the 1960s and 1970s, more and more American businesspeople and professors of management became interested in the style of management associated with Japanese firms. Early on, observers recognized that Japanese managers manifested an approach to management that was not Theory X, Theory Y, or Contingency Theory. At about the same time, two books appeared on Japanese-style management, which focused attention on Theory Z. The term *Theory Z* was coined by William Ouchi[5] in his book, *Theory Z: How American Business Can Meet the Japanese Challenge* (1981). Although it doesn't use the explicit term Theory Z, the book by Richard Pascale and Anthony Athos,[6] *The Art of Japanese Management: Applications for American Executives* (1981) deals with that theory. (Indeed, Ouchi and Pascale at one time in the 1970s conducted research together as colleagues.)

The basic propositions that characterize Theory Z are:

1. Decision making is a participatory consensual process; people place their fate in the hands of others since they hold compatible goals.

2. Commitment to working together is essential; therefore, there is much need for energy devoted to developing interpersonal skills which are necessary for collective deciding.

3. While decision making is collective, the ultimate responsibility for decisions still rests with one person.

4. A holistic orientation governs relationships among people in the organization; people are concerned with other people as whole humans, not as one role to another role (for example, manager to worker; clerk to floor supervisor); relations tend to be informal in a holistic orientation.

5. Open communication, trust, involvement, and commitment are instrumental objectives; compliance is an inadequate reaction to organizational policy.

6. Egalitarianism, which implies discretion and autonomy without close supervision, is fostered because the foundation, which is mutual trust, exists.

7. Loyalty, cooperation, high expectations, and motivation result when trust, commitment, interdependence, involvement, and self-direction flourish.

Theory Z sounds ideal. According to the two Theory Z books, the American firms which have already transformed themselves to this latest style of organization are far more successful than their counterpart firms in similar fields. Theory Z firms demand much from their managers and their workers, and this virtual total commitment is one which Theory X and Theory Y and Contingency Theory organizations do not have or promote. Theory Z requires that organizations give deep concern and careful attention to their fundamental beliefs—their basic philosophy. The basic philosophy that is to be openly arrived at and clearly and widely distributed once it is formulated must serve as an ongoing guide to interpersonal relations as major decisions are made.

In short, Theory Z holds that organizational life is a life of interdependence, and managers must establish organizational conditions that promote effective interdependent action. (See Figure 2-5.)

Implications for Supervision

For someone who reads McGregor, or at least more than just a list of the key points of his Theory X and Theory Y, it is immediately obvious that there is an explicit connection between motivation theory and organization theory. McGregor as well as Morse, Lorsch, Ouchi, Pascale, and Athos are organizational theorists who are aware of the contribution of psychologists in helping us to understand why people do what they do. It is in this light that we must build on the work of the four "theories" in this section.

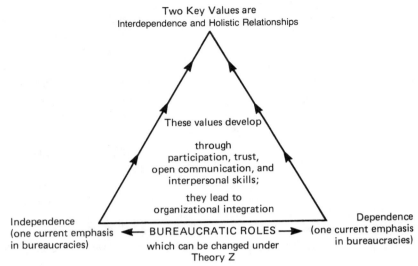

FIGURE 2-5. Values in Theory Z.

One basic point made by the three preferred theories of Theory Y, Contingency Theory, and Theory Z is that people have needs and the potential to satisfy those needs while at the same time satisfying the needs of the organization. This is a positive outlook as opposed to the essentially negative outlook of Theory X. According to the positive theories, you must keep in mind that if your teachers are not succeeding through their teaching to satisfy some of their needs but rather are passive and unwilling to work for the good of your school, you must look at what your school is like as you work with each teacher. You must accept that there is an interaction between the school's organization at that particular time and your teacher's negative behavior. All three of the positive theories emphasize this interaction. (See Figure 2-6 for a review of the interactional words characterizing these theories.) You must begin to see that the teacher's behavior is in some way the consequence of the school's organizational approach. This is similar to the point McGregor makes when discussing the disapproved behavior industrial workers manifest under Theory X organizations: the social scientist "is pretty sure that this behavior is *not* a consequence of man's inherent nature. It is a consequence rather of the nature of industrial organizations, of management philosophy, policy, and practice"[7] (speech, "The Human Side of Enterprise," 1957).

For example, let us suppose that Tom Smith, your eighth-grade science teacher, is the source of many discipline problems coming to your office and the reason for many complaints by parents. You can take the point of view suggested by Contingency Theory that Smith has a need to be competent but the fit between organization, competence in teaching, and Smith is not yet appropriate; that Smith is not happy or satisfied with his teaching; that Smith recognizes (and admits at least to himself) that a competent teacher is not the source of so much negative behavior even though he outwardly blames the situation on the students and their homes. You can work with Smith not on the symptoms but on the core of the problem—Smith's classroom behavior.

The key in working with Tom Smith is to build on his potential for and need to become a competent teacher. You can help him with the integration of lab experiments into study units on living cells or the earth's crust; you can help him establish alternative ways to group students for lab work and seat work; you can help him plan his lessons and units in order to improve the pacing of his teaching and the relevance of his material to that of other teachers in your overall eighth grade; you can help him to better understand

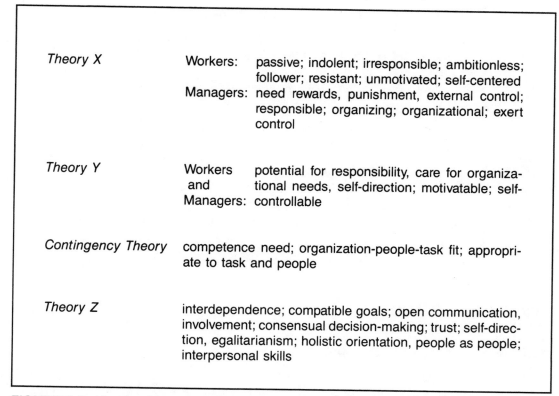

Theory X	Workers:	passive; indolent; irresponsible; ambitionless; follower; resistant; unmotivated; self-centered
	Managers:	need rewards, punishment, external control; responsible; organizing; organizational; exert control
Theory Y	Workers and Managers:	potential for responsibility, care for organizational needs, self-direction; motivatable; self-controllable
Contingency Theory		competence need; organization-people-task fit; appropriate to task and people
Theory Z		interdependence; compatible goals; open communication, involvement; consensual decision-making; trust; self-direction, egalitarianism; holistic orientation, people as people; interpersonal skills

FIGURE 2-6. Key words and terms on human administration and organization.

today's young teenager by talking over case studies with him and perhaps including another teacher or counselor who knows the students under study; and you can speak with Smith about how you can modify his assignments or schedule or your behavior in order to help him better work for the achievement of school goals. You can work with a positive perspective as you seek to satisfy Smith's potential as a whole human being and need for competence as a teacher. At the same time you can promote the school's goal of orderly learning by the students.

Another example: As a person in a leadership position and therefore at least partially responsible for the organizational approach currently used by your school, you can begin to examine that approach privately and with your fellow supervisors. You can ask: To what extent are you operating under Theory X? Theory Y? Contingency Theory? Theory Z? What really are the consequences—effects on teachers and supervisors—of your organizational approach? Which organizational approach is the preferred one for your school? What steps can you take to adjust your school to your preferred approach? How can you make your approach more positive in its effects on your entire staff, including yourself?

In his book on Theory Z, Ouchi lists thirteen steps for an American business to take if it wishes to move toward that theory. Keep in mind that Ouchi focuses on American, not Japanese companies, which have adopted Theory Z rather than the typical American organizational approach. These companies among the Fortune 500 include Hewlett-Packard, Intel, Dayton-Hudson, Rockwell International, and Eli Lilly Co. Perhaps you can utilize some of his steps to bring about change whether you wish to move toward Theory Y, Contingency Theory, Theory Z, or *Your Theory*.

The thirteen steps can be found at the top of page 46.

Step   1.   Understand the Type Z organization and your role

Step   2.   Audit your company's philosophy*

Step   3.   Define the desired management philosophy and involve the company leader

Step   4.   Implement the philosophy by creating both structures and incentives

Step   5.   Develop interpersonal skills

Step   6.   Test yourself and the system

Step   7.   Involve the union

Step   8.   Stabilize employment

Step   9.   Decide on a system for slow evaluation and promotion

Step 10.   Broaden career path development

Step 11.   Prepare for implementation at the first level

Step 12.   Seek out areas to implement participation

Step 13.   Permit the development of holistic relationships

NEGOTIATING CHANGE

The Principled Negotiation Approach

For some people negotiation is a dirty word; it raises images of unpleasant shouting matches between business magnates and radical labor unions officials. This is unfortunate. The field of negotiations, which includes, among others, labor negotiations, international negotiations between countries over war or border disputes, and legal negotiations over automobile accidents and divorces, has advanced way beyond the state of bilateral screaming. The ideas for improved negotiation found fruition in the work of the Harvard Negotiation Project under the directorship of Roger Fisher of the Harvard Law School.

Fisher, an international negotiator, professor of law, and co-author of the book *Getting to Yes: Negotiating Agreement Without Giving In,*[8] sets forth the characteristics of what he calls Principled Negotiation, or negotiation on the merits. This approach to negotiation is an alternative to the common mistake people make in negotiating, which is to focus on positions. Such a focus leads people to lock into their positions, to defend them, and yield unwise solutions. What is more, such a focus is inefficient in that negotiating then takes the form of bargaining over positions and slowly yielding concessions from an initial extreme position.

Before offering the four basic points of Principled Negotiation it is necessary to state *six preliminary items* explicitly:

1. Negotiation is *natural in life.*
2. Negotiation *takes place all the time* and whenever two parties must come to an agreement over some conflict, however minor.
3. Negotiations are judged by *three criteria:* a *wise agreement* should result (see immediately below); negotiations should be *efficient;* and negotiations should *improve or at least not damage the relationship* between the negotiating parties.

*The philosophies of the five Z companies mentioned above are included in an appendix of *Theory Z* by Ouchi.

4. A wise agreement has four characteristics: it meets the *legitimate interests* of each party to the extent possible; it *resolves* the existing conflict *fairly;* it is *durable;* and it takes *community interests* into account.
5. You can learn to negotiate successfully.
6. You can utilize principled negotiation in all aspects of your life, private and professional.

The strong implication of these six items is that as a supervisor working with teachers on the improvement of teaching and school conditions you can certainly and naturally employ the approach to negotiating developed by Fisher at the Harvard Negotiating Project. You can use it without feeling guilty or manipulative because there are "no tricks and no posturing." It is a straightforward and forthright approach that encourages all sides negotiating to act similarly.

Principled Negotiation consists of four basic points:

1. *People:* Separate the people from the problem
2. *Interests:* Focus on interests, not positions
3. *Options:* Generate a variety of possibilities before deciding what to do
4. *Criteria:* Insist that the result be based on some objective standard

Here is a workable, usable, sophisticated, and elegant alternative to the common approach to negotiating. The four points call your attention to the four essential elements of negotiation and also offer a capsule guide on how you should deal with that element. Obviously, each point deserves extensive elaboration; hence, Fisher wrote his book. Nevertheless, it is possible to comment on each briefly in regard to supervision in order to give an understanding of this improved approach to negotiating.

PEOPLE

As you negotiate with a teacher, keep in mind that the teacher is not your enemy. The teacher and you must be on the same side, two people examining a problem. It must not become a negotiation session in which you attack the teacher who retreats to a defensive, dug-in position to ward off any further emotional assault. Keep in mind that the teacher is a person who will react to defend himself if you attack him as a person rather than examine the problem situation. To keep yourself on target, solicit the teacher's perceptions of the problem you are discussing so that you will know his vantage point. Strive for open communications as you speak clearly, speak about your perceptions and emotions, and listen actively to the teacher's comments.

INTERESTS

As you negotiate with a teacher, do not lock yourself into a position or encourage the teacher to lock into a position. Neither of you might be willing to yield because you each might be too emotionally attached to your positions. You each may be afraid to lose face. Rather, look behind the problem to the interests of the teacher. Ask yourself, "What is it that this teacher wants deep down that motivates her?" "What interests do we have in common?" "What basic needs do the teacher's suggestions reveal?" As you seek answers to these questions you should set forth your own interests forthrightly so that you can focus on what solution can be reached rather than on whom to put blame for the problem.

OPTIONS

As you negotiate with a teacher, seek out a set of possible options that both of you can accept. This will require that you spend some time looking over your observation records and reports *before* even meeting with the teacher. You need to avoid judging these options and deciding on any given one before talking with the teacher; you need to seek a set of options in order to give choice and room for creative arranging; you need to believe that the problem is not the teacher's alone, not yours alone, but both of yours. With a set of options for both of you to begin with, you can more readily come up with a solution that will offer mutual gain to the teacher and you.

CRITERIA

As you negotiate with a teacher strive to involve fair and objective criteria which will not favor the teacher or you. The utilization of fair and objective criteria will take the burden off both of you to protect your statements and former ideas. For example, in regard to classroom interaction you can use such objective (or reasonably objective) criteria as: the number of explanation questions asked; the amount of positive reinforcement statements made by the teacher; and the number of times the teacher worked with a student at his or her desk during practice problem solving. Some quick brainstorming with the teacher will yield several ways to look objectively at the agreed-upon change. Such objective criteria will reinforce basic point number one by separating the teacher from the problem and offering you some concrete solutions to look at *with the teacher.*

Using the Supervision Window as a Prelude to Negotiation

The Supervision Window is the adaptation of the well-known Johari Window for purposes of supervising teachers. The Supervision Window is a two-by-two figure to show you that, for the teacher, there is known and unknown information, feelings, skills, and beliefs. (See Figure 2-7.)

Figure 2-7 shows the Supervision Window in its theoretical position—that is, all the quadrants are of equal size. This position does not suggest that what is shared between the teacher and you as supervisor (public quadrant) is the same size or amount as what is hidden from you by the teacher (private quadrant). Rather, the theoretical position is neutral and serves only to alert you to the existence of four interrelated sets of information, feelings, skills, values, and interests. As an initial position only, the quadrants are of equal dimensions.

As you prepare for your negotiation session with the teacher, consider the following questions: What type of things, especially interests, are shared by you in the *public* quadrant? What types of information do you have about the teacher but about which the teacher is *blind?* Are there problems that you believe exist but that the teacher doesn't know about or won't admit? (Blind quadrant.) How and under what conditions can you communicate this information to the teacher? What types of information, feelings, values, interests, and skills does the teacher *privately* have that you would like to know about? What would lead the teacher to make these things *public* by revealing them to you? How can we shrink the unperceived quadrant? What are, at this point, the relative sizes of the four quadrants?

	Known to Teacher	**Unknown to Teacher**
Known to Supervisor	1 PUBLIC	2 BLIND
Unknown to Supervisor	3 PRIVATE	4 UNPERCEIVED

The labels of the quadrants are from the teacher's perspective

FIGURE 2-7. The Supervision Window.

The use of the Supervision Window here is mainly to spur you to think about commonly shared things and uncommonly shared things. It is to serve as a way to avoid focusing on the teacher because you highlight information, interests, problems, values, skills, and feelings. This is the essence of basic points 1 and 2 of principled negotiation (page 47) and therefore a good prelude to your negotiation efforts themselves.

The "Supervisor's Guide for Facilitating Teacher Change"

To build on the concept and basic points of principled negotiation, you need a concrete way to begin the process of change. It is always tempting simply to order the teacher to change, but we know from theory—motivation theory, organization theory, negotiation theory—that you only can order compliance. You cannot order commitment, and most supervision issues involve commitment rather than mere compliance with rules of the school. It is for this reason that most of the time you must resist temptation to say to the teacher, in effect, "Change or else!" Compliance generally fades once surveillance ends and you don't have the time for eternal surveillance. You need teacher commitment—internalization—for long-term change.

The "Supervisor's Guide for Facilitating Teacher Change" (Figure 2-8) provides you with a framework for working with the teacher according to the principled negotiation approach. First, notice that the word used is *change* or *development,* rather than *improvement.* This is so because for many teachers, especially older and tenured teachers who see themselves as having "arrived," the word *improvement* has a negative connotation. It means that they are bad, inadequate, or weak as teachers, otherwise they would not need to "improve." It is unfortunate that some people take such a narrow perspective on teaching.

Supervisor _____ Date _____

Teacher _____

Aspect of Teaching under Consideration _____

1. *Current* question for the teacher as he/she asks it: "Should I change the way I teach?

   A.* If I do change, the following results are likely now:

      1. _____
      2. _____
      3. _____

   B.* If I do not change, the following results are likely now:

      1. _____
      2. _____
      3. _____

   *RESULTS OF <u>NOT CHANGING</u> NOW OUTWEIGH RESULTS OF CHANGING.

2. *Future* question for the teacher as he/she will ask it: "Should I change the way I teach?"

   A.** If I do change, the following results are likely:

      1. _____
      2. _____
      3. _____

   B.** If I do not change, the following results are likely:

      1. _____
      2. _____
      3. _____
         _____
         _____

   **RESULTS OF <u>CHANGING</u> OUTWEIGH RESULTS OF NOT CHANGING IN THE FUTURE.

3. To help the teacher arrive at a point in the future where he/she will decide to change because the results of changing outweigh the results of not changing, we (the teacher and I) must deal with what is important to both of us.

   A. The teacher and/or I should _____
   B. The teacher and/or I should _____
   C. The teacher and/or I should _____
   D. The teacher and/or I should _____

FIGURE 2-8. Supervisor's guide for facilitating teacher change.

Supervisor *Chris Johnson*   Date *Oct. 31*

Teacher *Pat Jones*

Aspect of Teaching under Consideration *Classroom Interaction with Students*

1. *Current* question for the teacher as he/she asks it: "Should I change the way I teach?

    A.* If I do change, the following results are likely now:

    1. *I'll feel uncomfortable conducting a class discussion*

    2. *I'll probably have trouble monitoring my behavior.*

    3. _____

    B.* If I do not change, the following results are likely now:

    1. *I can continue the status-quo – not rock the boat*

    2. *I won't have to worry about the boys upsetting the class.*

    3. *I won't have to spend time really preparing new lesson plans.*

    *RESULTS OF <u>NOT CHANGING</u> NOW OUTWEIGH RESULTS OF CHANGING.

2. *Future* question for the teacher as he/she will ask it: "Should I change the way I teach?"

    A.** If I do change, the following results are likely:

    1. *Chris will feel quite positive towards me*

    2. *I'll feel good that I'll still be able to learn new skills*

    3. *Some of the hidden pressures I feel during class will disappear*

    B.** If I do not change, the following results are likely:

    1. *Chris might get on my back and keep close tabs on me*

    2. *I'll feel that I'm the old dog that can't learn new tricks*

    3. *One of these days soon the kids or the parents or both will complain and really get after me about how they disapprove of all these fact-fact-fact questions.*

    **RESULTS OF <u>CHANGING</u> OUTWEIGH RESULTS OF NOT CHANGING IN THE FUTURE.

3. To help the teacher arrive at a point in the future where he/she will decide to change because the results of changing outweigh the results of not changing, we (the teacher and I) must deal with what is important to both of us.

    A. The teacher and/or(I) should *find a model for Pat to observe and begin to emulate*

    B. The teacher and/or(I) should *loan Pat my material on techniques of questioning from the Rutgers seminar*

    C. The teacher and/or(I) should *spread the word that Pat is involved in a new project so everyone will give recognition to Pat*

    D. The (teacher and/or(I) should *talk together and start working out a strategy*

FIGURE 2-9. Completed sample of supervisor's guide for facilitating teacher change.

Teaching is a complex profession and continually requires everyone to *develop* further. It is unfortunate but true that the word *improvement* causes some people to resist changing and that it turns out to be a counterproductive word.

Second, after you decide—based on previous conversations and observations—what aspect of teaching you want to consider, you should begin to think about the present. The Supervisor's Guide directs you to consider the advantages and disadvantages of changing (that is, developing) from the teacher's viewpoint initially. This is important, because it leads you to recognize and understand the teacher's interests. You need to consider and write out these interests carefully even though the teacher most likely has not and will not formally do this. You, as supervisor, need to recognize the teacher's interests so you can lead the negotiation efforts.

Keep in mind here that the potential results of *not changing* now outweigh the potential results of changing. We know this because the teacher is not changing now; the teacher needs some help in further development, as we all probably do; sufficient motivation to change is missing. Also, the teacher, as does everyone, has multiple interests and not one single interest. Therefore, you need not worry that you are not precise at this point in recognizing the teacher's interests. Rather, the objective here is to begin to understand the issue from the teacher's perspective.

Third, you need to move on to the future. You must move to the point at which the teacher will decide—alone or with you—to change. Here the potential results of changing will outweigh the potential results of not changing. Again, this is from the teacher's viewpoint, and your forecast need not be precise. The objective in this section is to lead you to consider the future, to consider what in the future will convince the teacher to change.

Finally, you must consider what action you should take in order to guide the teacher from the present reality to the future forecast. You probably will take some action alone, and this is the only action you can ever control; you probably will take some action together with the teacher; and you will try to lead the teacher, through your talks, to take some action alone. All three types of action are aimed at leading the teacher to the point at which change will be the most likely outcome of your efforts. You must focus on *action* that will *result* in change.

Figure 2-9 shows a completed form of the "Supervisor's Guide for Facilitating Teacher Change." Here, Chris Johnson uses the guide to work with Pat Jones according to the observations and reports presented in Chapters 3, 5, 6, and 8. Johnson focuses on classroom interaction and realizes that Jones will probably feel very uncomfortable conducting a class discussion in which there is not strong teacher control. Jones is accustomed to knowing just what the students will say in response to the questions asked. In a discussion, such tight control is not possible, and for someone not yet skilled in leading a discussion this can easily lead to fear and discomfort.

On the other hand, Johnson recognizes that Jones has the potential to change and wants to feel competent, recognized, and approved. With these recognitions of Jones's basic needs, Johnson writes out four actions that should be taken. By circling "I" in the first three, Johnson makes it clear that the burden is not on Jones to act. Rather, Johnson must take the initiative and clearly indicates so. Johnson wants to lead Jones to change rather than to force (as if it were possible, anyhow) change. Johnson responds to the significant question, "What should I do alone or do with the teacher in order to lead him or her to the future point where there will be motivation and willingness to change?" In short, "How can I help bring about the future I prefer?"

CREATING A TEACHER DEVELOPMENT PLAN

As mentioned in the preceding sections, it is necessary to think about long-term teacher motivation as well as short-term motivation. The "quick fix" is just not enough because as a supervisor you work with a teacher for a year, or three, or ten, or more. You must not avoid guiding a teacher in the hope that a potential problem will go away. There is not the mobility among teachers that existed two decades ago. As a result, the teacher who is in your school today will probably be there next year, too. Moreover, it isn't worth betting against the odds that the teacher will leave since a loss of your bet would leave the students and you with an unmotivated teacher who needs more help than before.

Once again, notice the absence of the word *improve* in regard to this plan. Just as in the previous section with the Supervisor's Guide for Facilitating Teacher Change, the word *improve* is absent here. Instead, the words *develop, grow, change,* and *progress* appear because they do not seem to have negative connotations with teachers. If for some reason these words have negative associations for your teachers, change the words you use. Use the words that have positive meanings for your teachers and avoid the others. The words are important; the metaphors do have their effect.

Characteristics of a Teacher Development Plan

Several key elements are necessary to make the development plan potentially effective (there never is a guarantee of success). In New Jersey, for example, the key characteristics are mandated by law. The Teacher Development Plan is/has:

1. In writing and signed by teacher and supervisor.
2. Filed in school records with a copy given to the teacher.
3. Explicit indication of deficiencies and/or areas of concern to be *developed* for professional growth.
4. Actions teacher is to take.
5. Actions supervisor and/or school is to take.
6. Timelines for implementation and review.
7. Measures to be used in assessing the teacher's development and the effectiveness of the plan. That is, procedures for assessing the teacher's progress toward meeting the objectives of the development plan.

Considerations and Actions

Simply providing for the foregoing seven characteristics is not enough. You need to consider five things, at least. First and foremost, since you are interested in long-term, effective development, you should create the plan *cooperatively* with the teacher. (In New Jersey, where such plans are required by law and required to be created by the supervisor and the teacher, a teacher recently won a grievance case, claiming that his supervisor never consulted with him about the plan handed to him to implement.) Cooperation in creating the plan is essential in order for you to be congruent with motivation theory, organization theories of Theory Y, Contingency Theory, and Theory Z, and principled negotiation. In short, you should be congruent with what is universally accepted in education as sound supervision. If you want the teacher to have a stake in the plan so that you can get beyond external compliance, you must create the plan cooperatively with your teacher. Otherwise, the development plan will be an incongruent, negative model for your teacher.

Second, you must consider the supervision approach that you have been employing with the particular teacher. The development must be consistent with the ongoing approach being used. If, for example, you have been mainly nondirective with Nancy Hartwick, a plan in which you take responsibility for 90 percent of the action seems out of balance. It would appear that with Nancy Hartwick, who has functioned well relatively independently of you along with two colleagues of hers, a directive approach is inappropriate. This leads to the next point.

Third, you must consider your teacher. For example, if you are working with a teacher who is new to your school, who is a recent graduate of a teacher preparation program, and who is nontenured, the timelines you seek to establish should take into consideration that you must reach a personal decision regarding tenure within a year or so. You need to arrange for more frequent reviews and conferences so that you have the necessary data to make rational recommendations about rehiring and recommending for tenure. On the other hand, if you are working with a ten-year veteran of your school whom you know well, you can arrange for a longer timeline and perhaps more informal checks along the way. In either case, the development plan can be fairly simple rather than complicated because the real value is in getting the teacher moving forward. There will be a natural spillover onto other aspects of the teacher's job, and this will create a synergistic effect.

Fourth, the key to the development plan is the action you both will establish as appropriate for that teacher to reach the agreed-upon objectives of the plan. The action should be positive action—that is, specific things you both will do. Emphasize the positive rather than the negative things you will stop or avoid doing. The action should be specific, concrete, and delineated in regard to what the teacher will do, what you will do, what you two will do together, and what the school will do to implement the plan. In short, you should specify who will take what action so that the teacher can develop.

The following *partial* list of fifteen "actions for professional growth" was generated through brainstorming when a group of supervisors convened for a morning "update" session in one school district:

1. Join or form a team for planning and teaching your subject.
2. Visit other faculty members to observe demonstration lessons.
3. Tape record three lessons and compare them, listening for qualities x and y (for example, questions, classroom climate, teacher movement, pattern of student participation).
4. Take a college course in subject field or guidance procedures or pedagogy.
5. Develop a new course or unit that integrates two themes.
6. Visit two other school districts and compare them with ours for creating classroom innovations.
7. Lead an in-service workshop for teacher and/or student teachers.
8. Be a demonstration teacher for visitors from other school districts and debrief with them regarding our school's approach to teaching.
9. Develop a handbook of school activities for mainstreamed special education students.

10. Prepare a series of assembly programs in conjunction with Community Resource People.

11. Conduct some action-research on achievement of the regular and gifted students in your classroom.

12. Apply for a State Education Department grant for research on our local history.

13. Develop an annotated reading list for your students regarding your environmental protection project and waste hazards.

14. Design a series of role-playing scenarios on communication problems between student and student, student and parent, and student and teacher; utilize these and then prepare a brief guidebook for other teachers on how they can use these scenarios.

15. Prepare a series of four half-hour video cassettes on classroom innovations for distribution by the regional A-V centers; you can lecture and/or demonstrate.

Many more items may be added to this list. By referring to it, you can locate some actions the teacher can take as a step toward continued professional development. You can use one or several items in combination to help the teacher move forward. Such motion will serve to motivate the teacher, and the accompanying by-products will in all likelihood lead to progress in and out of the classroom.

Fifth, once you have agreed on a plan for teacher development there remains one more critical part—review. You must consider how and when you will review the actions you both take. You will need to meet with the teacher to talk over the progress made according to the timelines you have set. In your conference to create the development plan and your subsequent review conferences you can employ the concept of educational "bridging." The term *bridging* is set forth by Gary Fenstermacher to mean "what one does when bringing completed or near-completed educational research to bear on educational practice."[9]

You can use *rules* to bridge education research and practice (for example, if the teacher maintains a high level of academically relevant interaction with the student, the student is likely to show a gain in achievement of a basic skill); or you can use *research evidence* to bridge (for example, when you began in September you averaged ninety questions per class session and now three months later you average but thirty-five; at the same time the number of student questions has tripled, and the telephone calls from parents have virtually disappeared; that defeats your initial skepticism about potential effect); or you can use *schemas* to bridge (for example, you can use a schema—a concept or structure which provides a way to "see" a phenomenon and a way to think about it—which will help the teacher to organize his thoughts about types of teaching strategies; you can suggest that there are three main types of teaching strategies which he can think about and consider using—presenting, enabling, and exemplifying; these three types are named for the principal activity of the teacher when interacting with students; or you can use the Supervision Window to help the teacher organize his thoughts about his interaction with other people).

In other words, your role in the conferences you have with the teacher in creating the development plan and in reviewing it will be to provide some "bridging" for the teachers. You probably will need to use rules, evidence, and schemas rather than rely on only one approach. Therefore, as you prepare for your conferences, you will need to begin to think about your role in providing bridges so that you can lead the teacher to further development.

Suggestions for Your Conference: Some Dos and Don'ts

The conference you have in which you create the development plan with your teacher is a significant one because you are thinking about the long run. What you establish with the teacher will set off activity for a semester or an entire year. It is for this reason that you must carefully prepare for and approach the meeting with the teacher. A list of suggestions follows. (See Chapters 4, 5, and 6 for further details on conferring.)

1. Preparation.
   a. Schedule your conference with the teacher for a time of day when you'll both be in a good mood and be relaxed. For example, not at 3:00 P.M. on Friday when most people are eager to go home for the weekend.
   b. Review previous observation and evaluation reports and prepare some initial remarks and "bridging" ideas.
   c. Prepare some recommendations of specific actions the teacher and you can do.
   d. Especially if you foresee some trouble or tough resistance from a particular teacher, role play at home with your family or at school with a trusted supervisor-colleague.
   e. Set up a warm environment in the conference room; provide snack and/or coffee-tea-cocoa; provide a clear conference table, not a desk.
   f. Ask the teacher to prepare by reading previous written reports.
   g. Ask the teacher to think about some possible avenues for further development as a professional educator.
   h. Review the material on motivation theory, organization theory, and principled negotiation.
2. Conferring
   a. "Psych" yourself for success by thinking of the potential benefits you will reap when the teacher makes good progress.
   b. State the purpose of the conference concisely and briefly when you begin.
   c. Try to avoid confrontation; use the four basic points of principled negotiation to lead you to success.
   d. Refer to previous written reports as you move along; keep on track by talking about relevant points in the reports.
   e. Remember that you are engaged in a joint endeavor with the teacher.
   f. Seek suggestions from the teacher and suggest modifications in order to fit them into an overall cohesive plan.
   g. Treat information and opinions from the teacher as confidential matter.
3. Possible Nonagreement
   a. Accept possible nonagreement as normal but temporary.
   b. Seek creative new suggestions through brainstorming.
   c. Take a break—an hour or even a day—if you have come to an apparent impasse.
   d. Involve a third person, if things are going very poorly, to insert a fresh look at matters.
   e. Keep your focus on a solution by looking forward rather than backward in terms of who or what is to blame for the temporary impasse.

4. Overall Don'ts
   a. Don't conceive of the development plan as a punitive device; don't suggest actions in order to "get even" with the teacher.
   b. Don't think of the teacher as an adversary; don't assume an adversarial position toward the teacher.
   c. Don't flaunt your power; think "cooperation."
   d. Don't talk too much; don't let your talking silence the teacher.
   e. Don't try to overwhelm the teacher with many and complicated actions for him to take; make progress and success possible; keep your eye on the long-term development of the teacher.
   f. Don't paint yourself into a corner or push the teacher into a corner where there is no face-saving way to get out.
   g. Don't arrange the room and furniture (the "turf") to work against the teacher. For example, don't sit behind a wide desk as it will serve as a barrier between the teacher and you.
   h. Don't complicate or worsen matters by expressing blame to the teacher for slow progress toward mutual agreement.

Illustrative Teacher Development Plans

Figures 2-10 and 2-11 present two teacher development plans from the same school district. Both follow the same form and use the same opening sentence stem: "We agree that as a way of continuing to grow professionally." According to the supervisors who negotiated these plans, this sentence stem appears in order to show specifically the double emphasis on mutuality and positive "professional growth" rather than emphasize the negative term "correction of deficiencies."

Neither of the two plans is complicated. In Figure 2-10, the science teacher will concentrate on current reports about school reform. He will read the reports and discuss them with his supervisor. The reading teacher featured in Figure 2-11 will do three related tasks—analyze tape recordings, discuss the results with the supervisor, and then report on the entire experience to her peers at a workshop at the end of the first semester. Both teachers, it is clear, will be doing some specific things alone and some things with the supervisor with definite timelines established for all concerned. It would be easy for the teachers and the supervisors to expand and embellish the plans, but obviously each person is satisfied with what is shown. Probably, each person is satisfied that the uncomplicated development will serve the purpose of long-term motivation and teacher growth.

Also, there is no evidence from the two plans themselves—nor should there necessarily be explicit evidence—why the teachers and supervisors chose to focus on keeping abreast of current literature on the one hand and analyzing classroom interaction on the other hand. The former concerns broad educational matters while the latter concerns the classroom interaction of that particular teacher. Nevertheless, both supervisors, we may infer, believe that these two teachers can develop further in these ways.

The two supervisors have agreed to some common activities with their teachers. One will meet several times to discuss the readings by the science teacher, and the other will meet with the reading teacher to discuss her analyses of the tape recording and to plan the workshop session. In both cases, the activities with the supervisor serve several

Washburn School District

PROFESSIONAL DEVELOPMENT PLAN FOR 19____/19____ (year)

Describe the action(s) planned to continue professional growth and/or correct deficiencies, including responsibilities of district and teaching staff member.

We agree that as a way of continuing to grow professionally, Mr. Kramer will keep abreast of the current developments, trends, and research related to his subject area through the reading of related professional literature. Specifically included are three books: Goodlad's *A Place Called School;* National Science Board's report *Educating Americans for the 21st Century;* and *A Nation at Risk* by the President's Commission. We will meet in six weeks to begin discussion of Goodlad's book and then set a time to talk over each of the other two, to be no later than the end of May. Assessment of growth will be mutually decided.

Teacher's Signature	Date	Supervisor's Signature	Date

FIGURE 2-10. Example of a teacher development plan for a junior high school science teacher.

purposes simultaneously—to give support, to show interest, and to keep track of the teacher's progress as the semester moves ahead.

Perhaps the key message of both development plans is their tone. There is a tone of cooperation with an emphasis on assistance without inferiority. The plans do not convey a tone that the teachers are being reprimanded or penalized. There is a sense of seriousness toward "continuing" development as a part of professional life in education. This tone is congruent with long-term teacher motivation for the betterment of our schools.

Washburn School District

PROFESSIONAL DEVELOPMENT PLAN FOR 19____/19____ (year)

Describe the action(s) planned to continue professional growth and/or correct deficiencies, including responsibilities of district and teaching staff member.

We agree that as a way of continuing to grow professionally, Ms. Wells will tape record a series of five classroom lessons, one every three weeks beginning September 12. She will analyze them on her own regarding classroom interaction and thinking skills. We will discuss each one before the next taping and decide what to look for in the next tape. The objective is to become more aware of classroom events, and in particular participation by boys. Ms. Wells will report on her experience at the annual district in-service workshop in January. We'll plan her report together. Self-assessment will be used here.

_____ _____   _____ _____
Teacher's Signature   Date   Supervisor's Signature   Date

FIGURE 2-11. Example of a teacher development plan for an elementary school reading teacher.

Another action plan appears in Figures 2-12 and 2-13. The supervisor and teacher together have filled out Worksheet A (Figure 2-12) in order to determine the needs of the teacher. Then in Worksheet B (Figure 2-13) the teacher suggests her own action plan for Indicator 708, which falls under the major area of Planning/Managing/Organizing, as indicated on Worksheet A. Notice that this action plan states the objective to be reached, four specific activities that will lead to the achievement of that objective, and some timelines to follow.

| School Year: 19XX-XX | **WORKSHEET A DETERMINING NEEDS** | Copy 1–Evaluatee Copy 2–Evaluator Copy 3–Supervisor |

Full time __X__   Part Time _____

Evaluatee __Gail McGuire__   School/Office __Lyndhurst Elementary__

Evaluator __Betty Alexander__   Position _____Principal_____

Supervisor __Peter Evans__   Position __Elementary Supervisor__

DIRECTIONS: This is a two-part worksheet. Worksheet A is to enable the evaluatee and evaluator to identify and agree upon needs of the former. Worksheet B is the space in which to write an objective and action plan for a particular need. On Worksheet A, the evaluatee lists the numbers of indicators, under each major area, which he/she feels represents a need. Do this in triplicate, with copies routed as indicated above. Evaluator and supervisor review the evaluatee's lists so that when evaluatee and evaluator confer (step 3), the two will be able to reach consensus as to the needs. The supervisor may wish to attend the conference if he/she wishes to recommend certain areas of need. Otherwise, the supervisor may communicate reactions to the evaluator and he/she will communicate them to the evaluatee. Concurrence can be indicated by circling the number of the indicator and by signing and dating Worksheet A.

MAJOR AREAS OF RESPONSIBILITY	For Evaluatee	For Evaluator	For Supervisor
100-Humanizing Instruction	102		
200-Providing for Individual Differences	202	201	
300-Using Materials and Resources		301	
400-Organizing Learning Activities	404	404	
500-Providing Favorable Psych. Environment	502	501	
600-Evaluating Student Progress	605	605	
700-Planning/Managing/Organizing		708	
800-Ethics/Attributes/Growth/Responsibilities			

Signatures:

Evaluatee _____   Date _____

Evaluator _____   Date _____

Used with permission of the Montgomery Country (Virginia) Public School System. Taken from Cooperative Improvement Evaluation Program.

FIGURE 2-12. Action plan: determining needs.

School Year: 19XX-XX	WORKSHEET B OBJECTIVE/ACTION PLAN	Copy 1–Evaluatee Copy 2–Evaluator Copy 3–Supervisor

Full time   X   Part Time _____

Evaluatee   Gail McGuire   School/Office   Lyndhurst Elementary

Evaluator   Betty Alexander   Position   Principal

Supervisor   Peter Evans   Position   Elementary Supervisor

DIRECTIONS: After agreement has been reached by the evaluatee and the evaluator on the indicators, the former will develop an objective and action plan for each need, using the following format. (Use a separate page for each objective and action plan.)

OBJECTIVE: (what/outcome/measurement)   Indicator #   708

Will make weekly lesson plans so that both aide and substitute teacher will be able to carry on class in my absence and will place plans in agreed-on place available to both. Achievement of this objective will be judged by 100% compliance as judged by principal.

ACTION PLAN (activities to achieve above objective)	Completion Date	
	Estimated	**Actual**
1. Will plan coming week's lessons.	mid-week	
2. File plans in agreed-upon place.	Friday/weekly	
3. Will check with aide as to adequacy of plans.	weekly	
4. Will check with substitute teacher, following absence, to ascertain how adequate the plans were.	following absence	

Signature:

Evaluatee _____   Date _____

Used with permission of the Montgomery County (Virginia) Public School System. Taken from Cooperative Improvement Evaluation Program.

FIGURE 2-13. Action plan: objective/action plan.

The performance criteria that follow describe the general duties and responsibilities of teachers. In those instances where specialized duties are performed, it may be useful to supplement the criteria with job descriptions. The major areas and indicators under each are numbered to facilitate the completion of the evaluation steps.

100 HUMANIZING INSTRUCTION
    101 Is aware of academic strengths and weaknesses of each child.
    102 Is aware of the home and community environments of each child.
    103 Appreciates each child as an individual of worth.
    104 Helps all children to recognize their potential, develop their abilities, and assume responsibility as members of the group.
    105 Respects each child as an individual.
    106 Respects the values of cultural groups in the community.
    107 Recognizes the aspirations of each child.
    108 Accepts divergent views and opinions of children.
    109 Manifests a pleasant attitude and responsive reactions toward children.
    110 Encourages active participation of all members of the class.
    111 Other (specify)
    112 Other (specify)

200 PROVIDING FOR INDIVIDUAL DIFFERENCES IN THE CLASSROOM
    201 Provides different achievement standards for individuals with varying abilities and past achievements.
    202 Provides different subject matter, materials, and learning experiences.
    203 Provides opportunities for pupils to work independently on meaningful and relevant tasks.
    204 Enables pupils to experience success.
    205 Counsels pupils as individuals and in groups.
    206 Other (specify)
    207 Other (specify)

300 MAKING USE OF APPROVED AND AVAILABLE INSTRUCTIONAL MATERIALS AND RESOURCES
    301 Follows the approved curriculum.
    302 Uses supplemental materials such as library books, reference materials, newspapers, magazines, etc.
    303 Utilizes audio-visual media.
    304 Uses demonstrations, dramatizations, and other classroom activities.
    305 Conducts field trips in conjunction with course objectives.
    306 Draws upon resource persons and school-related youth organizations.
    307 Uses individual and group projects in and out of school.
    308. Uses physical school environment to support learning activities.
    309 Uses initiative in providing instructional materials.
    310 Other (specify)
    311 Other (specify)

400 ORGANIZING LEARNING ACTIVITIES TO ACHIEVE SPECIFIC OBJECTIVES
    401 Develops needed skills.
    402 Understands specific concepts about learning process.

FIGURE 2-14. Performance criteria for teachers.

403 Guides learner in solving meaningful problems.

404 Formulates both short-and long-range goals and objectives.

405 Develops wholesome attitudes.

406 Prepares and presents productive learning activities.

407 Uses questioning techniques that focus on higher cognitive processes as well as encouraging comprehension and retention.

408 Other (specify)

409 Other (specify)

500 PROVIDING FAVORABLE PSYCHOLOGICAL ENVIRONMENT FOR LEARNING

501 Involves pupils, under teacher guidance, in planning and conducting class activities.

502 Balances pupil-teacher participation.

503 Provides a healthful and attractive physical environment.

504 Stimulates pupils to show pride in quality performance.

505 Is sensitive and responsive to psychological needs of pupils.

506 Other (specify)

507 Other (specify)

600 EVALUATING PROGRESS OF PUPILS

601 Emphasizes the application of knowledge to new situations.

602 Measures achievement in all areas of instruction.

603 Helps each student develop ability to evaluate own progress.

604 Includes test scores in appraising growth and needs of pupils.

605 Evaluates in terms of individual differences.

606 Communicates with parents regarding pupils' progress.

607 Other (specify)

608 Other (specify)

700 PLANNING, MANAGING, AND ORGANIZING

701 Keeps accurate records.

702 Prepares lesson plans and manages instructional program.

703 Prepares and manages budget allocations for which responsible.

704 Cares for school property.

705 Adheres to school and district policies and procedures.

706 Works cooperatively within teams and departments.

707 Delegates tasks and responsibilities.

708 Plans and organizes work so that substitute teachers and aides can function with a minimum of difficulty.

709 Safeguards the health and safety of students.

710 Maintains positive discipline and control in working with students.

711 Other (specify)

712 Other (specify)

800 PROFESSIONAL ETHICS, ATTRIBUTES, GROWTH, AND RESPONSIBILITIES

801 Maintains cooperative and ethical relationships with colleagues, administrators, supervisors, parents, and support personnel.

802 Supports decisions made in the best interests of the school and the school system.

803 Is careful in seeking facts and reason for decisions before offering criticisms of them.

804 Maintains a sense of humor.

805 Manifests enthusiasm.

FIGURE 2-14. (continued)

806 Accepts additional responsibilities.
807 Participates in in-service activities.
808 Engages in advanced studies.
809 Demonstrates poise, self-confidence, and tact.
810 Demonstrates dependability.
811 Maintains interest in the profession of teaching and in own professional growth.
812 Involves self in school and student activities beyond the classroom.
813 Other (specify)
814 Other (specify)

Used with permission of the Montgomery County (Virginia) Public School System. Taken from Cooperative Improvement Evaluation Program.

FIGURE 2-14. (continued)

The key to completing Figures 2-12 and 2-13 is a set of numbered performance criteria that the Montgomery County (Virginia) Public School system has previously adopted. The performance criteria appear in Figure 2-14 for your review and understanding of Worksheet A, where several needs are referred to by the evaluator and the evaluatee.

CHAPTER 2 ENDNOTES

1.   DEAN SPITZER, "30 Ways to Motivate Employees to Perform Better," *Training, the Magazine of Human Resources Development,* Vol. 17, No. 3 (March 1980): 51–56.

2.   DOUGLAS MCGREGOR, *The Human Side of Enterprise* (New York: McGraw-Hill Book Co., 1960).

3.   DOUGLAS MCGREGOR, *Leadership and Motivation* (Cambridge, Mass.: The M.I.T. Press, 1966).

4.   JOHN J. MORSE and JAY W. LORSCH, "Beyond Theory Y," *Harvard Business Review,* Vol. 48, No. 3 (May–June 1970): 61–68.

5.   WILLIAM OUCHI, *Theory Z: How American Business Can Meet the Japanese Challenge* (Reading, Mass.: Addison-Wesley, 1981).

6.   RICHARD PASCALE AND ANTHONY ATHOS, *The Art of Japanese Management: Applications for American Executives,* (New York: Simon and Schuster, 1981).

7.   DOUGLAS MCGREGOR, "The Human Side of Enterprise" (speech given for the Fiftieth Anniversary Convocation of the School of Industrial Management, Massachusetts Institute of Technology).

8.   ROGERT FISHER AND WILLIAM URY, *Getting to Yes: Negotiating Agreement Without Giving In* (New York: Penguin Books, 1983).

9.   GARY FENSTERMACHER, "On Learning to Teach Effectively from Research on Teacher Effectiveness," *Time to Learn* (National Institute of Education, 1980): 127–37.

3

OBSERVING THE TEACHING PROCESS

Teaching is a complex and even mysterious activity that the world's greatest thinkers have sought to understand. It has numerous dimensions, some of which are comparatively easy to understand and talk about. Others, such as the affective connection created between teacher and student, are difficult to grasp and to describe. As teaching is complex, the observation of teaching is necessarily complex. The observer must have some understanding of what teaching is and the skills needed to carry out his or her task.

Chapter 3 explores the concept of teaching as a first step in providing you with help with the skill of observing. The concept of teaching presented here is perhaps an ideal one. It is worth considering and striving for when it directs your attention to dimensions too often neglected in talk about teaching. With this concept in mind, the chapter explores the skill of observing in terms of it being different from other supervisory activities and of having multiple purposes simultaneously, as does every complex endeavor. This chapter also offers a set of simple and straightforward methods for observing teaching that are congruent with other tasks that you perform as a supervisor.

After reading this chapter, you should be able to:

- Understand the various dimensions of teaching as an activity.
- Distinguish observing from other supervisory tasks.
- Know several methods for observing classroom teaching.
- Describe the activity of teaching in regard to such dimensions as act, intention, triad of dynamic elements, context, manner, reason-giving, ethics, language, and interpersonal relations.
- Distinguish observing from the supervisory activities of inferring, generalizing, evaluating, and recommending.
- List at least four purposes of observing teaching.
- State at least two reasons for observing teacher actions in the classroom.
- List at least two approaches for obtaining specific data by observing teacher activity.
- Apply at least ten different methods of observing classroom teaching.

THREE LEVELS OF TEACHING

As a supervisor of a teacher's professional growth, it is necessary to have in mind a concept of teaching. After all, it is the teacher's teaching that you are primarily supervising. In order to help your teachers, you need to know about the teacher's essential activity. As a leader, you need to have a firm understanding of what teaching is and how it fits into the overall picture of schooling. To that end, this section offers a concept of teaching that will serve as one foundation for the supervisory ideas and activities that follow.

Occupational and Enterprise Levels

The word *teach* has different meanings depending on its use in conversation. We can even use the word in two different ways in the same sentence. For example, "George Jones teaches at Central School, but he does not teach on Monday afternoon since at that time he attends a special class at the university." From that sentence it is clear that the first use of "teach" refers to George Jone's occupation. We know that Jones teaches to make a living. He is a teacher and not a janitor or painter or nurse or salesperson or doctor or quarterback or pilot. The second use of "teach" in the sample sentence refers to the general enterprise of teaching, the overall cluster of activities that teachers perform, such as explaining, demonstrating, questioning, attending faculty meetings, taking attendance, and filing reports. It is not difficult to make the distinction between the two levels of meaning of the word *teach*.

Act of Teaching Level

The word *teach* has yet a third level of meaning. It appears in the following illustrative sentence: "Jones stopped talking about the World Series with his class and began teaching algebra." In this sentence, it is clear that "teach" excludes such activities as chatting with students, sharpening pencils, and distributing textbooks, all of which are classroom activities that a teacher legitimately performs. Here, "teach" refers to the very essential activities such as explaining, questioning, answering, comparing, and defining. This third level of teaching is the *act of teaching,* which is different from the occupational and enterprise levels referred to earlier.

We shall focus this section on the act of teaching. This does not deny the importance of treating the dimensions of teaching that make it a significant occupation in our society and distinguish teaching from other occupations such as engineering, painting, playing baseball, plumbing, and cooking. Nor does it deny the importance of the dimensions of teaching that lead a person to have a full, beneficial role in your school. Such dimensions would include, for example, the ability and skills to participate in faculty meetings, file reports on students, serve on a curriculum committee, confer with parents, and lead a student club after regular class hours. All of these are important institutional activities in making your school a smooth and effective organization.

Rather, by focusing on the act of teaching (or activity of teaching) we recognize what is absolutely essential for the teacher to be called a teacher and focus on the interaction between teacher and student. Here are the essential activities without which there would be no need for faculty meetings, attendance reports, and school dances. The act of teaching includes the activities of explaining the subject matter and of questioning students, and these are crucial for student learning. While you might hire a teaching aide to collect milk money, or take the roll, or mimeograph worksheets, you hire a teacher to explain, define, demonstrate, conclude, compare, deduce, justify, question, test, motivate, reinforce, and evaluate. That is, you hire a *teacher* to perform these activities, because they are the essential logical and strategic activities that are the core of teaching.

Teaching is an intentional act. A teacher teaches with the intention of bringing about student learning. The teacher's actions are not guarantees of success. What the teacher does constitutes teaching whether or not it results in learning. Furthermore, the manner in which a teacher acts is critical. Manner counts in teaching. Without an appropriate and acceptable manner, the act of teaching can be considered to be nonteaching. If the teacher intends to bring about learning but does so without respect for the student, without permitting the student the intellectual integrity to form an independent judgment, and without giving reasons and telling the truth, the acts can be labeled brainwashing, conditioning, or propagandizing rather than teaching. If the teacher humiliates and threatens the students or otherwise abuses them, such activity will not constitute *teaching* even if the student learns some subject matter. In short, for a person's acts to be considered as teaching acts rather than brainwashing, for example, they must be performed in an acceptable, intentional manner.

Teaching is a triadic and dynamic activity. It is triadic in that in teaching there is a complex set of relations established among the teacher, the student, and whatever subject matter is involved. (This subject matter can involve skills, knowledge, and values or some combination of these three elements.) This triad exists within the context of time and place. Moreover, the triadic activity is constantly changing. As the student learns and changes, the teacher changes over time personally and in relation to the student and the subject matter. That is, the set of triadic relationships is dynamic rather than static. It is for this reason that the teacher and you as supervisor must continually examine the situation. What was effective in September and October may not be so in February or May due to the dynamic changes occurring in the relationships among the three elements of the triad. Figure 3-1 shows the triadic relations within the time and place context.

Teaching involves primarily verbal language. This does not mean that the teacher's nonverbal actions are not present and do not count; however, when the teacher explains or questions—two vital teaching acts—the teacher uses verbal language. The teacher

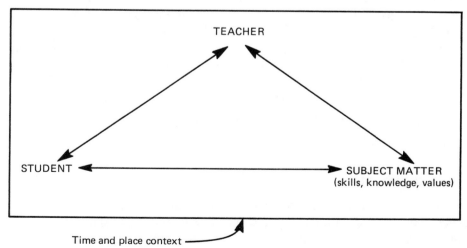

FIGURE 3-1. The triadic and dynamic qualities of teaching.

uses language: to teach definitions, facts, interpretations, generalizations, and concepts; to interpret and emphasize the demonstrations of the skills being taught; to correct, reject, accept, or praise student responses to questions; to encourage and prod students in their learning activities; to test and evaluate student achievement; to show respect, honesty, fairness, and equality of treatment; to express feelings of interest, warmth, and coolness; and to give directions and make assignments. In short, the teacher uses and needs language to teach.

The teacher also uses nonverbal language. Nonverbal language includes physical gestures such as pointing a finger to call on a student and shaking the head horizontally to indicate "No," and such actions as smiles and general demeanor, which convey messages in themselves about the teacher's values and attitudes. Teachers and students are continually sending nonverbal messages to each other, and these messages are important in teaching. Nevertheless, verbal language is the prime means of communication in teaching.

Teaching is a relationship that goes beyond the rational intellectual dimension that is central to teaching. Theoretically, it is possible for a student to learn from a teacher whom he thoroughly dislikes that, for example, $2 + 2 = 4$. However, we also know that for teaching to be sustained over a long period of time a positive interpersonal relationship is necessary. Through their actions, teachers must indicate their intention to respect the student, to minimize anxiety and threat, to establish mutual trust, and to encourage independence of thought. Teachers need to establish a positive interpersonal relationship with their students because teaching thrives on it and cannot exist without it.

Indeed, it is through this interpersonal relationship that the teacher is able to model the moral values—truth, respect, trust, cooperation, friendship, reasonableness, humaneness, and love—that are the foundation of teaching. They constitute the foundation that permits one person to seek the improvement of another person intellectually, socially, and morally. Hence, teaching requires good relationships as an essential and integral element of the activity.

In summary, teaching is an *activity* that is *intentional* regarding student learning; certain logical and strategic activities such as explaining and questioning constitute the essence of teaching; *manner* is central to teaching requiring a *positive interpersonal relationship* based on mutual respect and trust; teaching is carried on through *language;* teaching involves the use of *intelligence, reason-giving, and truth* as a way of promoting the cognitive and moral development of the student and recognizing the integrity of the student; teaching is a set of *triadic and dynamic* relationships that occur in a unique time and place context; and teaching is a *moral activity* that seeks the improvement of the student in the dimensions of skills, knowledge, and values.

DISTINGUISHING OBSERVING FROM OTHER SUPERVISORY ACTIVITIES

Illustrative Statements

As supervisor, you perform many activities in order to further the purpose of supervision, which was discussed in Chapter 1. While some people may claim that evaluating is most important because it is a culminating activity, others counter that observing is the most important activity because it serves as the basis of all your subsequent action. Whatever may be most important to you, no one denies that observing is critical to supervision. Indeed, observing is critical in every general activity, whether it is in social science, physical science, humanities, fine arts, law, or business. The key to understanding the role of observing is to distinguish observing from your other activities and identify its purpose.

An excellent way to understand observing is to consider ten statements made by supervisors in written reports, presented here in slightly revised form for our purposes. Although these ten statements are out of context, they identify observing, distinguish observing from other activities, and offer some working definitions. The ten statements are:

1. Seven students didn't bring in their homework.
2. You seem to like Mary.
3. You asked seventy-five questions in twenty minutes.
4. I suggest that you divide the class into three subgroups and work with them separately since you have trouble handling a large group of students.
5. Your organization was excellent.
6. It's apparent that the students didn't do their homework because they are confused.
7. You should ask fewer questions and become warmer toward the students.
8. You're a clock watcher.
9. The answer you gave to Rachel's question was good because it related the situation in Lebanon to previous Middle East situations.
10. Students in your class complete the workbook exercises early.

The ten statements differ in some essential ways. Statements 1 and 3 are observations in that they report what in fact happened in the classroom. They are descriptive; they are empirical, based on what the supervisor saw and heard. Statements 2, 6, and 8 are not observations, but inferences. They go beyond what the supervisor saw and heard; they present an interpretation and an explanation of what occurred. Statement 10 is a generalization. Statements 5 and 9 are evaluative, the former an opinion given without a reason to support it and the latter an opinion plus a supporting reason. Statement 7 offers a recommendation (advice; direction) and so does statement 4, but the latter contains a justification within it. (See Figure 3-2 for a listing of the five types of supervisory statements and their definitions.)

Let's take a closer look at each type of supervisory statement using the ten statements previously listed.

OBSERVATION

Statements 1 and 3 are observations of events. They are neutral, without any implication in them of evaluation, although many people might well feel an implied judgment. The only subjectivity is an editorial one—that is, because the supervisor made the statements in the first place, there is a message that the facts are worth consideration. Importance, however, does not automatically confer value, positive or negative. Just because a teacher asked seventy-five questions in twenty minutes, no one ought to assign a negative or positive weight to that fact. Given the conventional wisdom in force today about teacher questioning, people are tempted to say, "That's too many questions" and hence say, "That's not good teaching." There are reasons, however, for resisting the

1. *Observe.* To perceive or pay attention to; to gather items of information through our senses; to acquire data through sense perceptions

2. *Infer.* To go beyond immediate observations and to construct patterns as a way of predicting future observations and of explaining events; to extend and interpret what is observed; to go beyond the information given; to conclude based on observations

3. *Generalize.* To condense large amounts of data into a statement that covers all items; some generalizations have predictive value—e.g., "all humans are mortal"

4. *Evaluate.* To make a qualitative judgment; to rate in terms of good/bad, right/wrong, beautiful/ugly; to judge the value or worth of something; to offer a personal belief

5. *Recommend.* To suggest; to advise; to tell someone else what to do; to direct the actions of someone else regarding what should or ought to be done

FIGURE 3-2. Five types of supervisory statements processes in making supervisory statements.

temptation to assign a value—logical reasons and also pedagogical reasons stemming from the current research on teaching effectiveness.

INFERENCE

Statements 2 and 6 are inferences. They are based on observations, but go beyond them. Statement 2 shows that the supervisor has attached some interpretive and affective meaning to a series of events. Statement 6 shows that the supervisor is offering an explanation for some observed events. In both cases, the supervisor, by going beyond observation, steps onto slippery ground. The inferences do not permit the teacher to interpret or explain events on his own. The inferences not only deny the teacher the opportunity to think about events himself but also have the potential of offending the teacher by offering unacceptable interpretations. For this reason, it is best to return an inference to its observational base. For example, statement 2 can be modified to, "You said 'Thank you' only to Mary." Statement 6 can be modified to, "The students didn't do their homework." In each case, you can follow the statement with, "What do you think was the consequence of this?" or "What do you think was the cause of this?"

Statement 8 is an inference that deserves attention because it is quite different from another type of inference. Compare it with the most common type, as illustrated in "Your lecture apparently bored the students." This common type, type 1, concerns a specific event or object. This inference concerns a specific lecture but does not label the teacher as a lecturer. It merely goes beyond observation by saying something further about a single lecture. In type 2, illustrated by statement 8, the inference labels the person. This specific inference labels the teacher as a clock watcher, identifying a pattern of behavior. It is one thing to say, "You looked at your clock each time a student asked a question." It is quite different to say, "You're a clock watcher." The difference is significant.

To label a person—especially to give a person a negative label, which is the most common type of label people give others—is to depersonalize the situation. The labeled person is not seen as an individual but as a member of a class of people, one of a type to be known by associations rather than to be known as an individual. The effect on the labeled person is great; there is resentment about being tagged as a member of a negative category, about being seen as a person who is set in a pattern of negative behavior and who probably will not be able to change.

GENERALIZATION

Statement 10, a generalization, is based on observations, just as the statement "Students in your class completed the workbook exercises early" is based on observations. The difference between the latter statement and statement 10 is the "d" added to the word "complete." The latter statement is a generalization made from combining such observations as: Joe finished the workbook exercise early; so did Sam, Ellen, Charles, and Jane. Instead of saying, "Joe, Sam, Ellen, Charles, and Jane completed the workbook exercises early," the observer simply compresses the names and says, "Students in your class completed the workbook exercises early." This is a "condensing" generalization. However, the former, original statement 10 goes beyond this condensing of information by using the word *complete* in the present tense and thus creates a different type of generalization based on past events. It makes a statement about the present and future. This is a "predicting" generalization. It takes past events and creates a rule or principle that refers to all times and with which it is possible to forecast the future.

It is one thing for the supervisor to make a condensing generalization about past or present classroom events in that it does not have a predictive quality. It is quite another thing for a supervisor to make a predicting generalization about classroom events in that it does have a predictive value with some weight. The condensing and the predicting generalizations steal from the teacher the opportunity to note a pattern of events, and this is unfortunate because it is essential for the teacher to be the one to note the patterns in his own classroom. The predictive generalization goes even further, however, forecasting the future and possibly locking the teacher into a particular mind-set or expectation. In this way, it has a doubly negative effect on the teacher. As a supervisor, you must be alert to avoid making such statements.

EVALUATION

In statements 5 and 9, the supervisor evaluates the teacher. The difference between the two statements, however, is significant. In the latter, a stated reason supports the evaluation; in the former, there is none, only a stark opinion.

The evaluative word in statement 5 is "excellent," and it is very positive. Indeed, teachers are happy when they receive positive rather than negative evaluations from their supervisors. Nevertheless, this positive evaluation may not be helpful to the teacher seeking to improve.

Suppose, for example, that the teacher, Mary Morse, has been organizing her lessons the same way for five years. When she hears the supervisor's evaluation, she is pleased. However, she is not helped much at all with her plans to change her lessons. She wants to incorporate into her lessons some new ideas that she heard at a convention, but she does not know what she did specifically because she did not receive observational data. In addition, she does not know what it is that made her organization of her lesson "excellent." Since she does not know, she will have a hard time deciding what to change as she modifies her lesson plans.

These comments on the need for specificity and reason-giving as support for an evaluation do not in any way deny the supervisor the right or opportunity to evaluate the teacher. They only mean that the supervisor must distinguish between observing and evaluating (whether the evaluation has a reason attached or not) and that support for an evaluation is helpful while the lack of it may weaken the evaluation.

RECOMMENDATION

Statements 4 and 7 are evaluative, but they are disguised. With these statements, the supervisor says, in effect, "I believe that you should divide the class" and "I believe that you should ask fewer questions and be warmer." In this form, it is clear that these advisory statements are evaluative. However, they are obviously something more than an evaluative statement that says, "The weather is nice" or "I love summer sports." These statements tell the teacher what to do; they give advice, direction, recommendation, and suggestion. They are couched in polite language and are therefore softened somewhat. Nevertheless, since they come from a supervisor—not a peer—they convey a strong directive message to the teacher.

All of this analysis and commentary on supervisory statements emphasizes that what the supervisor says to the teacher is critical in regard to effecting change. Clarity of and sensitivity to language are necessary for effective communication and the establishment of a common ground for determining what action will lead to change. Setting forth distinctions is not mere hair splitting; it is necessary for reasonable communication and action.

THE PURPOSES OF OBSERVING

Your simple overall purpose in observing your teachers in their classrooms is to know and report to your superiors and board of education what happens there. In order to help a teacher continue to develop, which is one goal of supervision, it is necessary to know what the teacher does and does not do in the classroom—the area of prime importance for the teacher's job. This simple purpose is perhaps too broad to be helpful and needs to be broken down into smaller parts. Let's be specific about six purposes.

Detailed Reporting

When you observe a teacher, you can report in detailed terms what happened. This can be helpful because teachers are not particularly aware of what specific actions they perform in the act of teaching. For example, according to the research on teaching, teachers estimate that they ask between twelve and twenty questions per half hour of teaching. Yet, they in fact ask between 45 and 150. In confirmation of the more general condition of poor self-estimates by teachers, two researchers[1] conclude, "Thus, in practice, one is not advised to accept teacher reports of specific behaviors as particularly accurate. No slur is intended; teachers do not have practice in estimating their behavior and then checking against actual performance." When you report specific data, you can help teachers get a sense of reality which they do not have and which can help them to change.

Source of Awareness

The source of teacher change is awareness, as previously implied. (See Figure 3-3 for a principal's use of audio-taping during an observation visit to help bring awareness to her teacher.) Teachers need to be aware of what they do if they are to change or even to see the need to change. Once they are aware of their actions, they can consider the causes and consequences of them. For example, teachers, like supervisors, believe that student questions are essential for learning. Students who are confused should ask their teachers—and classmates—to clarify matters; students who are curious and concerned should ask questions for further knowledge; and students who are solving problems should ask questions to gather data and to learn procedures as a way of reaching solutions. Learning depends on the answers students receive to their questions. Despite the importance of student questions, however, teachers are simply not aware of the paucity of student questions. According to research on classroom interaction, students ask their teachers few questions; some research reports that about 2 percent and some that 4 percent of classroom actions are student questions.

When teachers bcome aware of this situation and *only* when they become aware of it can they set about changing it. They already hold the belief that students should ask questions and do not need to be convinced of the need. They need to be aware of what is actually occurring in order to change. Since they are not aware now, the situation persists. They don't feel a need to change because their perceptions are inaccurate. Just as awareness of your arm movements in swimming in necessary to improve your stroke, so is awareness necessary for a teacher to change classroom interaction.

Promotion of Dissonance

Another way to look at the purpose of observing is to use the concept of dissonance. Dissonance is an unpleasant feeling deriving from the discrepancy between a person's perception of or preference about behavior and that person's actual behavior. If you believe that X is occurring or should occur, but find that Y is actually occurring, you have dissonance. Two examples from the classroom will help. Suppose Thomas Troy perceives himself to be a teacher who asks about twenty questions an hour (this is what teachers generally estimate). When he becomes aware from your data that he *actually* asks about ninety-five questions an hour, he will experience dissonance. Suppose Nancy Davis desires (prefers) to ask approximately fifteen questions per lesson. When she becomes aware from your feedback that she actually asks about eighty questions per lesson, she also will experience dissonance. For Troy, there is dissonance because *perception of actual* and *actual* are discrepant. For Davis, there is dissonance because *preference* and *actual* are discrepant.

Dissonance creates tension in a teacher and is a motivating force for its own reduction. People do not want to feel dissonant; they seek to remove or reduce the feeling. When teachers Troy and Davis feel dissonant, they will have some motivation to change their behavior. Similarly, your teachers can get motivation to change their behavior from the data you report to them. You obtain the data when you observe them.

Status: ___ **Probationary**   ___ **Tenure**   ___ **Other**

The observation will be for a teaching segment of time no less than thirty (30) minutes, shall be reduced to writing, and delivered to the teacher observed within five (5) days of the observation. In addition, a conference will be provided upon request of either party.

Teacher _____   Observer _____

School/Location _____   Subject _____

Date _____

COMMENTS BY OBSERVER:

In the review lesson, students called on one another and assisted each other with corrections, but teacher remained very much in charge and repeated many answers. In the discussion that followed (on stories to be written) teacher elicited ideas from students but also injected many of his own.

At the principal's suggestion, the lesson being observed was also being audio-taped. Analysis of the data by observer and the teacher (who had listened to it before the conference) showed absolute congruence. The teacher was very conscious of the degree of his own input during the lesson.

The teacher is a very intelligent, cooperative, earnest and industrious teacher who has obviously worked very hard to give the students in his class the direction and guidance they need to achieve school success. He is also aware of the need to put students in charge of their own educational growth. The maintenance of a delicate balance between these two factors is literally the "art" of teaching, an excellent goal to pursue, and one in which this teacher has made some considerable progress.

Summary of performance:___ Satisfactory___ Needs to Improve___ Unsatisfactory

Signature of observer _____   Date _____

I have read and do/do not agree with the above.

Signature of teacher _____   Date _____

Used with permission of Mildred G. Ness, Principal, James P. B. Duffy School #12, Rochester, New York

FIGURE 3-3. Formal teacher observation form.

Observational data is firsthand data and more acceptable than hearsay, secondhand data you might report when you obtain it from students who chat with you in the halls.

There is ample evidence in regard to teaching that observing, which leads to awareness which in turn leads to dissonance, does lead to change. In a study conducted at Rutgers University and reported in the *American Educational Research Journal*, observers gave specific feedback to certain teachers of science, mathematics, social studies, and language. Those teachers who became aware of their specific behavior changed over a period of three weeks. "From the results of this study we may conclude that the behavior and self-perception of experienced, in-service teachers *can* be changed by invoking a discrepancy between a teacher's observed behavior and his own self-perception of his behavior and then making him aware of this discrepancy via verbal feedback. Thus, the teacher is seen to effect a change in his own behavior in the direction of reducing this discrepancy."[2] The conclusion of this study deserves restatement: teachers who received specific feedback effected *their own behavioral change* by reducing the discrepancy between how they actually behaved and how they believed they should behave.

Springboard for Conversation

Suppose you are not convinced by the above reasons of the need for observing—that is, you do not believe that awareness and dissonance will motivate your teachers to change. You still must start with observing the teacher teach. If you feel that a teacher needs to change and that awareness and dissonance are insufficient as indirect means, you certainly need to talk explicitly with your teacher about changing. However, such talk about change must be based on knowledge of what the teacher is doing currently. If you don't know specifically what the teacher is doing, you won't know what to change. Nor will you easily recognize change when it comes.

As you will see later in Chapters 5 and 6, you do not need to "lecture" your teacher about what is wrong and that change is necessary. You can present the data you have gathered by observing your teacher and ask your teacher to comment on the data. For example, you can ask, "Pat, what do these data mean to you?" In this way, you ask the teacher to talk about the data and to reflect on their meaning, probable consequences, and importance. Most often, the teacher will make comments that you can build upon in a discussion leading to the need for change. The teacher often will ask you for your comments on the data. Even if you feel awareness and dissonance are not enough, you need data as the stepping stone toward a discussion geared explicitly to leading the teacher to change.

Message of Caring

Your observing of the classroom serves an affective purpose. The classroom is the teacher's personal home ground. It is where the teacher works, where the teacher performs the primary duties he is charged to do. By observing the teacher teach, you convey a nonverbal message that you care to find out about what is essential to the teacher. You care about the central core of the teacher's life in the school. You communicate a positive message when you attend to what the teacher does. You indicate that what the teacher does is worth spending your time and effort to learn about. You show that you care, and this means something to the teacher.

Fulfillment of Job Description

Finally, by observing the teacher you fulfill your responsibility as a supervisor. There probably is a state regulation in your system requiring supervisors to observe their teachers. Even if there isn't, there no doubt is a local regulation by your board of education that you observe your teachers so that you can have the data to supervise them rationally and fairly—that is, with data you can confer with, evaluate, and guide your teachers in a sound manner.

In short, why do you observe your teachers? See Figure 3-4 for a listing of reasons.

WHAT AND HOW TO OBSERVE

What to Observe

To help the teacher, you need data that are important to him and to you. You will use these data as the basis of your subsequent personal conference. The question then is: What should you observe? The answer you offer must take into consideration that in your conference you will talk about such things as student achievement scores, student attendance, the role of teacher in the classroom and school, and teacher relations with students. The data on student achievement, for example, are available to you from school records, and, therefore, you need not observe the teacher teaching in order to gather such data. Besides, observing an ongoing session will not yield data on achievement anyhow. You might, then, wonder why it is necessary to observe a teacher teaching if crucial data are available to you whether or not you observe.

The answer centers on the recognition that you need to tie nonobservational data to what the teacher is doing. For example, if the students are scoring poorly on standardized math tests, you need to talk to the teacher about his actions that influence the students' scores. If you aim to suggest some possible and alternative ways to group

1. To know what is happening in the classroom.
2. To be able to report to others what is happening in the classroom.
3. To inform the teachers about details of their actions.
4. To help the teachers become aware of their actions since awareness is basic to change.
5. To create dissonance, which is a motivator for change.
6. To know what it is that needs to be changed in the classroom.
7. To gather data to serve as the foundations of discussions with the teachers about change.
8. To show the teachers that you care about what they do and that what they do is worth your effort to learn about.
9. To fulfill your legal requirement of performing sound supervision.

FIGURE 3-4. Reasons for observing teachers.

the students, you need to find out what the teacher is doing now. If you did not observe the teacher, you could not confer with him about specific current actions and future actions that you both believe are connected to student achievement. A resistant teacher could always say, "I do that already." In short, you need data on teacher actions that you will connect to other data—data about the teacher and data about the students. It is inappropriate to confer about unobserved data and then not relate those data to actions for which the teacher is responsible. By observing the teacher directly in the classroom, you can connect action with results and proposed future actions.

At this point, it is no doubt clear that you should observe the actions that are central to teaching. You should concentrate on such language activity of the teacher that *explains or defines the material being taught,* rather than classroom language activity, for example, about a new movie that the teacher and students have seen in common over the weekend. You should observe those specific activities that are central to classroom teaching and that the teacher should know about in detail because changes in them are significant to the teacher and students regarding other actions and results. You should observe the actions of the teacher that are integral to his manner of teaching and that indicate *respect and trust* because these two values are central values in teaching, as noted earlier. By concentrating on the central activities, you can observe what is significant in the classroom, and then you need not worry that you are not observing everything. Observing everything is impossible, in any case, because observing is by nature selective. The key issue in observation concerns *selecting what is essential.*

Furthermore, you should vary what you observe. Suppose your teacher has firmly established a positive classroom climate, as he should. In your next visit, you should not observe the classroom climate but should emphasize other activities of teaching such as the use of space or teacher questioning. This does not mean, obviously, that classroom climate is no longer important. However, if you wish to encourage continued growth, you are better off observing other activities since you wish to use dissonance to motivate further change.

The methods of observing contained in this chapter will provide you with a variety of ideas on what to observe. You will note that the emphasis is on the *teacher's own actions.* Focus on what the teacher does and is directly responsible for, such as teacher questions, teacher reactions to student responses, teacher physical position in the classroom, and teacher selection of students to participate in the classroom interaction. Since these are the teacher's own actions, the teacher can change them directly.

In general, there is little or no point in focusing on the way students sit in their seats, for example, since the teacher is not doing the sitting. The point of observing is to bring change in what the teacher does, and this change will come about most often by having the teacher become aware of personal actions. As a matter of fact, if you create awareness only of the students' actions you may well tempt the teacher to say, "But that's what they're doing. I don't control them 100 percent and I'm not really responsible for what the students do since so many outside factors influence them. What can I do anyhow? They act that way not because of me, but because of their home situation." Such a teacher reaction to student behavior may lead to entrenchment rather than change.

Nevertheless, there may be times when you should observe student actions. The criterion is the direct connection of the students' actions with the teacher's action. If there is a clear connection, it will be helpful for the teacher to be aware of student action. For example, you could observe the number of student questions over a two-day period. You could obtain data on the number of student questions related to teacher questions and to the teacher's solicitation of student questions. Your data might well show that the number of student questions increased when the teacher actively and patiently solicited them. Such data may create the motivation for the teacher to change his own actions since they are clearly connected to student actions.

The teacher can effect significant changes in teaching by changing personal actions that lead to changes in student actions. It is sensible and reasonable to expect a teacher to change only that which is controlled directly rather than that which, at most, is only controlled indirectly. Consider a parallel in sports. Lynda, a tennis player, cannot directly change her opponent's serve. She can only change her way of returning the opponent's serve. In recognition of her improved way of returning service, the opponent may change her own serve. Lynda must become aware of what she herself does and seek to change it. She can do no more than that. It is through her actions that she will change her opponent's actions.

How to Observe

The key to effective observing is concentration on specifics. If you are distracted by thoughts about a pressing meeting with your own superior, for example, then concentration on the teaching activities in the classroom may be particularly difficult—not impossible but difficult. Your mind may drift to thoughts about your forthcoming meeting or you may begin to think about the general situation. To facilitate and foster concentration, it is helpful to have paper and pencil available in order to take notes about specifics. Also helpful will be the use of an observation instrument to guide you in a systematic way. Such instruments are available in many sources, including *School Administrator's Handbook of Teacher Supervision and Evaluation Methods.*[3] However, you do not need anything fancy to serve the purposes of observing identified earlier. Simple devices, such as methods suggested here, will suffice.

Without the development of techniques for helpful, systematic observing, there is a good chance that your mind will drift. People need devices to focus their senses—especially the senses of sight and hearing that are the two most used senses in observing. Without a focus, people see everything but see nothing because the observations turn out to be too general. Thus, an observer might say in general to teacher Mike Troy, "You wrote on the chalkboard several times." This is not specific and probably will not cause the pinpointed awareness needed by Troy regarding his use of the classroom equipment.

In contrast, a statement by you to Troy with potential to raise awareness is, "You wrote on the board six times; each time a student gave the wrong answer you wrote it on the board; you did not write one correct answer on the board." Receiving this specific observation, Troy can draw on his knowledge of psychology to realize that in effect he is reinforcing the incorrect answers rather than the correct ones. Such a statement on your part to Troy can come only when you focus and concentrate on your objective for observing.

There are several techniques for focusing your observations.

A CHECKLIST

You can use a *checklist* of items you wish to note and make a mark next to each item each time you observe that item. For example, suppose you are interested in how a teacher asks a question. You could prepare a checklist, such as the one shown in Figure 3-5, to guide you.

	Frequency
1. Asks the class in general; no student specified.	
2. Selects the student and then asks the question.	
3. Asks the question and then selects the student.	
4. Asks the question to a specific student as a continuation of a previous remark; selection implied.	

FIGURE 3-5. Frequency checklist.

The checklist directs you to focus on the teacher and to jot down a mark next to one of the four choices listed for each question the teacher asks. If you find that the four choices are inadequate, you can modify the list by adding an overall miscellaneous fifth choice: other. Keep the list short and very easy to use whenever you observe a teacher question. Notice that for items 2, 3, and 4 in the checklist, you could easily add exactness by specifying boy or girl. You would then modify the checklist as shown in Figure 3-6.

TIME SAMPLING

A second technique is time sampling. Here, you decide on how long a time period fits your purpose and how often you wish to use that time period. For example, you could decide to observe teacher questions during a five-minute segment three times during the lesson or to observe during alternating two-minute segments (that is, two minutes observed and two minutes unobserved). With the observed segment, you could note just the frequency of teacher questions or you could use a checklist.

RECORD VERBATIM

A third technique is to record verbatim the selected type or types of speech. For example, you could record verbatim every teacher question without classifying or interpreting the questions in any way.

The observation record might look like this:

1. Who wrote this short story and when?
2. What did Mary do when she lost her way?
3. Who helped her?
4. If you were Mary, what would you have done? Would you have climbed the tree or what? I mean what do you think you would have done once you realized you were lost?

	Frequency	
	Boy	Girl
1. Asks the class in general; no student specified.		
2. Selects the student and then asks the question.		
3. Asks the question and then selects the student.		
4. Asks the question to a specific student as a continuation of a previous remark; selection implied.		

FIGURE 3-6. Modified checklist of frequency.

Of course, once you have the verbatim record of teacher questions, you must first use it alone or with the teacher in order to interpret it within the context of the classroom situation.

CATEGORIZE

A fourth technique is to categorize what you observe *after* you have finished observing. For example, you would observe teacher questions and record them verbatim in writing or on tape recording. Then, after reviewing all the questions, you would divide the questions into several categories depending on the situation. You would indeed have some notions of categories in mind from previous experiences, but you would not decide finally on categories until you examined all the current questions within the current context. In short, the categories would fit this specific situation.

Obviously, you will decide which of these four observation techniques to use and to modify depending on your particular situation. You will use what fits and feels comfortable to you in working with the teacher being observed. With each technique, there are ways to add specificity and complexity to the recording of your observations. The key to remember is that the observations are to help you in providing meaningful data for the teacher.

METHODS OF OBSERVING

With the purposes and specific conditions of observing in mind, you must choose a method for observing that you believe will yield data to help your teacher. This section offers you a series of methods for observing some areas significant to teaching, such as pedagogical verbal action, use of space and physical environment, nonverbal actions, and cognitive processes. This series is not a comprehensive group of methods for observing teaching in the classroom. Rather, it offers you some of the many methods possible. Consider it as a foundation and spur to your creativity when observing your teachers.

You can use the following methods as presented or design some new ones that better fit your situation. You can combine these with the observation forms already in use in your school. You can modify these methods in light of additional methods presented in other books and articles treating the topic of classroom observing.

In any case, it is up to you to use a method that will help you to help your particular teachers. You will use the data you gather when observing the teachers as the springboard for conferring about future development. As you tie these data to other data related to teacher action and student action, you will be talking about what is important in teaching.

Seventeen Methods

METHOD 1: FREQUENCY OF TEACHER QUESTIONS

For most classes, probably the most salient teacher action to observe is teacher questioning. This is so because teacher questions are central in and essential to teaching. With the exception of the traditional college lecture, teacher questions are frequent when teachers are talking with, rather than at, students. Therefore, let us begin with teacher questions. The simplest observing method is to count the number of teacher questions within a given time segment—say, three, five, ten, or twenty minutes. It is important to specify the length of time in order to calculate the number of questions asked per minute. This rate of teacher questions will be useful for comparison purposes currently and in the future.

A brief excerpt from an actual typescript follows. The excerpt is from a fifth grade lesson based on an article in *National Geographic* magazine.[4] Try reading it aloud at a normal teaching pace, making a tally mark for each teacher question. Better yet, ask two people to read the excerpt to you, one to be teacher and the other to be student. In this way you can simulate hearing "live" interaction.

So that we are looking for the same thing called "teacher question," keep in mind the following four criteria generally accepted by observers of teacher questioning:

1. A question occurs when a speaker *intends to elicit or request an oral response.* If the intent of the speaker is in doubt, it is helpful to see how the "target" person took the speaker's utterance. If the target person took the utterance as a question and responded, then the speaker has asked a question.

2. A question can be stated in any grammatical form—interrogative, declarative, or imperative. The key to identifying a question is *not the grammatical form but the intent of the speaker* to elicit or request a response.

3. Each question, *whether responded to or not,* is considered as a separate question. If a question is repeated or slightly rephrased during the same utterance or a short while later, then it counts as a *separate question.*

4. Calling on a person only to give permission to speak (that is, an *"acknowledging question")* is *not considered as a separate question.* For exlample, "Who is the President of the U.S.A., Tom?" is one question. If the teacher speaks after a student response and says, "All right. Mary?" or "Yes?" then there is no question counted.

Remember: whether you read the excerpt aloud or listen to it as read by someone else, keep track of the length of time as you mark a tally for each question according to the four criteria listed above.

EXCERPT

TEACHER: Now we covered culture, we covered customs, traditions, land per se. Correct?

JOE: Yes.

TEACHER: Now, first question. Do all people live in the same type of house? Do all people eat the same type of food? Do all people have the same customs? Do all people wear the same clothes?

BRIAN: No.

TEACHER: All right, no. Would anyone say yes? (pause) All right. Let's see if we can come up with reasons why all people don't live in the same house. Why not the same house all over the world?

SUZIE: Maybe they don't have enough money to pay for it or it's too far from where they work.

TEACHER: All right. Suzie, what happens if you have money to pay for it? What happens— are you referring to like in the same country they get very little money in the way of wages?

SUZIE: Yes.

TEACHER: All right.

ELLEN: People like different things, like they won't like what other people have.

TEACHER: You mean the type of house?

ELLEN: Yeah.

TEACHER: All right. Some other reasons, please.

MARVIN: People might want to decorate their houses different.

TEACHER: Yes.

MARGY: Depends on the weather.

TEACHER: What do you mean by the "weather"?

MARGY: Like if you want to have a cabin or a five room or...

TEACHER: All right. Mary?

MARY: Like in, like in Alaska it's a lot colder than Florida, and Alaska might have a thicker wall or something because it's colder there.

TEACHER: All right. The people that are with me for reading, how many of you remember the story of "The Rope"?

PETER: I do.

TEACHER: Why was, why was that type of house put on stilts? Peter?

PETER: Because it was in the water.

TEACHER: All right. Now what about food? Do we have the same food prepared differently in different countries?

SALLY: Yes.

TEACHER: Yes, in some countries they prefer this food this way; another country another way. What about clothing? Why different clothing?

MARY: Different weather.

TEACHER: Different weather, exactly. All right. In warm weather do you wear dark or light clothing?

BRIAN: Light, to reflect the sun; it doesn't attract that much heat.

TEACHER: Do you wear it tight or loose?

TOM: Loose.

TEACHER: Loose. Do they work their farms different in different parts of the world?

SUZIE: Yes.

TEACHER: All right. What do we have in our country?

RALPH: Machines.

TEACHER: Machines. What about some of these native lands? Do they have wooden tools?

RALPH: Yes.

TEACHER: Yes, all right. Does anybody want to describe one of these things? You haven't seen the article so use your imagination to tell me what they are.

ELLEN: They are like houses that people live in.

TEACHER: All right, you are going to call it a house that they live in; all right. Do you think this was shaped out that way? People shaped this out of this or this is what it came to be?

TOM: Probably a volcano's shaping it.

TEACHER: What do you mean by the shape of a volcano? Do you mean that this thing is the lava from the volcano?

TOM: Lava from the volcano.

TEACHER: Right, that's it. Now, the lava from the volcano comes from rocks?

TOM: Yes.

TEACHER: Once this rock is changed to lava and then it's changed to something like this. Is this softer material than the original rock?

TOM: Yes.

TEACHER: Yes. This is, these are homes and there's that word cave. You can see—see these doors; see the windows. Odd-shaped, aren't they?

SALLY: Yes.

TEACHER: Yes, all right. Now, this article was written by two...

According to the four criteria, you should have counted thirty-two questions. Even if you have a slightly different number, it is of little consequence here. You probably came close to thirty-two. (You can check, if you wish, by referring to Method 2 which lists the thirty-two questions verbatim.) The excerpt is four minutes long as timed from the tape recording of the actual session. A simple arithmetic computation yields the ratio of 8 questions per minute ($32 \div 4$). Later we shall deal with using this information with the teacher. For now it is sufficient to become familiar with this method of observing and the other points you are now alerted to as a by-product of using this method.

METHOD 2: VERBATIM RECORD OF TEACHER QUESTIONS

With this method you focus on teacher questions, as before, but here you write down each question in order to have a document to examine. A verbatim record of the thirty-two questions from the excerpt follows:

1. Correct?
2. Do all people live in the same type of house?
3. Do all people eat the same type of food?
4. Do all people have the same customs?
5. Do all people wear the same clothes?
6. Would anyone say yes?
7. Why not the same house all over the world?
8. Suzie, what happens if you have money to pay for it?
9. What happens—are you referring to like in the same country they get very little money in the way of wages?
10. You mean the type of house?
11. Some other reasons, please.
12. What do you mean by the "weather"?
13. The people that are with me for reading, how many of you remember the story of "The Rope"?
14. Why was that type of house put on stilts?
15. Now what about food?
16. Do we have the same food prepared differently in different countries?
17. What about clothing?
18. Why different clothing?
19. In warm weather do you wear dark or light clothing?
20. Do you wear it tight or loose?
21. Do they work their farms different in different parts of the world?
22. What do we have in our country?
23. What about some of these native lands?
24. Do they have wooden tools?
25. Does anybody want to describe one of these things?
26. Do you think this was shaped out that way?

27. People shaped this out of this or this is what it came to be?
28. What do you mean by the shape of a volcano?
29. Do you mean that this thing is the lava from the volcano?
30. Now, the lava from the volcano comes from rocks?
31. Is this softer material than the original rock?
32. Odd-shaped, aren't they?

With these thirty-two questions written down, you can offer some analysis and interpretation with the teacher in your forthcoming postobservational conference.

METHOD 3: TEACHER DIRECTIVES

Closely related to teacher questions are teacher directives in that they too elicit a response from the students. A teacher directive elicits, requests, or demands a student to do something mentally or physically. For example, a teacher may say, "Look at this map," or "Please read to yourselves page 23 in your textbooks," or "Pass your homework papers in." Teacher directives are worth observing because they indicate how and to what extent the teacher controls student behavior, especially when viewed in combination with teacher questions. For practice, return to the excerpt presented earlier and count the number of teacher directives.

You may have counted one, two, or three, depending on your interpretation here of how the teacher sounds to you. You may have noted the following:

1. You haven't seen the article so use your imagination to tell me what they are.
2. See these doors.
3. See the windows.

Let us assume that you counted all three. If so, then you now have in this excerpt the following frequency data:

Teacher questions: ℍℍ ℍℍ ℍℍ ℍℍ ℍℍ ℍℍ II

4 minutes

Teacher directives: III

METHOD 4: FREQUENCY OF STUDENT QUESTIONS AND DIRECTIVES

Teachers, as well as supervisors, are often rightly interested in student questioning as an indicator of motivation, concern, clarity, and curiosity. If you are not already aware of how many student questions and directives there are in the illustrative excerpt, count them now.

If you have counted the number of student questions and directives by tallying in groups of jots, your observation worksheet will look like this:

Teacher questions: ℍℍ ℍℍ ℍℍ ℍℍ ℍℍ ℍℍ II

Teacher directives: III

Student questions:

Student directives:

METHOD 5: TEACHER QUESTIONS FOR PRODUCTIVE THINKING

Over the years, there have appeared numerous ways to categorize teacher questions based on various dimensions of questioning, such as cognitive level, productivity, verification process, and openness. Of course, you may choose any category system that makes sense to you and that will be helpful to the teacher. You may design your own categories, modify an existing set (such as the one for supervisor questions offered in Chapter 7), or use one of the two systems appearing here as Method 5 and Method 6. These two systems have a long tradition of being useful and helpful.

The system based on productive thinking was developed and became popular several years ago when there was a great interest in creativity and creative students. The concept of productive thinking was initially applied to teacher questions by Aschner and Gallagher in their research[5] with gifted and talented students. These educators defined productivity as "consisting in those divergent, convergent, and evaluative operations whereby the individual draws upon available past and present acts, ideas, associations, and observations in order to bring forth *new* facts, ideas, and conclusions. Productive thinking, so defined, includes both the creative and critical-analytic dimensions of reasoning."

There are five main types of questions in the Aschner and Gallagher system, four related to the substantive material and one related to classroom management or routines. There are subtypes, but they are not necessary here. If you wish to break down each main type, it is just as well to do it personally based on the particular teaching session being observed. The following five main types of this system are based on productive thinking:

- *Cognitive-memory questions.* These questions elicit responses that are nonproductive; they are recall of previous material. These questions elicit answers that "represent the simple reproduction of facts, formulae, or other items of remembered content through the use of such processes as recognition, rote, memory, and selective recall." (For example, "How do you spell thyme?" "According to our text, what were the reasons for the popularity of the musical *Oklahoma* when it played on Broadway?")

- *Convergent questions.* These productive thinking questions elicit responses that require the respondent to merge diverse data productively. These questions elicit a response that contains more than mere recall or memory. "Convergent thinking represents the analyses and integration of given or remembered data. It leads to one expected and end-result or answer because of the tightly structured framework through which the individual must respond." (For example, "Explain why Anderson ran as an independent in the 1980 Presidential election?" "Compare the habitat of the frog with the rattlesnake's.")

- *Divergent questions.* These productive thinking questions encourage the elaboration of previous ideas, the drawing of implications, and the generation of new data and ideas, as well as spontaneity, originality, flexibility, and initiative. The questions seek a creative response and therefore often ask about contrary-to-fact situations in order to provide freedom for the respondent to answer them. "Divergent thinking represents intellectual operations wherein the individual is free to generate independently his own ideas within a data-poor situation or to take a new direction or perspective on a given topic." (For example, "Say more about your idea that there are three main phases in Picasso's works." "What would have happened in North America had Jefferson not purchased the Louisiana Territory?" "What were the implications of Nixon resigning rather than facing the public as President?")

- *Evaluative questions.* These productive thinking questions ask the respondent to express a personal opinion about some person, event, or policy; to estimate on the basis of a personal assessment of a situation or policy what probably will occur; and to offer a judgment or interpretation based on a previous statement. "Evaluative thinking deals with matters of judgment, value, and choice, and is characterized by its judgmental quality." (For example, "What's your opinion of this ballet dancer?" "Do you believe that the Freudian interpretation of *Hamlet* holds water?"
- *Classroom routine.* These nonproductive thinking questions elicit responses about the management of the teaching game and personal matters. (For example, "Do you want me to close the window?" "What page is the map on?" "Are you following me?")

When applying this system of categorizing questions, or any system, keep in mind the context of the lesson. It is the context that is the primary guide. Just the use of the word *why* does not indicate a convergent question since in the context the teacher may be asking the students to recall a reason given in the textbook or in yesterday's lesson. Therefore, since the context of the earlier excerpt is not known to us, it is not reasonable to ask you to categorize the teacher's thirty-two questions. This is especially important here because these thirty-two questions fall into the cognitive-memory and convergent categories with few in the divergent, evaluative, and routine categories. For this reason, a precise categorizing of the question is not possible. A rough categorizing is:

Cognitive/memory ⟩ 30 (at least)	
Convergent	
Divergent	1 (at most)
Evaluative	0
Routine	1

METHOD 6: TEACHER QUESTIONS FOR LOGICAL/COGNITIVE PROCESSES

This system for categorizing questions based on logical/cognitive processes derives from a philosophical position about questions and answers. This position states that answers make statements which are in essence truth claims. To categorize the question we ask how we would verify the expected response. This logical/cognitive approach was used (in a slightly different and more complicated form) in the research by Smith and his associates and Bellack and his associates in their research on classroom teaching. There are seven main types of questions in this system, only six of which appear in classrooms with any degree of regularity:

- *Definitional questions.* These questions elicit responses that define a word, term, or phrase. The respondent gives a label, or descriptive characteristics, or specific instances that tell how people have *agreed to use language* (for example, "What do you mean by 'sell short' in the stock market?" "What is air pressure?" "What is the word that we use to describe an object that children play with?")
- *Fact questions.* These *empirical* questions elicit responses that give facts based on *sense perceptions* of the world. The respondent gives *empirical data based on observations* and claims that something is true. That is, the respondent says that

something is indeed the case as known by our five senses. These facts can be specific or general and can refer to past, present, or future events. (For example, "Who won the Oscar last year for best female actress?" "Will it rain next Tuesday?" "What can you state in general about the great composers, Bach, Beethoven, and Mozart?" "Give a summary of the plot of Miller's *Death of a Salesman*.")

- *Relations among facts.* These *empirical* questions elicit responses that state *relationships among facts* by giving *comparisons, contrasts, causes and effects,* or *purposes.* The responses come from requests for *reasons or explanations,* often shown by such words as "why," "how," and "how come" in the question (for example, "Why did the police officer stop the traffic on the bridge?" "How do you fix a flat tire on a huge construction tractor?" "What's the difference between yogurt and sour cream?" "Why does the heart go thump, thump, thump?")

- *Opinion questions.* These *evaluative* questions elicit responses which offer a *personal value judgment.* The responses praise, blame, commend, criticize, or rate something dealing with attitudes, feelings, morals, personal beliefs, policies, or aesthetic matters. These questions do not explicitly request a reason or justification for the opinion to be given. (For example, "What is your favorite dance form— ballet, modern dance, square, or ballroom?" "Do you favor legalizing the smoking of marijuana?" "What is your attitude toward nuclear power for generating electricity?")

- *Justification of opinions.* These evaluative questions elicit reasons or explanations for personal opinions. The respondent *justifies* an opinion by giving a reason or purpose of the opinion and often—but not necessarily—also giving the criteria by which to assess the value judgment offered (for example, "Why do you support the equal rights amendment?" "What are your reasons for preferring opera over all other kinds of music?")

- *Metaphysical questions.* These questions are rare in most classrooms. They elicit responses stating *metaphysical or theological* statements. The respondent offers beliefs based on *faith* and deal with God, the after-life, the soul, or other such matters (for example, "What happens to righteous people when they die?" "Do you believe in God's mercy and compassion?")

- *Classroom routine.* These are not logical-cognitive questions about the topic under study, or a related topic, or even a digression. These are questions which elicit responses about classroom management, the flow of the interaction, and personal matters (for example, "Do you want me to close the window?" "What page is the map on?" "Are you following me?" "Did we do that already?")

Although this logical/cognitive system depends on knowing the context of the teaching situation, it does not do so as much as the productive thinking system presented in Method 5. Therefore, re-read the excerpt and categorize the 32 questions according to the seven definitions given above.

After each question in the following list is found the number of the type of question it is as defined according to the logical/cognitive process:

1. Correct? (7)
2. Do all people live in the same type of house? (2)

3. Do all people eat the same type of food? (2)
4. Do all people have the same customs? (2)
5. Do all people wear the same clothes? (2)
6. Would anyone say yes? (2)
7. Why not the same house all over the world? (3)
8. Suzie, what happens if you have money to pay for it? (3)
9. What happens—are you referring to like in the same country they get very little money in the way of wages? (2)
10. You mean the type of house? (2)
11. Some other reasons, please. (3)
12. What do you mean by the "weather"? (1)
13. The people that are with me for reading, how many of you remember the story of "The Rope"? (7)
14. Why was that type of house put on stilts? (3)
15. Now what about food? (2)
16. Do we have the same food prepared differently in different countries? (2)
17. What about clothing? (2)
18. Why different clothing? (3)
19. In warm weather do you wear dark or light clothing? (2)
20. Do you wear it tight or loose? (2)
21. Do they work their farms different in different parts of the world? (2)
22. What do we have in our country? (2)
23. What about some of the native lands? (2)
24. Do they have wooden tools? (2)
25. Does anybody want to describe one of these things? (2)
26. Do you think this was shaped out that way? (2)
27. People shaped this out of this or this is what it came to be? (2)
28. What do you mean by the shape of a volcano? (1)
29. Do you mean that this thing is the lava from the volcano? (2)
30. Now, the lava from the volcano comes from rocks? (2)
31. Is this softer material than the original rock? (2)
32. Odd-shaped, aren't they? (2)

You may disagree somewhat with the categories selected because the context is not 100 percent clear to us. It is not important if there is some minor disagreement at this point. If we examine the categories selected we have the following frequencies:

1. Definitional   =   2
2. Facts: Specific and general   =   23
3. Relationship Among Facts   =   5
4. Opinions   =   0
5. Justification of Opinions   =   0
6. Metaphysical   =   0
7. Routine   =   2

COMMENTS ON METHODS 5 AND 6

The importance of teacher questioning is great. For this reason, Methods 5 and 6 and any other system you use for classifying teacher questions deserve emphasis in observing the classroom.

By observing the types of questions asked, the observer gathers data on the manifest aims of the teacher regarding how to involve the students in thinking. Although most teachers rightfully advocate that their aim is "to get students to think," they are not aware of the types of thinking they in fact elicit from the students. And students do the kind of thinking that their teachers elicit from them. So, if the teacher is eliciting only or mainly nonproductive thinking (see Method 5) or mainly facts (see Method 6) the range of thinking done by the students will be narrow. Furthermore, the type of thinking elicited may not be in keeping with the espoused type of lesson the teacher wishes to conduct with the students.

When we look at the data gathered about teacher questions from Methods 5 and 6 together, we get a deeper insight into the earlier excerpt. We already know from Method 1 that the teacher asks eight questions a minute. Now, we recognize that related to rate of question asking is the fact that the questions primarily elicit factual responses that are probably mostly nonproductive thinking. Certainly, the student performs few definitional processes and no evalutive processes. Also, there is little if any divergent productive thinking by the students. What we get, therefore, is a series of quick questions in the empirical mode of thought that the student can and does answer in a brief phrase. The observer must ask, "Is this what the teacher desires? Is the teacher aware of what types of question he is asking? Is this what I as supervisor prefer for this teacher?"

METHOD 7: TEACHER EVALUATING A STUDENT RESPONSE

In addition to asking questions, the teacher must field student responses to the questions asked.

There are many ways to field a student response, including evaluating the response as good or bad, indicating that the response is correct or wrong (and this carries with it an implied evaluation of good or bad), acknowledging the responses in a neutral manner, asking a follow-up question, launching a new topic in light of the response, and so on.

There are two clusters of ways for a teacher to field a student response to a question. The first one deals with how the teacher evaluates a response. Some types of evaluative fielding comments that a teacher makes orally to a student response follow:

1. *Positive-mild:* "Okay," "All right," "Hm-hm," and teacher repeats the student's response.
2. *Positive-strong:* "Correct," "Yes," "Excellent," "That's right," "Good answer."
3. *Qualification:* Teacher expresses reservation about the response ("Yes, but…," "However," "That's only one way," "Maybe," "Yes and no").
4. *Negative.* "No," "Wrong," "Uh-uh," "Nope," "That's not even a possible answer").
5. *Acknowledgment:* Teacher does not evaluate the response, only *acknowledges or accepts* it into the discourse as something stated by the student as a response ("Thanks," "I'll write that on the board"). Sometimes a teacher's "Hm-hm" may sound

like an acknowledgment rather than a positive-mild evaluation. The line between mild evaluation and acknowledgment is difficult to draw. To promote consistency, it is better to designate all "hm-hm" comments as positive-mild.

6. *No evaluation:* Teacher does not evaluate or acknowledge the response; teacher does something else (for example, teacher asks another question, calls on another student, launches into a new topic or activity, or extends the response by expanding on it with new information).

NOTE: Enthusiasm or the lack of it, as expressed by the speaker's tone of voice, may lead the observer to switch a comment from positive-mild to positive-strong and vice versa (for example, "All right," with a loud and emphatic tone is considered as positive-strong). If there is a positive-mild and a positive-strong comment in the same teacher fielding move, the move is considered to be positive-strong.

With these six possibilities in mind, return to the excerpt and observe how the teacher orally fields the student responses to his questions.

The following is a list of teacher fielding moves from the excerpt:

1.   Now, first question.... (6)
2.   All right, no... (1)
3.   All right... (1)
4.   All right. (1)
5.   You mean...? (6)
6.   All right... (1)
7.   Yes. (2)
8.   What is...? (6)
9.   All right... (1)
10. All right... (1)
11. Why was...? (6)
12. All right... (1)
13. Yes, in some... (2)
14. Different weather, exactly... (2)
15. Do you wear...? (6)
16. Loose... (1)
17. All right... (1)
18. Machines... (1)
19. Yes, all right... (1)
20. All right... (1)
21. What do you...? (6)
22. Right, that's it... (2)
23. Once this rock... (6)
24. Yes... (1) (1 or 2 depending on the meaning of "yes"; tally it as type 1 since it appears from context to be only a repeat of the student's response.)
25. Yes, all right... (1)

When we convert this to a frequency count, we get the following information for Method 7 regarding teacher evaluative fielding comments:

1. Positive-mild   =   14
2. Positive-strong   =   4
3. Qualification   =   0
4. Negative   =   0
5. Acknowledgment   =   0
6. No evaluation   =   7

METHOD 8: TEACHER BUILDING ON A STUDENT RESPONSE

After the student responds to a teacher question, the teacher must field that response in some way. Very often the teacher evaluates the student response, as we see from the data gathered about the excerpt.

In addition to evaluating, the teacher can and does often make other remarks. The teacher can make these fielding moves before an evaluative or acknowledging comment, after an evaluative or acknowledging comment, or apart from an evaluative or acknowledging comment:

1. *Expands* the response; teacher adds on, embellishes, extends, modifies, or explains the response further in some way; this expansion is more than just a repeat of the response.

2. *Asks a question* for clarification of the response; (for example, "Did you say Reagan followed Carter?" "What do you mean by 'real war?'") Note that the clarification deals with the *words* of the response and not the meaning of the response in general.

3. *Asks same question again;* teacher seeks additional response to previous question (for example, "What else?" "Another one, please, Bill." "I'll repeat the question. What causes lightning?").

4. *Asks another question;* teacher pushes the material forward in some way; includes challenging and probing; includes asking for reasons for facts or opinions or other statements made in previous response (for example, "Now why *did* Russia invade Afghanistan?" "How come leaves turn color in autumn?").

5. *Structures;* teacher launches new activity or new topic; teacher halts/excludes activity or topic.

6. *Other.*

With these six fielding possibilities in mind, return once again to the excerpt and observe how the teacher builds on the student response. If there is only evaluating, do not mark a tally. If there is more than one thing the teacher does, write the appropriate number for each thing.

The same twenty-five teacher remarks from Method 7 are listed again. This time, the numbers following each entry refer to the types of teacher building remarks for Method 8:

1. Now, first question... (5, 4, 4, 4, 4)
2. All right, no... (3, 5, 4)
3. All right... (4, 2)
4. All right... (no tally because it is evaluative only)
5. You mean...? (2)

6. All right... (3)
7. Yes... (no tally because it is evaluative only)
8. What do...? (2)
9. All right... (3)
10. All right... (4)
11. Why was...? (4)
12. All right... (4, 4)
13. Yes, in some... (1, 4, 4)
14. Different weather, exactly... (4)
15. Do you wear...? (4)
16. Loose... (4)
17. All right... (4)
18. Machines... (4, 4)
19. Yes, all right... (4, 6)
20. All right... (4, 4)
21. What do you...? (2, 2)
22. Right, that's it... (4)
23. Once this rock... (1, 4)
24. Yes... (1, 6, 4)
25. Yes, all right... (5)

When we convert this to a frequency count, we get the following information for Method 8:

1.	Extends the response	=	3
2.	Questions: clarification	=	5
3.	Questions: additional response	=	3
4.	Questions: new material; probes	=	24
5.	Structures	=	3
6.	Other	=	2

METHOD 9: TEACHER FIELDS A STUDENT QUESTION

Methods 7 and 8 deal with teacher fielding moves of student responses. Method 7 refers to teacher fielding moves of student questions. Since we have already noted that the students in the excerpt did not ask any questions, it will be impossible to ask you to practice this method here. Nevertheless, it is possible to show some types of fielding moves you can identify at another time. The following is a list of 10 fielding options:

1. Teacher responds directly and answers the question.
2. Teacher returns the question back to the questioner (for example, How would *you* answer that question?)
3. Teacher relays the question to another specific student or to the class as a whole (for example, "Elana, would you please answer that question." "Does anyone want to answer Jonathan's question?")
4. Teacher rejects the question (generally because it is irrelevant) and continues on with the lesson (for example, "That's irrelevant here." "That's getting us off the topic.").

5. Teacher waits silently for the questioner or another student to answer.
6. Teacher launches into a new topic or activity as a way of answering the question (for example, "Let's pick that up now and now talk about it further and you'll see what happens.").
7. Teacher praises the question and then answers it (for example, "That's a great question at this point.").
8. Teacher seeks clarification of the question and then subsequently answers the question (for example, "When you speak of causes of the gasoline shortage, what do you mean by 'causes'?").
9. Teacher asks a question(s) so that the student can come up with an answer to it.
10. Teacher delays the question to a later part of the lesson or later time in the marking period (for example, "I'll answer that question later this week when we discuss the rise of Adolf Hitler.").

If the teacher does more than one of these fielding options, mark a tally for each one.

COMMENT ON METHODS 7, 8, AND 9

In the educational literature, there has been a general emphasis on how the teacher asks questions and structures the classroom interaction. Certainly questioning and structuring the lesson are important. Nevertheless, a significant part of any communication between two people is the feedback element each person gives to the other. It is this feedback element that is the focus of Methods 7, 8, and 9. If the teacher tells the student that his question is insightful, the student will feel satisfied and probably seek to ask another question when the situation feels appropriate. If the opposite is true, the result may be devastating for future participation by the student. It is for this reason that it is helpful to the teacher to become aware of his fielding behavior by way of your observations of the classroom.

METHOD 10: TEACHER WAIT-TIME

By now, the concept and research on wait-time are familiar. Nevertheless, wait-time is a fresh idea for many educators and still a vibrant one for those who have known it for years. Teacher wait-time refers to the amount of time a person waits after asking a question before speaking again. For example, the teacher asks a question, waits, and then begins to ask another question or calls upon another respondent when the student originally asked the question remains silent. Teacher wait-time also refers to the amount of time a teacher waits after a student responds to a question or reacts to another student's remarks before that person speaks again. For example, the teacher asks a question, a student responds, the teacher waits, and then the teacher speaks again. A brief illustration will help clarify the two types of wait-time

TEACHER: When was V-J day? (Wait-time 1) When was World War II over in the Pacific area against the Japanese? (Wait-time 1)
STUDENT: I guess it came soon after the bombing of Hiroshima. (Wait-time 2)
TEACHER: Okay, and when was that? (Wait-time 1)

That is to say, there is a wait-time after the very first teacher question, and it is called wait-time 1. Since the student didn't respond fast enough, the teacher proceeded to ask another question. There is another wait-time 1. Now, the student responds, and there is another wait-time; this wait-time after a response is called wait-time 2. Then the teacher speaks again, giving a positive-mild evaluation of the response (see Method 7) and then asking a third question.

We need to ask how long was each of the four wait-times by the teacher (three wait-times 1 after the questions and one wait-time 2 after the response). There is no accurate way to measure wait-time when using a typescript. The observer must hear the teacher in order to measure the wait-time. In general, we speak about short wait-time and long wait-time. Short wait-time is up to three seconds and long wait-time is over three seconds. The observer without a stop watch must listen carefully to estimate the teacher's wait-time. The point is to determine whether the teacher has long wait-time or short wait-time after asking a question (wait-time 1) and after hearing a student speak (wait-time 2). The reason for this determination relates to the intriguing research on wait-time which will be presented shortly. Notice that if a student responds immediately to a teacher's question, this does not count as teacher short wait-time. Similarly, if a student speaks immediately after another student has spoken, this does not count as teacher short wait-time. On the contrary, most of the time a student speaks after another student precisely because the teacher has long wait-time. Teacher short wait-time is recorded only when the teacher speaks within three seconds after asking a question or after hearing a student speak.

Since you cannot determine the teacher wait-times for the written excerpt, the data for that excerpt follow in Figure 3-7. These data come from a determination of each of the wait-times after listening to the tape recording of that section of the lesson. That is, this teacher never once had long wait-time; he only had short wait-time.

	Long	Short
	OVER 3 SEC.	**UNDER 3 SEC.**
Wait-time 1 (after question)		卌 II
Wait-time 2 (after student speaking)		卌 卌 卌 卌 IIII

FIGURE 3-7. Tally sheet for wait-times.

COMMENT ON METHOD 10

Wait-time is a measure for determining the teacher's patience, listening ability, and willingness to involve the student in the teaching game. The research on teacher wait-time is both intriguing and convincing. Research shows that the average teacher waits one second after asking a question (wait-time 1)—that is, if a student does not begin a response within one second, teachers usually repeat the question, or ask another question, or call on another student to respond. Also, after students respond (wait-time 2) teachers usually wait slightly less than one second before speaking again.

According to the research conducted by Rowe[6] and Lake,[7] when teachers increased their wait-time to 3 to 5 seconds (long wait-time), the following significant results occurred:

For students

- The length of student responses increased.
- The number of unsolicited but appropriate responses increased.
- Failure to respond decreased.
- Confidence as reflected in fewer inflected responses increased, that is, fewer responses have the tone of "Is that what you want?"
- The incidence of speculative thinking increased.
- The incidence of offering alternative explanations increased.
- More evidence followed by or preceded by inference statements occurred.
- The number of questions asked by students increased and the number of (science) experiments they proposed increased.
- Teacher-centered show and tell decreased, and student-student comparing increased.
- The number of responses from "slow" students increased so that there was a greater variety of students participating.
- The incidence of students responding with congruent and more complex answers occurred (that is, ascend modal congruence increased).
- The incidence of conversation sequences increased (that is, sequences involving three or more related utterances increased in number).

For teachers

- Teachers became more flexible in their discourse.
- Teachers asked fewer questions.
- Teachers increased the variety of their questions.
- Teachers improved their expectations of performance of "slow" students.

In short, the results show that a slight change just in the pacing of the talk, done by increasing the teacher's wait-time, led to changes in pedagogical roles and cognitive performance. Students started asking more questions and participating more, as well as offering alternative explanations, increasing speculative thinking, and offering more complex responses.

METHOD 11: TEACHER SPEAKS AFTER WHICH GENDER?

It is possible and fruitful to chart the sequence of many events occurring in the classroom. Method 11 is one example of recording the sequence of a particular type of event, and it deals with the relationship of the teacher to the males and females in the class. Here we observe the following four possibilities during a lesson where there are no guests or audiovisual aids.

1. Teacher after female student.
2. Teacher after male student.
3. Student after female student.
4. Student after male student.

Of course, it is possible to expand each of the "student" types above if you wish. For example, instead of just "student after male student," you could have "male student after male student" and "female student after male student." You might want to do this if you find that there is much cross-discussion going on in the lesson. Generally, the specific breakdown is not necessary.

Try this method with the earlier excerpt. Notice that if the teacher only calls upon a student to speak but says nothing else after a previous student has spoken (for example, "Jeff?"), then do not count this as "teacher speaks." Count this as "student-after-student." With these possibilities in mind, your frequency count should look like this:

1. Teacher-after-male   =   13
2. Teacher-after-female   =   12
3. Student-after-male   =   0
4. Student-after-female   =   0

METHOD 12: TEACHER SPEAKS TO WHICH GENDER?

With this method, we observe the teacher speaking to the students. Two possibilities are immediately obvious, but the items for observing are a bit more than that:

1. Teacher speaks to male.
2. Teacher speaks to female.
3. Teacher speaks to class or group.
4. Not clear.

Although it may be difficult to do from a written excerpt, try this method with the excerpt. Indicate to whom the teacher speaks each time the teacher asks a question, talks substantively, gives a directive, scolds or criticizes a student, or evaluates a student. If a teacher says, "Joe, what is the formula for water?" and then says, "Good" after Joe's response, mark a tally twice under "Teacher speaks to male." If the teacher is expanding on a point in general, mark a tally under the category for the class as a whole.

The frequency count from the excerpt is as follows. There may be some slight disagreement stemming from a disagreement about how often to mark a tally. A minor difference is unimportant here, however.

1. Teacher speaks to male   =   12
2. Teacher speaks to female   =   13
3. Teacher speaks to class or group =   13
4. Not clear   =   3

METHOD 13: TEACHER CALLS ON VOLUNTEERS

With this method, we observe the teacher calling on students to speak. This is not always as easy as it might appear, however. The possibilities are shown in Figure 3-8. No data for the excerpt appear here since it is impossible to mark tallies based on the written script alone. The observer must see and hear the teacher personally to use this method.

	Student	
	MALE	**FEMALE**
Teacher calls on a volunteer		
Teacher calls on a nonvolunteer		
Teacher doesn't call on a student (student speaks out)		
Not clear		

FIGURE 3-8. Tally of teacher calling on students.

COMMENT ON METHODS 11, 12, AND 13

It is certainly possible that a particular teacher will favor boys over girls during classroom interaction and favor volunteers over nonvolunteers. Yet seldom do teachers who favor boys over girls realize that they do so. Furthermore, seldom do teachers who do so realize that they speak following virtually every student who speaks. Nevertheless, the consequences of the teacher speaking after every speaker are immediate because the opportunity for a student to speak is lost, diminished, or at best delayed each time the teacher speaks. Thus, teacher talk after a student speaks has a direct impact on the degree of verbal participation in the lesson. The degree of verbal participation is important because of the positive correlation that exists between student participation and achievement.

From the data gathered by Methods 11 and 12, it is clear that the teacher in the excerpt does not favor boys over girls or girls over boys. His (the teacher is a male) treatment of the students is much the same. He speaks immediately after the boys as well as the girls and talks to them almost equally. The striking data show that not once does a student speak after another student has spoken. The class interaction is very much like a Ping-Pong game between the teacher and the students. The teacher is on one side of the net with all the students together on the other side. After a student hits the ball, the teacher hits it and possibly, but not generally, the same student hits the ball back. This excerpt is not like a volleyball game where the players on one side of the net may hit the ball three times before allowing the other team to return the ball. In this excerpt, the teacher speaks after each student, thus prohibiting student-student interaction simply because he enters the discourse quickly (remember that he has short wait-time) each time a student finishes. At one point, the teacher did not even wait for the student (Margy) to finish but cut her off in the middle of a response.

METHOD 14: LOCATION OF THE TEACHER

With this method, we observe where the teacher sits or stands during the lesson. To observe the teacher's location, it is necessary for the observer to draw quickly a simple and operational map of the classroom. (See Figure 3-9.)

With the map in hand, the observer chooses a time limit. If the teacher is particularly mobile, then the observer should choose a five- or ten-second time period. If the teacher, on the other hand, is fairly stationary, a twenty- or thirty-second time period or more is appropriate. The observer simply counts silently and marks a number every twenty seconds, for example, to indicate the sequence of the teacher's positions. The numbers indicate where the teacher is in relation to the students during the lesson.

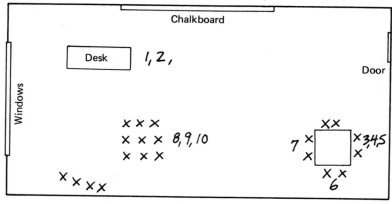

FIGURE 3-9. Operational map of the classroom.

METHOD 15: LOCATION OF STUDENT CALLED ON BY TEACHER

With this method, we observe the location of the students whom the teacher calls upon to speak. It is possible to use the same map as in Method 14 and simply tally each time a student speaks during the entire lesson or segment of it. Another way is to draw a map of the classroom and divide it into student zones in a way resembling a professional basketball court. Such a map might look like Figure 3-10.

The observer, with such a map, marks a tally to indicate the position of the student called on by the teacher. At the end of the observation period, the observer can leave the map as it is in the raw state or total up the frequencies for each of the three student zones in a chart, as shown in the top section of Figure 3-11.

The observer can even divide the room into two vertical halves to yield a right and left part for each of the three zones. The frequency count chart would then be shown as in the bottom of Figure 3-11.

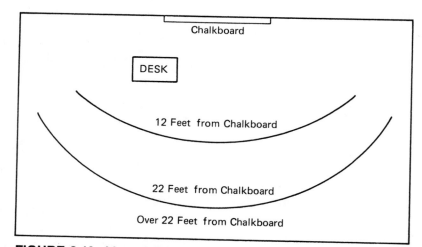

FIGURE 3-10. Map of the classroom.

	Frequency
Front (12') zone	
Middle (22') zone	
Far (22 + ') zone	

	Frequency	
	Right	**Left**
Front (12') zone		
Middle (22') zone		
Far (22 + ') zone		

FIGURE 3-11. Location of student (tally sheet).

METHOD 16: TEACHER NONVERBAL ACTIONS

With this method, we observe the teacher's nonverbal actions as they appear. We observe such items as frowning, smiling, and laughing. This method uses a checklist of nonverbal behaviors and requires the observer to check off each item as it appears. The observable items of importance are shown in Figure 3-12.

It is important to remember that you can and should modify the items in the system to suit your given situation. When you do so, keep in mind that it is important not to make the list very long or else you will have trouble marking tallies as the observation period proceeds.

Nonverbal Action by Teacher	**Tally here each time item appears**
1. Smiles	
2. Frowns	
3. Laughs	
4. Uses chalkboard	
5. Uses other A-V equipment	
6. Raises voice level (shouts; yells)	
7. Pats student on shoulder, etc.	

FIGURE 3-12. Checklist of teacher's nonverbal actions.

COMMENT ON METHODS 14, 15, AND 16

With these three methods we concentrate on the nonverbal actions of the teachers. We do so to broaden our perspective and also to follow the research on nonverbal actions that is growing as well as demonstrating new insights on teaching. For example, in an article on the physical environment of the school, Weinstein shows that a "front-center seat facilitates achievement, positive attitudes, and participation at least for those somewhat predisposed to speak in class."[8] In another study concerned with zones of distance from the teacher, researchers concluded that "the form and content of teacher-pupil interaction may be related to pupil distance from the teacher. As pupils were seated closer to the teacher, they were more likely to be involved in the decision making (permissive factor) and question answering in the classroom. Conversely, the further pupils were from the teacher, the more likely they were to be lectured to and less likely to participate in classroom decision making."[9] In short, nonverbal actions by the teacher directly affect classroom interaction.

Although the teacher's verbal action is more obvious and somewhat easier to observe objectively, teacher nonverbal action is always present and influences the students. The teacher who never moves from behind the desk has a different rapport with his students from the teacher who "rubs shoulders" with his students by working with them at their desks. Also, a teacher who smiles and laughs sends a different message to the students from one who frowns and shouts. While teachers can hear themselves talk and possibly monitor their verbal action through internal feedback, they need help in gaining critical information about their nonverbal action. If a teacher unconsciously does not call on students in the far right zone of the classroom, for example, then an awareness of this tendency or habit will be important to the teacher.

METHOD 17: TEACHER AND STUDENT TALK

With this final method, we come perhaps full swing to the simplest and oldest observation method. The observer, after deciding on an appropriate unit of measurement of three, five, seven, ten, fifteen, or twenty seconds (depending on the switching of speakers), marks a tally to indicate who is talking at the end of the time unit. Probably a five- or seven-second time unit is the best unit to use for ease of tallying and the gathering of helpful information. You can use a shorter time unit if there is fast interaction between teacher and student. Or, you can use a longer time unit if there is slow interaction. (The data for the earlier excerpt, based on a five-second time unit, are shown in Figure 3-13.)

COMMENT ON METHOD 17

It is patently obvious that if students do not participate orally in the lesson it is most difficult for them, at any age level, to maintain interest and achieve the objectives of that

| Teacher speaking | ~~THL~~ ~~THL~~ ~~THL~~ ~~THL~~ ~~THL~~ ~~THL~~ ~~THL~~ ||| |
| Student speaking | ~~THL~~ ~~THL~~ | |

FIGURE 3-13. Tally at end of five-second time unit.

lesson. A straightforward measurement of who is talking at the end of every time unit yields vital information because teachers generally have a poor estimate of how much they talk—dominate the verbal interaction. The data from the excerpt show the large differential between teacher and student talk. Keep in mind that the category of student talk must then be divided by twenty to thirty in order to compute how much the average student talks in comparison with the teacher.

Summing Up

The seventeen methods presented in this section are not the only ways for you to observe the teacher teaching. They are only a small sampling of what is possible for you to do. The methods are rather effective and bring a focus to observing the classroom. They yield data that will be helpful to your teachers.

You should try these methods and modify them to suit the particular situation that exists with your teachers. After using these methods, new ideas will come readily as you and your teachers decide together on what next to observe as part of the teachers' continual striving to find ways to develop professionally. You can and should persist in gathering specific data through observing the classroom directly rather than relying on indirect remarks made by teachers in the faculty room, or by students in the halls, or by parents on the telephone. Direct observation with a focus on specifics has no substitute. The results become evident in the postobservational conference.

CHAPTER 3 ENDNOTES

1. COLIN M. HOOK and BARAK V. ROSENSHINE, "Accuracy of Teacher Reports of Their Classroom Behavior," *Review of Educational Research,* Vol. 49, No. 1 (Winter 1979): 1–11.

2. BRUCE W. TUCKMAN, K. M. McCALL, and R. T. HYMAN, "The Modification of Teacher Behavior: Effects of Dissonance and Coded Feedback," *American Educational Research Journal,* Vol. 6, No. 4 (November 1969): 607–19.

3. RONALD T. HYMAN, *School Administrator's Handbook of Teacher Supervision and Evaluation Methods* (Englewood Cliffs, N.J.: Prentice-Hall, Inc., 1974).

4. JONATHAN S. BLAIR, "Keeping House in a Cappadocian Cave," *National Geographic,* Vol. 138, No. 1 (July 1970): 127–46.

5. JAMES J. GALLAGHER and MARY JANE ASCHNER, "A Preliminary Report on Analyses of Classroom Interaction" and "Addendum: Secondary Classification Categories," reprinted in *Teaching: Vantage Points for Study,* edited by R. T. Hyman (Philadelphia: J. B. Lippincott, 1974), 181–97.

6. MARY BUDD ROWE, "Science, Silence, and Sanctions," *Teaching Science as Continuous Inquiry* (New York: McGraw-Hill Book Company, 1973), 240-76.

7. JOHN H. LAKE, "The Influence of Wait-Time on the Verbal Dimensions of Student Inquiry Behavior" (Doctor dissertation, Rutgers University, 1973).

8. CAROL WEINSTEIN, "The Physical Environment of the School: A Review of the Research," *Review of Educational Research,* Vol. 49, No. 4 (Fall 1979): 580.

9. DOUGLAS M. BROOKS, S. B. SILVEN, and M. WOOTEN, "The Ecology of Teacher-Pupil Verbal Interaction," *The Journal of Classroom Interaction,* Vol. 14, No. 1 (1978): 41.

4

PREPARING

TO CONFER

WITH TEACHERS

As a supervisor, holding a conference with a teacher is as basic to your job as exercise and a nutritious diet are to good health. The way you confer serves as a model for the teacher on how to interact with and treat students. If you are prepared for the conference, are strategic and tactical during it, and are reflective after it, the teacher can—and probably will—use you as a model. This fact adds to the importance of the conference in supervision.

You can confer with a teacher about many things, not only about a classroom observation. You can confer about telephone calls you have received from parents, about the teacher's behavior at the school dance or graduation picnic, about the teacher's application for a sabbatical leave, or whatever. Yet, none of these, except observation in the classroom, requires you by tradition, by school regulations, or by contract with the teacher's organization to confer with the teacher. Nothing gets to the heart of the teacher's job as does observation in the classroom. Therefore, since the principles of conferring are the same no matter what the impetus, we shall restrict ourselves in this chapter to conferring about classroom observation.

Chapter 4 deals with the relationship between observing and conferring. The need for congruence between observing and conferring will be established. Then ways to prepare for the conference will be offered so that you can achieve your objectives.

After reading this chapter, you should be able to:

- Understand the need for congruence in and preparation for the conference.
- List at least three reasons why a conference is needed after an observation.
- Describe the importance of congruence between an observation's purpose and a conference's purpose.
- State at least ten actions to take in preparing for a conference.

THE RELATIONSHIP BETWEEN CONFERRING AND OBSERVING

Despite the current literature's call for preobservation conferences between supervisor and teacher, there are few such conferences. The reason may be a disagreement with the literature as to the efficacy of preobservation conferences, or it may be the lack of time supervisors and teachers have in their busy schedules, or both. In any case, the commitment to preobservation conferences seems not to exist at the present time among most supervisors, although the preobservation conference can be beneficial.

A supervisor's personal judgment about the workability and suitability of a preobservation conference in his or her particular situation is important; therefore, this chapter's conception or description of preobservation conferences does not infer that they are absolutely necessary to sound supervision. Helpful, yes; absolutely necessary, no.

Reasons for Having Postobservation Conferences

The postobservation conference, the most common type of supervisory conference, is desirable and necessary for four reasons:

1. The teacher wants to know what the supervisor observed and what are his or her reactions to the collected data. This is a natural, normal response to having someone, whether a peer or superior colleague, come to observe a teacher teach.

2. You, as supervisor, want to report to the teacher what you observed. You want to do this because, by doing so, you manifest your concern for the teacher and students, you alert the teacher to data he or she may not be aware of, and you indicate what you consider to be important. All of these actions are important because they allow you to put in practice what you believe and express it to your teacher. The nonverbal message of these actions is a strong and positive one not to be considered lightly.

3. Reflection brings meaning to experience; raw data is not enough for the teacher or for you. When you talk about what you observed, the teacher and you discover together the meaning of the data you have collected. In a conference, you connect the data to previous events and investigate the implications of those data for the teacher and students. An analogy will help here. Let us suppose that a kindergarten teacher takes his students to the zoo. They see snakes, lions, elephants, seals, and birds. The teacher has the pedagogical obligation either at the zoo or upon returning to school to discuss what the children saw and experienced on the field trip. The meaning of the experience at the zoo comes out as the teacher and students talk about the different types of animals, their physical characteristics, their unique feeding requirements, and their habitat requirements. The teacher cannot rely on the students to debrief themselves.

It is necessary for every person to reflect on experience in order to acquire an understanding of it. For example, it is the teacher's job to guide his or her students in reflecting about their field trip to the zoo. So, too, with the teacher and you. You both need to talk about what you have observed so that you can arrive at an understanding of what it all means. Observation data are necessary, but not sufficient; reflection makes your classroom visit complete.

4. Face-to-face communication establishes connection between people. When you speak to someone face-to-face, you engage in verbal and nonverbal communication simultaneously in a strong way. You communicate with your eyes, face, hands, and body as well as your voice. You reach the other person individually. He becomes more than just a name, as he is when you write a memo, and more than just a voice, as he is when you speak together on the telephone. You establish a connection with that person that emphasizes the meeting of two concerned people. The other person is not distant or anonymous, or just a member of some category of person. He is, rather, a live, unique being. It is this connection that is the foundation of the supervisory relationship, what allows you to help the teacher to change, and what allows the teacher to allow you to help him.

Establishing Congruence Between Conferring and Observing

THE NEED FOR CONGRUENCE

It should be self-evident and obvious that your approach to conferring should be congruent with your approach to observing. If you observe with the purpose of making the teacher aware of what is occurring in his classroom as he interacts with his students, you must follow up in your conference by emphasizing the function of reporting. It makes no sense at all to observe, for example, how the teacher fields student responses to the teacher's questions and then to chastise the teacher with an angry voice about what the teacher did when he wasn't even aware of the whole notion of fielding responses in the first place. It makes no sense to observe with one purpose—alerting the teacher to what is happening—and then to confer in a way—criticizing—which negates that purpose. Rather, it is reasonable for you to follow through with your purpose, to confer with the teacher in a way that encourages change in teaching. This occurs when the teacher becomes aware of key aspects of interaction between the students and him- or herself.

EFFECTIVE COMMUNICATION

In order for effective communication to occur, the receiver of a message must receive and interpret the message in the way the speaker intended. If, through some "noise" on the communication channel, the listener interprets the message not as intended, the communication process has a flaw. The flaw may be in the clarity of the message as spoken or written, or in the hearing acuity of the listener, or in a misinterpretation of the speaker's tone of voice, or whatever. The flaw need not necessarily be in the speaker's message, as is so often implied by our continued advocacy of clear speech. Communication is a two-direction process in which sender and receiver, speaker and listener, interact actively, although it may appear on the surface that only the speaker is active.

As speaker, you need to consider who the listener is. You must personalize the message in such a way as to suit the teacher, as receiver, in the attempt to convey the desired intention. You must consider voice tones, as well as other nonverbal elements that exist simultaneously with every verbal message. You must recognize that your very role as supervisor gives greater intensity to the words you speak to the teacher. Words that you might say to your spouse or friends or colleagues take on a different meaning when spoken to a teacher during a supervisory conference. Further, words mean something different to the successful, confident, tenured teacher than what they mean to a struggling, inexperienced, nontenured teacher even though they may be the exact same words.

For this reason, you must be alert to the need for establishing and maintaining effective communication with the teacher. You must speak clearly and directly, trying to avoid phrases and tones that might lead the teacher to make inferences regarding hidden purposes and intentions. You must try to keep the channels of communication open and free from "noise"—that is, any disturbance that hinders transmission of the messages sent between the teacher and you. If a particular teacher reacts negatively to frequent conferences on your "turf" (that is, your office), you must make other arrangements by changing the meeting place for sending messages.

VERBAL AND NONVERBAL MESSAGES

You must be sensitive to the language used and the nonverbal messages conveyed in the interaction that occurs during a conference. Suppose that you have gathered data about the teacher's questioning activity. At the beginning of the conference, you report to the teacher, for example, that she has asked thirty-two questions in four minutes and that thirty of the thirty-two are of the nonproductive cognitive-memory type. The teacher hears the message and then sits silently without saying a word. You must not infer from the teacher's silence that she doesn't understand the message or that she is angry. Rather, her silence may be a sign that she needs time to think about the powerful data you have just given her. She may be dealing with the dissonance you have created in her between her beliefs about what she should be doing as a teacher and the actuality of her actions. You must, therefore, allow for her silence and after a short while request her comments.

If your objective for observing the teacher was twofold—to gather data in order to alert the teacher to what is occurring and to discuss the teacher's interpretation of the data with her—you must keep that objective in mind when you confer. Create congruence between conferring and observing by reporting the data and by being careful not to go beyond this without the teacher's participation. Remain committed to your original intention so that the teacher can be personally involved in change as she becomes aware of her own actions. Encourage the teacher to accept the data, reflect on them, express her comments aloud, and discuss with you the implications for the future. You cannot be congruent if you alone expound on the meaning of the observational data. If only *you* express interpretations about the meaning of the data, the teacher loses the opportunity to promote her own reflection and responsibility for change. Indeed, for congruence between observing and conferring, the teacher must become involved with the data during the conference by interpreting them and participating in the decision as to what changes, if any, she needs to make in light of them.

You might offer an interpretation at the request of the teacher and then perhaps compare it with the teacher's. This is a healthy procedure to follow. However, if you observe the teacher and then you alone interpret the data, the teacher suffers. The teacher loses the rich opportunity to search for meaning personally, and it is this type of search that leads to significant change. When a supervisor interprets and generalizes for the teacher, there occurs an intellectual robbery that victimizes a collaborative approach to supervision. In effect, when you interpret for the teacher without her comments and participation, you convey a negative message. Through your action, you nonverbally say, "You are not able to understand what you're doing, but I can because I am better than you. That's why I'm the supervisor in the first place. I am competent, but you are not."

It goes further. The message conveyed concerns not only cognitive competence but also interpersonal trust. You are also saying, "I don't trust you to think about what you're doing and to change. To make sure that you get some interpretation, I'll give you mine. This way, I'll know that you've heard what you should hear." This message is deflating; it eliminates the possibility of collaborative supervision by destroying the element of trust between two people who seek mutual gain. Trust is necessary, and with it you and the teacher both gain because only when the teacher improves do you benefit.

A negative message stemming from the lack of congruence also attacks the teacher's self-respect because self-respect cannot flourish in an environment where trust and a sense of intellectual ability are absent. Self-respect, like trust, is necessary for improved teaching. If you do away with a teacher's self-respect, the likelihood of change for the better evaporates just as water on a bather's back does after a swim in the ocean on a hot, dry summer day.

ESPOUSED THEORY AND THEORY IN USE

The idea of congruence between conferring and observing (that is, between intent to implement a particular approach to supervision and the carrying out of that intent) is related to a more general idea. According to Harvard psychologist Chris Argyris,[1] there are two kinds of human behavior theories: (1) an espoused theory of action, which "people hold about how they behave toward self and others," and (2) a theory-in-use about action, which is inferred from people's behavior and "does predict their behavior." People state their espoused theories easily and reliably, but these theories do not serve as good predictors of their actual behavior. People are not generally aware that their espoused theories are poor predictors nor are they aware of the theories-in-use that do account for their behavior quite well. A theory-in-use governs a person's behavior whether or not it is in conflict with the person's espoused theory.

When a person's espoused theory is incongruent with the theory-in-use, the effect is a lack of understanding of the action that takes place. For example, Ellen Evans, a supervisor, espouses a theory that says that it is advisable for her to observe a teacher, Anne Adams, and to report the collected data to Adams and to discuss Adams' comments with her. Evans believes that her espoused theory accurately predicts her behavior in the postobservation conference with Adams. However, Evans is unaware that what actually occurs in the conference is incongruent with her espoused theory. Evans begins by reporting the data but shifts to offering explanations for Adams' behavior without getting Adams actively involved. Then she directs Adams to change her teaching behavior along specific avenues. Evans' behavior is best understood not by understanding and accepting her espoused theory as a collaborative supervisor, but rather by understanding her theory-in-use, which is based on Evans' self-concept as a directive "boss."

If Evans is unaware of her theory-in-use and unaware that her espoused theory does not account for the kinds of interaction she engages in during a conference, she cannot understand why Adams reacts as she does—as a resistant, unmotivated, defensive, conforming, somewhat uncooperative, and annoyed teacher. Evans' behavior may be governed by a set of assumptions and factors that are in direct conflict with what she believes explicitly. To help Evans and Adams, as supervisor and teacher, Evans must bring her espoused theory into line with her theory-in-use so that the action she takes matches her intentions.

To demonstrate the need for congruence, in any type of professional situation, Argyris[2] shows the effect of incongruence between espoused theory and theory-in-use among faculty members in the alternative schools that flourished during the late 1960s and early 1970s. According to Argyris, people established alternative schools out of their dissatisfaction with the effects of the hierarchical and bureaucratic organizational structures of the traditional schools. When these educators began their alternative schools, they espoused new theories of action, but their actual behavior was guided by their theories-in-use, which were still suited to the old structures they had abandoned. Without a theory-in-use congruent with their expectations for their alternative schools, the faculty continued to behave in a way that conflicted with their new environment. The net result was the fairly rapid degeneration and failure of the alternative schools. What is more, the faculty could not account for the deficiencies and failings of the way the alternative school functioned. They could not comprehend why their interaction with students, parents, and other educators remained essentially the same as in their former schools once the initial novelty and enthusiasm palled. In a footnote, Argyris makes a significant comment about espoused theory and theory-in-use, which emphasizes the need for you to confer with your teachers with care: "In the field of education, the incongruity appears to be high."

GUIDELINES FOR PREPARING FOR THE CONFERENCES

You can only prepare well if you can anticipate what might occur during the conference. Your preparation serves to allow you to face what might occur and to deal with it appropriately. Preparation can serve to cause certain things you want to occur to occur in fact and can serve to avoid or eliminate certain other things that you don't want to occur. Let us, then, briefly present in broad strokes the characteristics of an average conference as held today and that we will seek to improve on in several ways.

1. The supervisor meets with the teacher the same or next day after observing him or her.

2. The supervisor and teacher meet in a private place (probably the supervisor's office).

3. The teacher is somewhat anxious—nervous, uneasy, and somewhat eager—because generally conferences have been times of criticism and evaluation by the supervisor (the superior) of the teacher (the subordinate). There is no way to deny the unequal relationship between supervisor and teacher.

4. The supervisor has the responsibility to get the conference going and to set the agenda as well as the tone.

5. The supervisor and teacher talk about the class session, starting with how the teacher felt about the lesson and continuing with what the supervisor criticizes as needing correction.

6. There is a tendency for the supervisor to dominate the talk as the teacher yields to the supervisor's authority. The supervisor has a tendency to talk about negative items and to justify comments on them. There is a tendency to talk less about positive items than negative ones and little tendency to justify positive comments.

7. The teacher waits on each word, looking for some praise and encouragement from the supervisor so that he or she won't be totally deflated. If the supervisor criticizes him or her, the teacher may well be defensive or simply agree to what is said in order to appease the supervisor. Internalization and commitment probably are absent.

8. The teacher looks to the supervisor for suggestions or directives regarding what changes to make in order to please the supervisor or just to get him off his or her back. Or, the teacher looks to the supervisor simply because he or she has always looked to the supervisor in the past.

9. The supervisor ends the conference in a friendly way after making suggestions for change.

The foregoing list of characteristics describes the average conference as often held today. Some of the nine characteristics are positive, and you will want to continue them in general (items 1 and 2, for example). However, you will want to change others in order to effect change (items 6 and 8, for example). The following thirteen guidelines will help you in both aspects.

Keep in mind that these guidelines for preparing for the conference are offered with a concept of what the conference itself ought to be like. Thus, you will probably find it helpful to re-read this section on preparing for the conference after you read the chapters on holding the conference. (That is, after you understand what you are preparing for, these preparatory guidelines will make even more sense.) What follows is not a sequence of steps because it is impossible to create one that will apply to everyone. Rather, it is an intertwining cluster of suggested actions. The effect of these actions will be a calm, sensible approach rather than an angry or impetuous one, and this calm approach has a high probability of being constructive to a sound supervisory relationship.

1. Decide on what features of the teaching session you will observe and offer data about them to the teacher. Ideally, your decision should be based on an agreement you reached with the teacher at your preobservation conference, or at your last postobservation conference as you looked ahead, or at the beginning-of-the-year conference that you held to lay out your overall plans. If at all possible, what you decide to observe should offer some variety for the teacher in order to get a range of views about his classroom. For example, if at one point you have collected data about the teacher's questioning, during your next observation you might well look at questioning for a short time as a follow-up. You might well supplement this by collecting data on the teacher's use of space or on the social-emotional climate of the classroom.

2. Create or choose an instrument that will guide you in collecting the desired data. You don't necessarily need a formal one, as used by researchers, although you certainly can use one if it suits your purposes. You can do well with an informal instrument, be it one offered in Chapter 3 or a variation of one offered there, or one of your own creation. It is important to come to the conference with data that you can present to the teacher to help him to learn what happened in his class session. If you are interested in discussing his questioning activity, for example, you may profitably use observation methods 1 and 6, as suggested in Chapter 3. Or, you can modify these to suit your specific purposes.

3. Review your observation notes, making sure you have data in a form you can present to the teacher. It's important that before you begin to talk with the teacher, you look over your notes to have an overall view of the data and some sense of what they indicate. Try to put them in a form that you can show to your teacher for a lasting impression. It is one thing, for example, to hear "forty-nine substantive questions and eight routine questions," and another to see written on paper:

Cognitive/memory	ℍℍ ℍℍ ℍℍ ℍℍ ℍℍ ℍℍ ℍℍ ℍℍ ǀ	= 41
Convergence	ℍℍ ǀ	= 6
Divergence	ǀ	= 1

Evaluative I = 1
Routine   ~~TTTT~~ III = 8

4. Prepare in writing some awareness questions that you can ask about the data you have collected. Write these in your notes for your use only.

5. In light of the data, your awareness questions, and the teacher's anticipated responses to them, consider which type of conference you think would be most appropriate. Think of how you will conduct the conference. Prepare a strategy by modifying one offered in Chapter 6. Suppose you plan to give the data on questioning presented in guideline 3 above and you believe that the teacher will sit there silently as if transfixed by disbelief. You must now plan what you will do. If you think that it is best to conduct an awareness conference, you must plan on being silent for a while and then say something like, "It seems to me that you need more time to think about these data. Get back to me tomorrow or the next day so we can plan together where we go from here." If, however, you believe that a correction conference is in order, you must plan how you might shift to that type. You must plan on saying something like, "If it's okay with you, let's take a look at those data together. We probably can come up with some alternatives to what you did. What do those data mean to you in terms of consequences you didn't anticipate?" This question or its equivalent will probably elicit an explicit verbal response; it can entice the teacher into a discussion exploring alternatives that may eliminate what he didn't find satisfactory. On the basis of what he says, you can ask him for some possible solutions, comment on them, and together agree on some steps for implementation.

6. Decide on what constitutes acceptable behavior regarding the data to be reported. If the data in your opinion show the teacher's behavior to need change, you must know what will be considered acceptable because the teacher may well ask you. For example, if you think that eight routine questions and forty-nine substantive questions in less than thirty-five minutes are too many, you should have an idea about how many questions you consider acceptable. Be sure that you can describe the acceptable behavior in observable, operational terms.

7. Decide on some suggestions that you will probably receive and accept from the teacher or that you will make to the teacher regarding actions that will lead to acceptable alternative behavior. You need to have some idea ahead of time as to what actions the teacher can take that will effect change. This is true for a session with positive data as well as negative data. The teacher needs alternatives for successful actions lest he get into a rut where those successful actions turn sour. If you believe that the data are negative, you especially need alternatives for the teacher since some change is necessary. Suppose you plan to present the data on questioning given in guideline 3 and you believe that they are negative. You might consider the following suggestions: The teacher should prepare a strategy including about five key cognitive-memory questions to aid in reviewing the details of the story to be discussed. Upon completion of those questions, the teacher should shift to a series of about three convergent questions for analysis before shifting to other matters. During this time, the teacher should encourage student questions. Write down these suggestions in your notes for your use only.

8. Plan which option you will take if the teacher resists your observational data. When you present your data, the teacher may resist, making it impossible for you to proceed with your plans. Decide if you will move ahead unilaterally and make recommendations. (For details on the options available to you, see the section on teacher resistance to observational data in Chapter 6.) For example, you may decide to shift and proceed unilaterally, offering recommendations in a directive way rather than to proceed in a collaborative way.

9.   List some probable successful outcomes of the conference. This will aid you in achieving a positive viewpoint about the conference. You might jot down something like: "He'll be sensitized to the questions he asks and what the students have been saying; he'll recognize that his lesson is a barrage of questions rather than opportunity for the students to discuss the material they read." This will also give you a basis for encouraging and praising the teacher if you feel the data are negative. You don't want a thoroughly negative conference.

10.   Plan a couple of pertinent things you can say to or do for this particular teacher that will help improve the climate of the conference. In order to have an effective conference, you need a climate that promotes interaction. That is, you need a climate that will help the teacher feel at ease so that he can concentrate on the purpose of the conference. The very nature of a conference may have the teacher nervous, and you need to consider how you can show the teacher that your intention is to help him, not destroy him. You can make some comments, for example, about his personal participation in school life or his successful relation with one of the students. In this way, you can be specific, show that he is of special value, and remove some of the tension he may feel about the conference.

11.   Arrange for an appropriate meeting place that will allow you both to discuss the data openly and without distractions. You might meet in the teacher's classroom, the faculty room, the conference room, or your office. Suppose you think that the conference will be one in which the teacher is quite likely to be upset because the data you have collected are most negative or the evaluation you plan to give will probably lead to the teacher not being rehired. Plan, then, *not* to conduct the conference in your office. Plan to use the teacher's classroom or the faculty room or an conference room, if you have one available. You do want to be able to end the conference when appropriate and leave. You cannot do this if you use your office. If you use the teacher's room or a conference room, you can gracefully get up and leave. The teacher can remain if he chooses to. All of this is not possible if you use your own office. So arrange the meeting room with thoughts about what might occur during the conference.

12.   Arrange for privacy, no interruptions, and a stretch of time that will permit completion of the conference. With privacy, no interruptions from secretaries, colleagues, or telephone calls, and an adequate stretch of time, you can conduct and complete the conference in one sitting. You convey the nonverbal message that your conference is important. These arrangements are especially necessary if you will be reporting data that the teacher will probably interpret as negative. This is in accord with the maxim: Praise in public; criticize in private.

13.   Conduct a simulated conference if you are inexperienced, nervous, or insecure about a particular conference. Simulate with close colleagues, or friends, or family at home a day before the conference. This will illuminate points for you to reconsider and treat in a special way. Simulations are excellent for the opportunity to learn without the threat of failure or the possibility of causing damage. In our society, we conduct many simulations such as those for helping NASA astronauts, car drivers, airplane personnel, surgeons, and trial lawyers. We even have laws mandating simulation. For instance, we have laws requiring fire drills for students and lifeboat drills for ship passengers because legislators recognize the value of simulation. With simulation, you can err without losing face and feeling embarrassed. If you fail or make a mistake, you can proceed to correct the error with another trial run. You can prepare by practicing the basic awareness conference. You also can try out each of the other types of conference by requesting the "simulation teacher" to make certain statements and requests. With experience gained from simulation, you can be prepared to hold a conference where congruence with your espoused theory of conference action will be manifest.

If you plan to conduct an evaluation conference, evaluating the teacher based on several observation sessions, you should gather your notes, data, and reports from all of the sessions. You need to prepare more formally for such a conference in terms of your review and analysis of your past conferences and reports so that you will be able to justify your evaluations. You will need to have with you all the previous documents so that you can reply specifically to any questions by the teacher regarding your evaluation.

CHAPTER 4 ENDNOTES

1. CHRIS ARGYRIS, *Theory into Practice: Increasing Professional Effectiveness* (San Francisco: Jossey-Bass, 1975).
2. CHRIS ARGYRIS, "Alternative Schools: A Behavioral Analysis," *Teachers College Record,* Vol. 75, No. 4 (May 1974): 429–52.

5

CONFERENCE SKILLS AND ASSESSMENT APPROACHES

Conducting a conference is a complex task because it requires the use of skills that may go unnoticed to a naive participant or observer. Conference skills are essentially oral skills, which can be identified and learned. Although you are "only" talking with a teacher, you must be skillful in your talk so that you lead the conference to achieve its goals. Your conference talk is not like the talking you do when you casually converse in the cafeteria line or at the coffee urn in the faculty room. Your conference talk is more deliberate as you put your leadership skills to use.

Since you have a goal for your planned conference, you should also assess the conference in some formal way. You should do more than think about the conference after it ends, because it is helpful and even legally desirable to have some written record of what happened during the time you spent with your teacher. It is in this light that Chapter 5 outlines a set of conference skills and assessment approaches.

After reading this chapter, you should be able to:

- Understand the conference skills and assessment approaches.
- Describe six conference communication skills.
- Apply the six conferring skills at opportune times during the conference.
- Apply four different approaches for assessing a conference with a teacher.

CONFERENCE SKILLS

Conference skills are essentially oral communication skills, and for that reason not visible or tangible. Yet conference skills are concrete in that you can learn them, practice them, and review them in your mind or with the aid of a tape recorder. The skills you utilize in a conference are similar to those used in leading a group discussion, or participating in a committee meeting (as chair or committee member), or conducting a faculty meeting. Although the details may change slightly, the essence of these skills is basically the same in all of these settings.

There are six conferring skills: contributing, questioning, focusing, opening/closing, crystallizing, and supporting. You do not use these skills in any particular order no matter how the conference starts because there is no way to predict perfectly how an interactive conference will proceed. All six are integrally related to each other. The following order of presentation, therefore, is somewhat arbitrary.

Contributing

When you are *contributing* to a conference, you are making comments about the topic at hand. For example, when you report observational data based on your visit to the teacher's classroom, you are contributing. You also are contributing when you offer some alternative ways to organize the students, or to phrase questions, or to arrange the furniture. You are contributing when you explain your own goals for the school and your expectations of the teacher's role as a member of the faculty. You also are contributing when you make recommendations on how the teacher and you should proceed in your supervisory roles (for example, scheduling another conference for next week) or when you comment on the teacher's apparent anger at the last faculty meeting.

There always are opportunities during a conference to contribute. Indeed, if you are not careful, you will do virtually all of the contributing, and this will inhibit the teacher from contributing, which is necessary in developmental supervision. If you contribute too often and too much, you will stifle the teacher. This would be unfortunate since the teacher's contributions create a sense of ownership and responsibility for the conference.

Examples:

A. *YOU (Supervisor):* I gathered the data about the three special ed students as we agreed last time. I used a sign system to check off what they were doing every minute. Take a look at them.

B.   *YOU:* For the future, we should see if the change in student participation continues.

TEACHER: When do you think we should look at this again—November? December?

YOU: Let's do it at the end of the first full week in December. That'll be enough time to assess stability but way before the Christmas vacation fever.

TEACHER: Okay. That's fine with me. Good idea and a good time.

In example A, you contribute by presenting the data the two of you have agreed to examine at your previous conference. You tell what type of data they are, but you wisely stop short. You do not give any analysis or interpretation of the data on your own. You rightly give them to the teacher for him to comment on. This is a correctly restrained use of the skill of contributing.

In example B, you raise the idea of checking on the stability or permanence of the change in student participation that has occurred. The teacher picks up on the idea and asks for your judgment as to when the two of you should review the situation. Your response sets the time and the teacher agrees. In this brief exchange, you have contributed in the procedural realm significantly by suggesting the reassessment and the time for it. Again, the exchange shows an interaction that calls for the teacher's participation as you take clues from the teacher regarding the appropriateness of your contributions.

Questioning

The skill of *questioning* is the most well-known and well-used skill in education and at the same time the most delicate one to master. It is for this reason that an entire chapter of this book (see Chapter 7) is devoted to it. There is no reason, therefore, to present a long review of questioning here. Suffice it to say that you should question with care because of the many nonverbal messages that accompany a supervisor's question.

The five types of questions, explained in more detail in Chapter 7, are:

- Awareness
- Information seeking
- Delving
- Divergent
- Interpretation/evaluation

Examples:

C.   *TEACHER:* As I see the data I did most of the questioning; the kids asked very few.

        YOU: Did you plan to ask more or less than fifty-seven questions on the story? (Awareness)

D.   *TEACHER:* These data on questioning are really revealing. They tell me a lot about myself that I didn't know. Very interesting.

        YOU: On a scale from 1 to 10, with 10 as high, what would be your self-rating regarding your interaction pattern today? (Interpretation/ Evaluation)

In each of these two examples, you ask questions based on what the teacher says. In example C, you seek to make the teacher further aware of what actually occurred; in example D, you ask the teacher to do some self-assessing. Thus, you can proceed to effect change and measure it against what the teacher answers to your question.

Focusing

Due to the drift caused by associations in the remarks of the teacher and you, the conference may tend to go astray. When this occurs, you will need to put it back on course. You do this by *focusing.* When you focus, you direct the conference to its intended course or direct it onto another path that is desirable at that time. With a remark here and there, you steer the conference so that you both can achieve your goals.

Examples:

E.   *TEACHER:* I assigned the homework on that story last Thursday, and some students still haven't done it.

        YOU: The connection of the homework and the data is important here. Let's talk about homework a bit in relation to the number of questions you asked.

F.   *YOU:* The type of question you ask in the beginning of the lesson will influence what you can reasonably ask later on. For example, if you've asked for and gotten lots of information, you can legitimately ask for an explanation to account for all the facts.

TEACHER: Well, if I give them the facts, that may help them. When I taught in the junior high school, there was a rule of thumb: Give 'em the facts fast, and then explain them slowly. So I just have kept that up.

YOU: You're shifting ground on me here a little. First talk about questioning the students and then we'll pick up on your role in explaining things.

In example E, you focus on the connection between the data and the homework assignment. The teacher has mentioned homework, but you take the step to emphasize it. You also state the reason. That is, the connection between the assignment and the homework is important. In example F, you are talking about how one question or set of questions permits the teacher to ask other questions properly later on—to build one question on another—which is the fundamental idea of what constitutes a questioning strategy. The teacher picks up on the notion of explanation and talks about how he explains things to the students. There is a connection, but you redirect the conference to the topic of questioning, indicating that explanation by the teacher is a topic to be picked up after a while. You focus by redirecting and postponing a topic.

On the one hand, it is important to let the teacher talk so that there is an open atmosphere present to foster the exchange of ideas. When the teacher freely expresses the matters on his mind, you also have the opportunity to diagnose his position. On the other hand, if you allow the conference to drift (either due to the teacher's comments or your own), you risk spending too little time on the topics of importance that you have prepared for that day. You need to set limits and keep on target for your mutual benefit. It is this tension between open, free exchanges and targeted comments that requires you to use the skill of focusing delicately. The balancing between the two possibilities requires sensitive use of this skill of focusing.

Opening/Closing

For many people, it is difficult to begin a conference, or at least the section of the conference where the main part takes place. For others, closing a conference is difficult. They just don't know how to say, verbally or nonverbally, "Enough!" In general, what can be said about *opening* a conference applies to *closing* a conference, in a symmetrical way. Closing is not the same as ending or stopping. For this reason, it is unfortunately an overlooked and undervalued skill.

Examples:

G.   *YOU:* Jane, we'll talk about my observation this morning, but first we should look at the goal sheet we drew up at the end of last year. I made a copy for you since I didn't expect you to bring yours.

H.   *YOU:* The first thing I think we need to do is to listen to the tape you made. Then we can begin to compare where you are now in February with where you were in October. Is this okay with you?

In example G, you indicate that the main topic for the conference will be the observation. As a prelude to that and probably as a way of understanding in a context of overall development, you state that you'll start off with a look at the goals established earlier. There is no question what direction the conference will take. As supervisor you have assumed the responsibility for organizing and directing the conference. This is certainly a reasonable position to take in general and reasonable here in particular because the two parts—review of the goal sheet and discussion about the observation—are so sensible. The key element will be the quality of your conference exchanges, so there is no reason to fuss here about who chose these two sensible parts.

In example H, you make a definite suggestion and preference. Here you check it out with the teacher. The teacher probably will go along with your suggestion, especially since the suggestion is reasonable. If there is any question in your mind about the desirability of the procedure to follow or if you want to emphasize the participation of the teacher in the conference, it is best to check your suggestion with the teacher. Once you get the conference going, you can keep it on track through your skill of focusing.

Closing the conference is related to *opening* it. To close a conference you make a conscious effort to tie things together and set the stage for future work. In short, you recapitulate and launch. This is quite different from just ending or stopping the conference. Sometimes because of a time constraint a conference must just end. Maybe the cause is the bell signaling the end of the period or maybe it is someone knocking on the door to see you. But such an ending is most often unsatisfying in contrast to an appropriate closing where you recapitulate the key points of the conference and launch yourselves into the next step of your supervisory activity.

Example:

I.

YOU: Well, Gary, our time is finished according to the clock. Let me summarize by saying that the data indicate you've made some definite progress toward performing as expected. We agreed that you need to continue working on specific fielding of student responses. So, if you'll work on that, that'll be fine with me. But now let's set a date for my next observation.

TEACHER: I'd like it to be soon as a checkup. How about in the end of this month again, the 29th or 30th?

In example I, there is no doubt at all that the conference is at an end. You mention the clock and also that you are going to summarize, another clue that the end has arrived. After your summary, you raise the topic of the next observation as a launching into the future. The teacher completes the launching by setting the specific time. If you now stand up, you say nonverbally that the conference is concluded. The message is clear; the conference has come full circle since the end is tied to the beginning, and there is a sense of knowing what you will do in the future.

Crystallizing

When you are *crystallizing*, you state the essence of what the teacher has said or what the two of you have been saying together. Often you crystallize when you give a summary, but the mere recitation of a series of points raised does not constitute crystallizing. Crystallizing most often goes beyond reciting or summarizing because you get at the underlying meaning of what has been said or what has happened. You will use some of the words already spoken and most likely will add some of your own as a way of expressing your understanding of the situation.

Examples:

J. *YOU:* Allow me to state what we've been saying. The basic idea here is your attempt to build up the students to the point where they can function on their own in the lab. Therefore, you've emphasized procedures and taught them self-checking rules. And you've held trouble-shooting sessions at their request.

TEACHER: That's right; that's my aim—to help them be fairly independent in the lab.

K. *TEACHER:* I think that this emphasis on observational data is crazy.

YOU: Are you saying that you're annoyed and that there are better alternatives—for example, I should evaluate you without visiting you or evaluate you based on hearsay information from parents by way of their kids?

TEACHER: That's what I was saying, but I don't think I want to say that anymore.

In example J, you explicitly indicate that you will crystallize the thrust of your entire conference up to that point. You do so, and the teacher agrees with you, adding his own brief goal. In example K, you crystallize just one remark of the teacher. The teacher is peeved about your visits to his classroom to gather data. You pick up the tone and suggest what the meaning of his statement could be. You suggest that he is annoyed and that he is looking for alternatives to your disturbing his classroom. You identify his feeling and give him two possibilities. When you have finished crystallizing, he realizes the message he sent to you. He withdraws these because he recognizes that observation data are preferable to no data and hearsay data. You were able to crystallize his messages effectively.

One important technique is present in example K—the question at the end of your crystallizing. The use of the question to check with the teacher to see if your crystallizing is apt is most important when you get involved with the emotional tone of statements. It is not critical to use a checking question when talking about a series of events, but it is desirable when dealing with feelings. By using the question, you allow the teacher the opportunity to correct your interpretation of his feelings, a sensitive matter at all times. In this example, the teacher has no disagreement with your interpretation.

Supporting

When you encourage the teacher, praise the teacher, and relieve tension during the conference so that effective communication can continue, you are being supportive. Supporting is often accomplished through nonverbal means. For example, you can support a teacher through laughter and even by the way you place the chairs during the conference. It is one thing to sit behind a wide desk separated from the teacher and another thing to sit cross-corner at a coffee table or conference table where you can both look at documents at the same time. The latter position creates an atmosphere encouraging open communication and is thus supportive, while the former does just the opposite. Active listening is a nonverbal way to be supportive of the teacher.

Examples:

L. *YOU:* The kinds of questions you asked today are the very ones we're advocating. The progress you've made is great and I'm really proud of what you've accomplished these past few months.

M.   *TEACHER:* What I've said to myself all day in anticipation of this conference is difficult to say now.

YOU: Well, take your time and try hard since it must be important to you. I'm listening.

TEACHER: What I'm trying to say is that I'm very angry at you for the way you dealt with Jimmy yesterday. Apparently,...

In example L, you are supporting by the words of praise you speak to the teacher. Such words are always well received by everyone. In example M, you are supporting in that you assure the teacher that you want to hear what is on his mind. The teacher is struggling to tell you something, and you encourage him to speak out on what is important to him. You indicate your attentiveness and patience, and this action is supportive. As supervisor, you are in a special relation with your teacher that influences to a large degree how that teacher feels and behaves not only in the school but out of the school as well.

The studies of teachers at work all show one thing—teachers want support from their supervisors more than anything else available to them. Support comes in many ways—from backing a disciplinary action taken by the teacher in regard to a disruptive student to recommending a merit increase in pay for excellence in classroom teaching. No matter the situation, the teacher seeks support, and giving support during a conference, which is a situation involving close personal interaction significant to the very core of the teacher's job, is a skill important for you to apply.

Summary

If you apply these six skills described and illustrated while you implement your plans (see Chapter 4), you will be able to conduct a fruitful conference. The purpose of using these skills is to provide for affective and smooth communication between the teacher and you. The purpose is not manipulation of the teacher since that implies a negative quality in your conference. Rather, the application of the six conference skills is to help you both achieve the legitimate goals of the conference, the primary one being the improvement of the classroom performance of the teacher. You can practice these skills one at a time in nonconference, social settings where there is much less requirement for you to apply these skills successfully. With concentration and practice you can learn these skills well enough to use them for the mutual benefit of the teacher and you.

ASSESSING THE CONFERENCE

Just as you took time before the conference to prepare for it, now you must take time after to assess it and to take stock. As supervisor, you need to step back and assess the conference in terms of what was accomplished, what was not accomplished, how well you employed the six conferring skills, what was omitted, what might have been discussed, and what did not work out well at all. Not every conference is a total success, but, on the other hand, not every conference is a total failure. In looking back at the conference, you have the opportunity to learn from it and to make plans for the future. Here are several approaches for assessment:

Notes

The simplest, but least directed, way to assess the conference is to sit down and write out some notes giving your thoughts about the conference. It is necessary to write things out since you will want to refer to your reaction in the future. Memory alone will definitely not suffice. You can write your notes any time after the conference ends. To do so within a short time after the conference ends has the advantage of writing while your memory is fresh. This is similar to a debriefing that astronauts perform after a space flight. They are debriefed before any other events occur so as not to cloud their knowledge of their experience of flight in space.

To write notes after waiting a short while has the advantage of allowing you to gather your thoughts and cool down from an emotional experience, especially if the conference was one in which you met with resistance from the teacher. By waiting a while, you can be more of an observer and less of a participant. You can perhaps see the conference more clearly when you have some distance from it. By analogy, you can see a pointillist painting better by moving away from it than by standing close where you can see only the thousands of individual dots that the painter has put on the canvas. Naturally, you must be your own judge as to when you can and should write your notes if you use this approach.

Post-Conference Reaction Form A

This form guides you in your assessment of the conference. It is a simple, effective form in that it guides you to give an overall judgment and then to give specific positive and negative elements that support your judgment. It also leads you to give yourself suggestions for improvement that too often are neglected but needed in assessment. This aspect asks you to consider your own development just as you did for the teacher during the conference.

If at all possible, you should ask the teacher to fill out this Post-Conference Reaction Form A also. This will provide you with additional information since it is certainly possible that the teacher and you have different perceptions of the conference. With the reaction of the teacher in hand, you can better understand what happened. Therefore, you can better decide on what steps you might take now in order to improve future conferences that have as their purpose helping the teacher continue to grow.

Figure 5-1 is a blank Form A. Figure 5-2 has been filled out by the supervisor who conducted the correction conference cited in Chapter 6. Notice that although the supervisor rated the conference as "5," closer to "outstanding" than to "poor," there are still lingering feelings of dissatisfaction. The supervisor realizes that the conference could have been better. The form is good in the respect that it leads to thoughts of improvement. It does not let the supervisor remain with the status quo. Two suggestions are written down, although the second one may not work out since third parties in a conference are rare. However, at least an attempt will be made.

Post-Conference Reaction Form B

This assessment form offers you an alternative with some advantages over Form A. This form requires you to draw only nine circles since the questions are all in yes/no form

Supervisor _____   Date _____

Teacher _____

1. OVERALL I think this conference was
   (circle the appropriate number from 7 to 1)

   Outstanding: 7   6   5   4   3   2   1   :poor

2. The things I LIKED BEST about the conference are:

3. The things I LIKED LEAST about this conference are:

4. TO IMPROVE the next conference I suggest:

FIGURE 5-1. Post-conference reaction form A (blank).

Supervisor_____M. Lebrean_____   Date____Jan. 19____

Teacher_____J. Trannert_____

1. OVERALL I think this conference was
   (circle the appropriate number from 7 to 1)

   Outstanding: 7   6   ⑤   4   3   2   1   :poor

2. The things I LIKED BEST about the conference are:

Joe, for the first time, agreed to read some material counter to his point of view; reluctantly but will read it. He didn't fight back when I gave some suggestions to him on how to get unattached from his desk.

3. The things I LIKED LEAST about this conference are:

He seemed resistant; he's still fighting the school and his involvement in it. We didn't talk about his relationship with the students—very different for boys and girls.

4. TO IMPROVE the next conference I suggest:

1. We meet informally first just to discuss the article I loaned him.
2. I try to get him to talk more—maybe ask him if he would like someone else to join us. Maybe he'll open up?

FIGURE 5-2. Post-conference reaction form A (filled in).

along a sliding scale from 1 to 5. There is space to write notes in order to write some specifics. For this reason, this is an easy form to use with your teacher. That is, you can ask the teacher to fill out this form without imposing on him.

You can use this form immediately upon ending the conference. Ask the teacher to take a minute to fill it out as you do, and then compare your responses with his. The comparison is always instructive for both the teacher and you. During your debriefing comparison, you can request specifics from the teacher as you note your similar and different responses. You also can use this form after the conference by asking the teacher to fill it out and return it to you the next day. Then on your own you can compare your two sets of responses.

The disadvantage of this form is its lack of specificity and neglect of the future. While it asks you to rate your positive feelings, for example, it does not specifically require you to state what in the conference caused those positive feelings. Nor does it ask you to look at what actions could lead to improvement. The disadvantages do not, however, cancel out the advantages. Rather, it is a matter of gaining one thing while losing another. Fortunately, you do not need to choose forever between Form A and Form B. You can use one form with one conference and the other with a second conference in order to get the advantages of both while working with a particular teacher. In this way, you can benefit from the advantages of both forms.

Figure 5-3 is a blank Form B, and Figure 5-4 is a sample of one filled out by the supervisor who conducted the reinforcement strategy cited in Chapter 6. Figure 5-5 shows a form completed by the teacher with whom the reinforcement conference was held. It is apparent that, in general, the supervisor and teacher share similar perceptions of their conference. Both thought the conference was necessary, for example, and both were tense. For different reasons, both reacted unexpectedly during the conference.

On one item the two conferees differed. Whereas the supervisor found the conference not to be difficult (see item D), the teacher did find the conference difficult. The teacher's note gives the reason: No teacher likes a conference. The message is clear: There is always tension for the teacher in a conference no matter what type of conference is held. The teacher is under stress because what will happen in the conference is unknown ahead of time. The sophisticated and astute supervisor will always keep this in mind, otherwise an understanding of the teacher's behavior will be unattainable. The use of this form provides a continued reminder to the supervisor that the teacher may well have a different view of the conference no matter how the conference progressed.

Conference Category System

The Conference Category System has been developed by Professors Richard Kindsvatter and William Wilen[1] of Kent State University in Ohio. With this system, you can gain feedback about conference behavior as related to nine skill areas of the conference: climate building, target setting, questioning, commenting, praising, nonverbal communicating, balancing, sensitivity, and closure. The system offers you another excellent way to gain information about yourself from either your own use or the teacher's or both. If the teacher and you fill out an analysis form, you can analyze it together, as suggested with the use of the previous two forms.

Figure 5-6 shows a blank Conference Category System Analysis Form. (This is a modified form with the permission of Professors Kindsvatter and Wilen.) Notice that the form has the unique feature of providing a double analysis. In column A, under

Supervisor _____   Date _____

Teacher _____

    Respond to the items which you feel are *appropriate*. Circle a number representing your viewpoint for each item along the scale from 1 (Yes) to 5 (No).

	<u>YES</u> <u>NO</u>	<u>SPACE FOR NOTES</u>
A. Do you feel that this conference was necessary?	1 2 3 4 5	
B. Did you react as you thought you would?	1 2 3 4 5	
C. Do you feel that your position was understood?	1 2 3 4 5	
D. Was this a difficult conference for you?	1 2 3 4 5	
E. Do you feel that anything worthwhile was accomplished?	1 2 3 4 5	
F. Do you have positive feelings about this conference?	1 2 3 4 5	
G. Do you have negative feelings about this conference?	1 2 3 4 5	
H. Were you tense during this conference?	1 2 3 4 5	
I. Was this conference helpful to you?	1 2 3 4 5	

FIGURE 5-3. Post-conference reaction form B (blank).

Supervisor_____S. Braun_____   Date ___Nov. 24___

Teacher_____Leslie Nolan_____

Respond to the items which you feel are *appropriate.* Circle a number representing your viewpoint for each item along the scale from 1 (Yes) to 5 (No).

	YES	**NO**	**SPACE FOR NOTES**

A. Do you feel that this conference was necessary?   ①2 3 4 5

B. Did you react as you thought you would?   1 2 3④5   I was surprised about asking L. to present w/ me. I really didn't have it in mind before the observ.

C. Do you feel that your position was understood?   ①2 3 4 5

D. Was this a difficult conference for you? 1 2 3 4⑤

E. Do you feel that anything worthwhile was accomplished?   ①2 3 4 5

F. Do you have positive feelings about this conference?   ①2 3 4 5

G. Do you have negative feelings about this conference?   1 2③4 5   Maybe I imposed & pushed too hard. Not sure.

H. Were you tense during this conference?   1②3 4 5   When I asked about presenting w/ me

I. Was this conference helpful to you?   1②3 4 5

FIGURE 5-4. Post-conference reaction form B (completed by supervisor).

Supervisor_____Braun_____   Date _November 24_

Teacher_____Nolan_____

Respond to the items which you feel are *appropriate.* Circle a number representing your viewpoint for each item along the scale from 1 (Yes) to 5 (No).

	YES	**NO**	**SPACE FOR NOTES**

A. Do you feel that this conference was necessary?   ①2 3 4 5

B. Did you react as you thought you would?   1 2 3④5 Didn't expect to be asked to talk to adm.

C. Do you feel that your position was understood?   1②3 4 5

D. Was this a difficult conference for you?   1②3 4 5 Who likes conferences?

E. Do you feel that anything worthwhile was accomplished?   1②3 4 5

F. Do you have positive feelings about this conference?   1②3 4 5

G. Do you have negative feelings about this conference?   1②3 4 5 More work now to prepare for next week

H. Were you tense during this conference?   ①2 3 4 5

I. Was this conference helpful to you?   ①2 3 4 5 Glad to know that I'm making the rounds

FIGURE 5-5. Post-conference reaction form B (completed by teacher).

FIGURE 5-6. Conference category system analysis form (blank).

ANALYSIS SCALES

	A. Occurrence	**B. Effectiveness**
SUPERVISOR _____	1. Not evident	1. Not effective
	2. Slightly evident	2. Slightly effective
TEACHER _____	3. Moderately evident	3. Moderately effective
	4. Quite evident	4. Quite effective
DATE _____	N Not applicable	N Not applicable

Categories (Parts A&B Correspond to Occurrence and Effectiveness in the Analysis Scale)	**A. Occurrence**	**B. Effectiveness**
1. *Climate:* A. Supervisor made comments specifically intended to affect the climate. B. Supervisor's statements released tension and contributed to fruitful communication. Supervisor used expressions of support and encouragement, stated in a comfortable, relaxing tone.		
2. *Target Setting:* A. Supervisor set the conference agenda, including purpose and procedures. B. Supervisor clearly explained the purpose of the conference and the procedure to be followed. Supervisor gave the teacher the opportunity to comment on the agenda and to make other suggestions. The resulting agenda was attended to.		
3. *Questioning:* A. Supervisor asked questions matching the conference's purpose (e.g., to raise awareness, seek clarifying information, explain events, implement change). B. Supervisor asked questions thoughtfully and purposefully to encourage the teacher to reflect, analyze, and evaluate. Supervisor posed questions to probe, clarify, and focus matters in order to move beyond the obvious and mundane.		
4. *Commentary:* A. Supervisor provided feedback information, clarified ideas and teaching criteria, and made suggestions. B. Supervisor's remarks were appropriately descriptive and minimally judgmental. Comments were appropriate, substantive, and helpful.		
5. *Praise:* A. Supervisor praised and encouraged specific actions. B. Supervisor praised teacher's performance and ideas judiciously and authentically.		

FIGURE 5-6. (continued)

6. *Nonverbal:* A. Supervisor took specific nonverbal actions intended to promote good communication (e.g., made eye contact, arranged furniture without barriers). B. Supervisor communicated interest and enthusiasm nonverbally through appropriate body, facial, and hand expressions. Supervisor's speech was animated. Supervisor made good use of the conference space and furniture.		
7. *Balance:* A. Supervisor encouraged and created balanced, two-directional communication. B. Supervisor was a patient and attentive listener, eliciting teacher talk and involvement.		
8. *Sensitivity:* A. Supervisor's actions showed consideration of teacher's particular professional and personal needs. B. Supervisor was alert to emotional and conditional factors, to verbal and nonverbal cues. Supervisor responded appropriately to teacher's need. Supervisor avoided self-saving behavior.		
9. *Closure:* A. Supervisor summarized or asked teacher to summarize main points and outcomes. B. Supervisor in a clear way reviewed (or asked teacher to do so) the conference's purpose and outcomes—understanding, solutions, plans, and especially commitments—and ended the conference at an appropriate point.		

Occurrence, you score to what extent the nine components were evident in the conference. In Column B, under Effectiveness, you rate your skill in perfoming in these nine areas. Thus, you have two kinds of data, performance and evaluative. If the teacher also completes the form, you have two perspectives on these two kinds of data.

A brief description of the nine component skill areas follows to further aid you in understanding the categories. The descriptions are excerpted from the work of the authors of this system and supplement those found in the analysis form itself.

1. *Climate:* "Human feelings, attitudes, perceptions, and predispositions always influence interaction....Climate building, of course, is the application of good human relations principles to the conference setting."

2. *Target Setting:* "At the outset of the conference the topics to be discussed should be mentioned...Both parties should have an opportunity to suggest items to be discussed. A few moments should be spent agreeing on these and ordering them on the agenda."

3. *Questioning:* Questioning "is probably the most important means for pursuing the conference objectives. Questioning is also the predominant factor in determining the conference 'style' and competence of the supervisor."

4. *Commentary:* "The astute and sensitive supervisor will make comments that mirror the teacher's behavior, essentially distilling and clarifying that behavior so the teacher can focus on and examine it...the supervisor should describe rather than evaluate, as much as possible."

5. *Praise:* "Praise and encouragement are powerful means of positive reinforcement...praise is an indispensable strategy...praise and encouragement must be perceived as authentic by the teacher, growing naturally out of the interaction within the conference...Praise is most effective if it is specific."

6. *Nonverbal Communication:* "Tacit messages are communicated through body language...The most effective conference occurs when verbal and nonverbal communication reinforce each other...nonverbal communication authentically reflects a supervisor's real attitudes...it should be carried out with full awareness and with deliberate purpose."

7. *Balance:* "A productive conference requires two-way communication and the supervisor is responsible for balance in that communication....For optimum transfer of conference outcomes to classroom practice, the supervisor should generally do less talking than the teacher since insight occurs most readily when the teacher identifies his/her own behaviors, analyzes data, and conceives means for improvement."

8. *Sensitivity:* "The supervisor should approach the conference with certain predispositions: the intent to establish a warm climate, to use nonverbal cues, to provide praise and support, and to attempt to transcend the teacher's spoken ideas to a level of feeling and meaning that lies beyond....The area of sensitivity separates the merely competent supervisor from the supervisor who is inspiring."

9. *Closure:* "Closure reinforces the important conference outcomes. Closure also clarifies the extent to which the purposes of the conference have been achieved....The conference should culminate in a commitment to some resolution or course of action....closure usually involves summarizing the target topics, with a restatement of and mutual agreement on outcomes."

Figure 5-7 is an analysis form for the Conference Category System as completed by the supervisor who conducted the evaluation strategy cited in Chapter 6. Figure 5-8 is one filled out by the teacher who participated in the evaluation conference. The supervisor and teacher are in virtual agreement; the differences are slight. The teacher has given slightly higher scores for the conference than the supervisor. Apparently, the supervisor and teacher know each other and have established a good working rapport. Nevertheless, the teacher's completed form provides excellent feedback.

Summing Up

It is important that the supervisor take concrete steps to make the conference congruent with the purpose of observation and with the overall objectives of supervision. Conferring with the teacher is a necessary element in the supervisory process and care is

ANALYSIS SCALES

	A. Occurrence	B. Effectiveness
SUPERVISOR _____	1. Not evident	1. Not effective
	2. Slightly evident	2. Slightly effective
TEACHER _____	3. Moderately evident	3. Moderately effective
	4. Quite evident	4. Quite effective
DATE _____	N Not applicable	N Not applicable

Categories (Parts A&B Correspond to Occurrence and Effectiveness in the Analysis Scale)	A. Occurrence	B. Effectiveness
1. *Climate:* A. Supervisor made comments specifically intended to affect the climate. B. Supervisor's statements released tension and contributed to fruitful communication. Supervisor used expressions of support and encouragement, stated in a comfortable, relaxing tone.	3	3
2. *Target Setting:* A. Supervisor set the conference agenda, including purpose and procedures. B. Supervisor clearly explained the purpose of the conference and the procedure to be followed. Supervisor gave the teacher the opportunity to comment on the agenda and to make other suggestions. The resulting agenda was attended to.	4	4
3. *Questioning:* A. Supervisor asked questions matching the conference's purpose (e.g., to raise awareness, seek clarifying information, explain events, implement change). B. Supervisor asked questions thoughtfully and purposefully to encourage the teacher to reflect, analyze, and evaluate. Supervisor posed questions to probe, clarify, and focus matters in order to move beyond the obvious and mundane.	4	4
4. *Commentary:* A. Supervisor provided feedback information, clarified ideas and teaching criteria, and made suggestions. B. Supervisor's remarks were appropriately descriptive and minimally judgmental. Comments were appropriate, substantive, and helpful.	4	3
5. *Praise:* A. Supervisor praised and encouraged specific actions. B. Supervisor praised teacher's performance and ideas judiciously and authentically.	3	4

FIGURE 5-7. Conference category system analysis form (completed by supervisor).

6. *Nonverbal:* A. Supervisor took specific nonverbal actions intended to promote good communication (e.g., made eye contact, arranged furniture without barriers). B. Supervisor communicated interest and enthusiasm nonverbally through appropriate body, facial, and hand expressions. Supervisor's speech was animated. Supervisor made good use of the conference space and furniture.	3	3
7. *Balance:* A. Supervisor encouraged and created balanced, two-directional communication. B. Supervisor was a patient and attentive listener, eliciting teacher talk and involvement.	3	3
8. *Sensitivity:* A. Supervisor's actions showed consideration of teacher's particular professional and personal needs. B. Supervisor was alert to emotional and conditional factors, to verbal and nonverbal cues. Supervisor responded appropriately to teacher's need. Supervisor avoided self-saving behavior.	3	3
9. *Closure:* A. Supervisor summarized or asked teacher to summarize main points and outcomes. B. Supervisor in a clear way reviewed (or asked teacher to do so) the conference's purpose and outcomes—understanding, solutions, plans, and especially commitments—and ended the conference at an appropriate point.	4	4

FIGURE 5-7. (continued)

needed to assure a conference's success. Preparation for the conference, like preparation for teaching, is necessary in order to implement the various strategies and tactics available.

As the supervisor who is responsible for conducting the conference, you need to select or modify a conference strategy and use tactics which generally lead to an effective conference. This means that you must use the six conferring skills carefully and at appropriate times. The "mix" in your use of skills is your unique style.

In order to check on your effectiveness you should assess the conference. Several assessment methods are available to you, formal and informal, each of which offers you a way to set your own sights on future development in this matter of conferring. Just as you seek to lead the teacher to further growth you need to help yourself to develop, and the assessment forms can help you in this important effort.

ANALYSIS SCALES

	A. Occurrence	B. Effectiveness
SUPERVISOR _____	1. Not evident	1. Not effective
	2. Slightly evident	2. Slightly effective
TEACHER _____	3. Moderately evident	3. Moderately effective
	4. Quite evident	4. Quite effective
DATE _____	N Not applicable	N Not applicable

Categories (Parts A&B Correspond to Occurrence and Effectiveness in the Analysis Scale)	A. Occurrence	B. Effectiveness
1. *Climate:* A. Supervisor made comments specifically intended to affect the climate. B. Supervisor's statements released tension and contributed to fruitful communication. Supervisor used expressions of support and encouragement, stated in a comfortable, relaxing tone.	4	4
2. *Target Setting:* A. Supervisor set the conference agenda, including purpose and procedures. B. Supervisor clearly explained the purpose of the conference and the procedure to be followed. Supervisor gave the teacher the opportunity to comment on the agenda and to make other suggestions. The resulting agenda was attended to.	4	4
3. *Questioning:* A. Supervisor asked questions matching the conference's purpose (e.g., to raise awareness, seek clarifying information, explain events, implement change). B. Supervisor asked questions thoughtfully and purposefully to encourage the teacher to reflect, analyze, and evaluate. Supervisor posed questions to probe, clarify, and focus matters in order to move beyond the obvious and mundane.	4	4
4. *Commentary:* A. Supervisor provided feedback information, clarified ideas and teaching criteria, and made suggestions. B. Supervisor's remarks were appropriately descriptive and minimally judgmental. Comments were appropriate, substantive, and helpful.	4	3
5. *Praise:* A. Supervisor praised and encouraged specific actions. B. Supervisor praised teacher's performance and ideas judiciously and authentically.	3	3

FIGURE 5-8. Conference category system analysis form (completed by teacher).

6. *Nonverbal:* A. Supervisor took specific nonverbal actions intended to promote good communication (e.g., made eye contact, arranged furniture without barriers). B. Supervisor communicated interest and enthusiasm nonverbally through appropriate body, facial, and hand expressions. Supervisor's speech was animated. Supervisor made good use of the conference space and furniture.	4	4
7. *Balance:* A. Supervisor encouraged and created balanced, two-directional communication. B. Supervisor was a patient and attentive listener, eliciting teacher talk and involvement.	4	3
8. *Sensitivity:* A. Supervisor's actions showed consideration of teacher's particular professional and personal needs. B. Supervisor was alert to emotional and conditional factors, to verbal and nonverbal cues. Supervisor responded appropriately to teacher's need. Supervisor avoided self-saving behavior.	3	3
9. *Closure:* A. Supervisor summarized or asked teacher to summarize main points and outcomes. B. Supervisor in a clear way reviewed (or asked teacher to do so) the conference's purpose and outcomes—understanding, solutions, plans, and especially commitments—and ended the conference at an appropriate point.	4	4

FIGURE 5-8. (continued)

CHAPTER 5 ENDNOTE

1. RICHARD KINDSVATTER and WILLIAM W. WILEN, "A Systematic Approach to Improving Conference Skills," *Educational Leadership,* Vol. 38, No. 7, (April 1981): 525–29.

<table>
<tr><td>

6

</td><td></td></tr>
<tr><td></td><td>

CONFERENCE STRATEGIES AND TACTICS

</td></tr>
</table>

Conferring with your teachers is just as necessary in supervision as observing them. It is not enough to make observations mentally or even in note form for yourself. You must convey these observations to your teachers. If you do not speak with the teachers about your observations, the value of observing disappears.

In order to talk with your teacher profitably, you need to be clear about what types of conference you can conduct. Once you have decided, preferably with the teacher, which type will serve you both better, you then need to know how to proceed. You need some plan for your conference in terms of what to do and when to do it. A conference strategy offers you a guide to a clear and profitable conference.

Chapter 6 deals with the various types of conferences you can conduct and the strategies and tactics you can use to help achieve your goals.

After reading this chapter, you should be able to:

- Understand the various kinds of postobservation conference and the implementation strategies and tactics that are available to you.
- List four types of conference classified according to supervisor and teacher purpose.
- List three sources of dissonance that the teacher feels when receiving your observational data.
- Use one or more options to cope with teacher resistance to observational data.
- Use four general strategies for holding a conference.
- List at least six positive and four negative tactics that can be used during a conference.

FOUR TYPES OF POSTOBSERVATION CONFERENCE

Before you can plan your strategy for the postobservation conference it is important that you review the alternatives open to you. Although you may have in the past restricted yourself to essentially one type of conference, it is necessary to recognize that there are actually several different types of conference that you can hold with your teacher. Here are four types of conference classified according to purpose.

Awareness

In the awareness conference you give your collected observation data to the teacher. The purpose of such a conference is to make the teacher aware of what occurred during the class session. Awareness is the basis of all change. You can ask some awareness questions to the teacher to help him clarify his own heightening of awareness, not offer a challenge or criticism. Your questions should focus on the teacher's action itself rather than on its consequences so that the teacher recognizes positive, mental, or negative aspects of what occurred. For example, you might ask the teacher such questions as: "Did you plan to ask more, or fewer, or the same amount (41 out of 49) of cognitive-memory questions about the story you discussed?" "Did you deliberately speak immediately after each boy spoke?" Be careful that you yourself do not get involved in more than reporting and focusing on the data. Your main aim is awareness, not praise or criticism; sensitivity, not analysis or judgment.

Correction

In the correction conference, you help the teacher develop alternatives for reducing or eliminating those aspects of teaching that the teacher deems unsatisfactory. You explore with the teacher what the consequences and preconditions were for the unsatisfactory approach. Together you seek solutions to the problems identified by the teacher. The focus is on what the *teacher* feels needs correction, and, therefore, on what he is willing to change. This helps the teacher to seek his own solutions through your collaboration with him. Once the ineffective actions have been identified and labeled, you can offer your own analysis, explanations, and suggestions for new behaviors to be implemented. Due to the overall context of collaboration with emphasis on the teacher, the recommendations you make do not detract from the value of the teacher seeking his own solutions. On the contrary, collaboration supports self-help.

Reinforcement

In the reinforcement conference, you acknowledge that the teacher's espoused theory of teaching action is congruent with his theory-in-use. After presenting the data to the teacher, you analyze the data with the teacher to determine the consequences and pre-conditions of the effective approach. You explore with the teacher just how his actions jibe with his beliefs and how they contribute to his effectiveness. Together, you generate alternatives to what was deemed effective. In this way, you publicly recognize that the teacher is a professional person performing well and help the teacher maintain excellence. You facilitate the teacher's professional and personal development by drawing up a list of potential activities and challenges that the teacher can tackle. Such alternative activities and challenges provide continued motivation to perform as a teacher whose actions and ideals are congruent.

Evaluation

In the evaluation conference, you rate the teacher, passing judgment on how the teacher has taught based on several observations. You comment on the progress or lack of it that the teacher has made over a span of time. This type of conference is a summary one and grows out of several specific previous conferences. In this sense, it is not a postobservation conference about a single class session. Rather, it examines several class sessions and enables you to evaluate explicitly the overall progress of the teacher.

Comments on the Four Types

The four types of conference are general. In each, there is a main point that should be clear to the teacher. To try to accomplish many things in one conference is to overload the teacher, which results in a feeling of confusion or helplessness in the face of the situation. Surely, few conferences are pure in type, but the overlaps should be monitored and kept down in order to keep the purpose clear to the teacher and yourself. When there is a shift in type within a conference, it should be noted and made clear.

First, you must choose which type of conference to hold based on the situation. Second, you need to *decide with the teacher* the direction and focus of the conference. You can raise the question explicitly at the beginning of the conference if you wish: "Mike, take a look at these data I collected. Then let's see where we go from these. It would be good if you'd pick out some parts of the lesson to talk about—positive or negative—and make some comments for us to explore." Or: "Mary, here are some data to look over. I'd rather that you begin to analyze them and comment. I will do so to if you want me to. Let's take a minute to decide which way we want to proceed." Try to keep each conference as much of a joint effort as possible so that the teacher feels that he has a stake in determining his own destiny.

From these types and comments it is clear that the basic conference focuses on heightening awareness as a context for giving the teacher data you have collected. In it you restrict your purpose and comments to alerting the teacher to what occurred. Your basic premise is that for the teacher to change he needs to know the facts about his teaching so that he can draw valid conclusions about his performance. All other conferences are in essence expansions of the awareness conference—that is, each conference begins procedurally with awareness and then moves through varying steps. At the same time, each conference moves, if desired, from awareness to correction, or reinforcement, or evaluation.

TEACHER RESISTANCE TO YOUR OBSERVATIONAL DATA

Why the Teacher Resists Your Data

Before presenting specific conference strategies, it is necessary to deal with the topic of teacher resistance to the data you collect because there is a good chance that you will be presenting data that will indicate the need for change. Indeed, you may be presenting the data precisely because you believe that change is necessary. Yet your teacher may resist. He may deny the truth of your data.

Resistance is understandable in that the teacher, consciously or unconsciously, recognizes that change is necessary. Resistance arises because you have raised dissonance in the teacher. *Dissonance is the discrepancy between a person's perception of or preference about his behavior and his actual behavior. Dissonance is also the discrepancy between a person's preference about his own behavior and someone else's preference about that person's behavior.*

According to Leon Festinger, the noted researcher on dissonance and author of the book *A Theory of Cognitive Dissonance*,[1] dissonance is a motivating force for its own reduction. That is to say, when a person feels dissonant, there is motivation for him to reduce the dissonance. Dissonance is a tension that people seek to reduce or remove once they are aware of it.

The data that you present to the teacher may create dissonance, as shown in Figure 6-1.

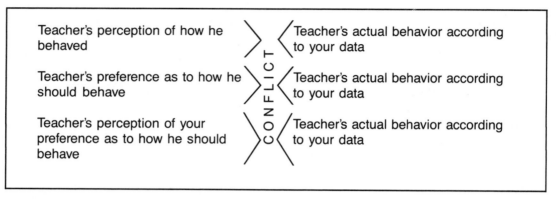

FIGURE 6-1. Examples of dissonance.

One, two, or all three situations may be causing the teacher to feel dissonant.

Our research shows that when teachers receive *specific feedback* they will change their behavior in order to reduce dissonance. Only when there is high dissonance do teachers change their self-preferences. Even so, they still must cope with your proferences, and these they cannot change easily. They may try, however.

There also are other possible sources of dissonance. One of these is the teacher's realization that *his* preference conflicts with *your* preference as to how he should behave. This is shown as:

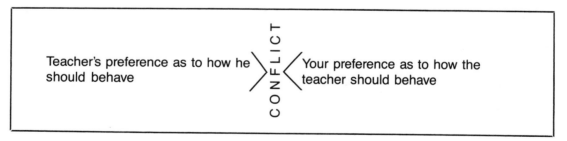

This conflict arises because the teacher realizes that the two preferences are not the same. The data only trigger the realization; they do not cause it. The teacher may even feel the conflict before he sees the data. The conflict exists prior to your observing the teacher.

The resistance that the teacher manifests is one way to deal with the dissonance he feels. In general, there are several ways a teacher can deal with the dissonance:

THE TEACHER CAN REJECT OR BLUR THE INCOMING DATA

By claiming that the data are not valid or true, the teacher can reject the data. By claiming that the data are too general, for example, the teacher can blur the data. In either case, the teacher does not accept the data. Since the data do not now apply to him, the teacher effectively removes the dissonance. Since there is no dissonance felt, there is no need to change.

THE TEACHER CAN CHANGE HIS BEHAVIOR

The teacher changes his behavior so that his new behavior becomes consonant with your preference or his own preference, whichever is the dominant preference. By changing his behavior, the teacher removes the dissonance. Behavior changes to match the preference.

THE TEACHER CAN CHANGE HIS PREFERENCE OR TRY TO CHANGE YOUR PREFERENCE

The teacher, now alert to what he is in fact doing, changes his preference about what he should do. By changing his preference to match his behavior the teacher removes his dissonance. The teacher can also try to convince you that what he is doing is what you should expect and prefer him to do. By changing your preference to match his behavior the teacher removes his dissonance. In either way, preference changes to match the behavior.

There are consequently three methods that teachers use to remove the dissonance they feel. Resistance to accepting your data, the first one mentioned above, is indeed *one* method for teachers to use but not *the* method you desire because it does not lead to change. Rather, it maintains the status quo.

These comments about dissonance bring to mind the story of a young man and a psychiatrist. One day, a young man burst into a psychiatrist's office.

"May I help you?" asked the psychiatrist.

"I don't know if you can," said the young man. "I don't know if you can help me because I'm dead."

"You're dead?" asked the doctor in order to be sure of what he heard.

"Yes, I'm dead. I died several weeks ago," said the man.

"Tell me what you've learned since dying," said the psychiatrist, trying to calm the patient.

"Well, I've learned that dead men don't bleed."

"Is that so?"

"Yes, it's true; dead men don't bleed."

The psychiatrist requested that the young man come over to his desk. When he did, the doctor took a sharp pin from the desk and pricked the man's finger. Blood flowed from the finger onto the desk blotter.

"What do you say about that?" asked the doctor.

The young man stared at another drop of blood on his finger and said, "I guess I was wrong: dead men do bleed."

As supervisor, you must recognize what the teacher is doing when you confer with him. (Consider how the "dead" young man resisted the data from the psychiatrist's brief demonstration.) The teacher may be rejecting the data as one way of removing dissonance so that he will not have to change. He does not want to change because change may be threatening to him and because it may require him to learn new skills, exert new types of effort, or spend more time planning for teaching. In short, change may be unpleasant or threatening, and the teacher may not want to get involved with it, just as the "dead" young man did not.

How to Deal with Teacher Resistance

Your aim is to help the teacher find a different way to remove the dissonance your data create in him. Specifically, you want him to change his behavior to match his own preferences or your preferences for him. To do this, you must be quite firm in your own knowledge that the data you have collected are valid. That is, the data are data that the teacher should accept.

Let us assume that you present data with the hope and expectation that the teacher will accept them and comment on the implications for change that he sees in them. However, in spite of your expectation let us assume that the teacher rejects them. You must then present the data again with a tone that is confident and not angry. If you become angry, you will only add fuel to the fire. Anger is inappropriate once you recognize that the teacher is using his rejection of the data as the method for removing the dissonance. If the teacher again rejects the data, you have several options, one of which you must take. You cannot, however, proceed in the same way you would have had the teacher accepted your data and thereby the need to change.

You should shift into one of the following options:

PROCEED UNILATERALLY

Comment to the teacher that you recognize that he is rejecting the data. Nevertheless, you accept the data for what they are and what they mean to you. Tell the teacher what the data indicate to you. That is, indicate through your interpretation of the data what changes are in order for the teacher to bring his behavior in line with the expectations you (and probably he himself, too) have for him. Be firm as you indicate specifically how the teacher can change his behavior to lead to consonance.

SHIFT TO ANOTHER TYPE OF COLLABORATION

Your initial intention is to collaborate with the teacher in discussing ways to change the teacher's behavior as the method of removing dissonance. Obviously, you cannot collaborate in this way because the basis is the acceptance of the data. Therefore, you need to have data that the teacher will accept. You now must direct the teacher to gather data that he will accept. You can suggest that the teacher gather his own data by recording himself on a video or audio tape. Or, you can suggest that the teacher have a fellow teacher observe him and report data to him. In short, ask the teacher to collaborate with you in the data collection phase of supervision rather than in the data analysis phase.

SCHEDULE ANOTHER OBSERVATION

You can cordially although reluctantly agree to collect additional data for the teacher. If the teacher says, "Well, that's just not the way I regularly teach. I had a headache today. You should visit me when I'm up to par" or some other equivalent dodge, ask him to set up another visit when you can see his teaching in a different light.

Perhaps the teacher will indeed behave differently because he was off his regular pattern. Perhaps he will deliberately modify his behavior even though he will not publicly admit it to you. In either case, the teacher will change his behavior, and that is your aim. You must not lose sight of your overall goal. Indeed, when you observe his changed behavior, you must reinforce it so that he will have the motivation to continue that new behavior.

COMBINE TWO OR THREE OF THE OPTIONS

Suggest, for example, as you offer your own interpretations, implications, and recommendations (the first option) that the teacher tape record himself perhaps to see what you have just seen (the second option). Or you can combine the first and third options so that you can begin to shift the teacher to change his behavior as the means of removing the dissonance he feels.

Keep these options in mind as you read through the conference strategies which follow. The conference strategies flow with the assumption that the teacher does not resist. If the teacher does resist, you may have to leave the strategy to pick up one of the other options. Notice in the first illustrative conference dialogue under the awareness strategy that the teacher offers some initial resistance but does accept the data. The supervisor does not need to leave the strategy in order to cope further with the resistance.

FOUR STRATEGIES FOR HOLDING THE CONFERENCE

The key to holding a helpful conference is congruence between observing and conferring so that an open learning situation between the teacher and you can occur in an atmosphere of trust. The positive self-image and self-respect of the teacher must be established and supported. The principles of learning that apply to the teacher-student relationship and that include the establishment of a positive interpersonal relationship apply equally well to the supervisor-teacher relationship. You must keep in mind that the teacher is in effect learning how to teach from you by virtue of being engaged in a situation where modeling is occurring. By extrapolating from what he sees you do in an interpersonal encounter, the teacher learns how to relate not only to you but to his students as well. In this sense, you are teaching the teacher how to act. Indeed, teaching is one of the tasks you have as supervisor, and the conference offers you perhaps the best opportunity to teach.

Preparation and a strategy for implementation of your main items and objectives are essential. *A conference strategy is a carefully prepared plan involving a sequence of major actions designed to achieve a supervisory goal.* Your supervisory goal is shown by the type of conference you intend to conduct with your teacher. That is, if you intend to correct unsatisfactory behavior by the teacher, you will use one strategy. For a conference that seeks to generate alternatives to acceptable behavior, you will implement a different strategy. The purpose of strategy is to provide you with a framework to guide your actions so that you don't lose sight of your goal in the ongoing complexity of an interactive conference.

The following four strategies for you to use are organized according to purpose of the conference. Each is general, so you will need to modify it to suit your purposes with a particular teacher in a particular conference. Something always occurs to lead you to improvise—to add, subtract, and change what you have done previously. This is as it should be. Each strategy provides only the basic framework for you to follow. You will always need to be flexible.

Awareness Strategy

The awareness strategy (see Figure 6-2) helps you to alert the teacher to what happened in his or her class session. Your purpose is to sensitize the teacher to the data and allow him to determine what steps to take in light of his own interpretation of the data. This strategy serves as the basis of the other three strategies. It is the basis for all the strategies because awareness is the essential ingredient for change. Before a teacher—or anyone else—can change, he must be aware of what he is doing.

Note that with this awareness strategy you as supervisor emphasize the offering of collected data for the teacher to reflect upon. You do not comment on the data nor ask the teacher to explain, justify, or interpret the data to you. If you ask any questions, you do so to make the teacher aware. You may have to prove to or assure the teacher that the data are valid because the teacher might not want to accept them. The data might be so incredible to the teacher that they are suspect. Or, the teacher may be so defensive about the data that he refuses to accept them because instinctively he knows that the implication is that he needs to change. The teacher may not accept the data, then,

Supervisor	Teacher
1. Establishes positive climate by verbal and nonverbal action*	1. Feels comfortable enough to talk openly about his teaching**
2. Presents data to the teacher	2. Learns what occurred along specified dimensions as observed
3. Waits for teacher's comments	3. Thinks about meaning of data
4. Asks awareness questions, if feels it necessary, to elicit teacher's reaction to data	4. Talks about observational data and possibly what they mean to him
5. Sets follow-up steps	5. Proposes or agrees to what he'll do next based on data offered
6. Ends conference	6. Ends conference
*Praises and encourages; maintains good climate as appropriate in Steps two through six	**Feels hopeful and good about some behavior; continues to be willing to talk about his teaching

FIGURE 6-2. Awareness strategy.

because he doesn't want to experience the unpleasantness and discomfort associated with changing long-established behaviors.

A dialogue following this awareness strategy between a supervisor and teacher illustrates several points.

SUPERVISOR: Well, Pat, I'm glad to hear that your hay fever attacks have subsided. For a while there I thought you would have to take a few days off. I've never seen anyone use more Kleenex in a faculty meeting as you did on Friday.

TEACHER: Thanks, me too. I was really miserable. This year has been a very bad one for everyone with allergies. But I'll survive, I guess. Tough, real tough. And what a sore nose I have. Oh well, we hay-feverites are blessed in other ways to compensate. Now, if I could only—

SUPERVISOR: No, I refuse to take your allergies. Sorry.

TEACHER: So am I.

SUPERVISOR: Well, as you know I took some notes while you were teaching today. Since we were talking last time about the importance of questioning, I jotted down some notes on that and another aspect of your recitation, too. I haven't written the notes up formally since I was at the assembly last period; besides, I wanted to talk with you first. Here's the notes I took (*hands Pat the sheet*).

Pat J.   10:15-10:50   10/16

Questions

Cog.-Memory   THL THL THL THL THL THL THL THL I

Converg.   THL I

Diverg.   I

Eval.   I

Rout.   THL III

TEACHER: Thanks, Chris.

SUPERVISOR: Look 'em over and maybe we'll talk about it.

TEACHER: Okay (*Pause.*) Oh!

SUPERVISOR: Pardon?

TEACHER: Nothing. I was just thinking to myself. I don't know, are you sure this is me? I can't believe it. Are you sure?

SUPERVISOR: Sure as I'm Chris Johnson. Did you plan to ask more or less than 57 questions on that runaway story?

TEACHER: Much less; it's so hard to believe that I asked that many questions on that short story. But what really gets me is not the 57 total, but the 41 memory. And I always consider myself a "lit." teacher, teaching the sophomores to think, finally. I'm shocked if you can assure me those numbers are right.

SUPERVISOR: They are; I marked down each question as you asked it. I remember, for example, as a cognitive-memory question, "Where was Nancy headed when she left home?"

TEACHER: I remember that one, too. I'm beginning to get nauseated in addition to being shocked. No one should ask 41 memory questions on that story; the whole story's not worth it. Do I get a D on my report card for today, Chris?

SUPERVISOR: No, just a score of 41 memory questions, 6 convergent, and…

TEACHER: Okay, okay, so you won't tell me that I made a no-no.

SUPERVISOR: There's no need to tell you you were awful today. What would you gain? What would I gain? You know what's good teaching. No point in it. When can I see you again, Pat, so we can compare the two lessons?

TEACHER: Anytime starting tomorrow. I need to settle my stomach today. What about that other stuff you said you observed?

SUPERVISOR: Maybe you've got enough to plan with already. You're a super open-minded person for not fighting the 41 tallies. I wish everyone was as open as you.

TEACHER: Thanks. Okay. Whatever it is, talk to me tomorrow about those other tallies, will you?

SUPERVISOR: It's a date; coffee time during 3rd period? (*Stands up*)

TEACHER: Fine. Are you leaving? You haven't told me what and how I should do now?

SUPERVISOR: If you want, I'll be glad to help you plan your discussion of your next story. Do you want me to help you plan or do you want to work on it on your own?

TEACHER: Let me try it on my own this time. If I blow it again, then we'll plan together. I'll take a rain-check on this rainy day. Do you really think I can do it?

SUPERVISOR: No—I don't *think* you can do it; I *know* you can. See you for coffee tomorrow at 3rd period. By the way, where did you buy those shoes? They're good-looking.

TEACHER: Believe it or not, through some mail-order house. Saw the ad in the newspaper last month. Great buy. I'll bring in their catalog tomorrow.

SUPERVISOR: Thanks—gotta run. I have a parent coming in to see me. See you tomorrow.

Let us look at this dialogue. The supervisor, Chris, opens the conference with some personal ice-breaking comments on the teacher's allergies problems. These opening comments personalize the conference, and give Chris the opportunity to show that their relationship is more than a professional one. Chris cares about Pat's personal health, and rightly so. Chris ends the conference with a personal note, too, making a complimentary remark about Pat's shoes. Pat responds in a positive way by agreeing to bring in the mail-order catalog. The point of all of this is to create the basis for a good conference climate.

From the opening personal remarks, the supervisor moves into the presentation of the observation data. Chris first informs the teacher that the focus of the observation grew out of a previous conference, thus establishing the justification for collecting data on Pat's questions. Chris shows Pat the notes taken without any additional oral or written comments other than the offer to talk about them. The supervisor then gives the teacher ample time to look over the notes. As is common with many teachers who are unaware of their behavior, Pat has a hard time accepting the data and therefore seeks assurance that the data are from that observation session. The supervisor, without defensiveness in recognition of the teacher's need of assurance, gives that assurance in a friendly and understanding manner with "Sure as I'm Chris Johnson." Even when asked a second time about the data, the supervisor does not become angry and offers the reassurance that the teacher obviously needs. The key is that the supervisor stays with the data and does not drift off in anger or insult into other matters.

To focus the teacher's attention on the number of teacher questions, the supervisor asks an awareness question concerning the number of questions asked. The teacher responds and then expands by stating that the total number of questions is of less concern than the number of cognitive-memory questions. The supervisor has succeeded in creating dissonance between Pat's espoused theory of teaching that has as its purpose to cause students to think reflectively about literature and Pat's theory-in-use of teaching that has as its purpose to ask students to recall information about material read. It is in recognition of this success in creating dissonance that the supervisor does not offer any other data to the teacher during the conference. Chris does not want to overload Pat who has just accepted some data and comes to an important realization. The supervisor agrees, however, to give the teacher the data the next day upon request.

Even when the teacher asks for an evaluation, the supervisor side-steps the chance to give one. The teacher recognizes the side-step move immediately. The supervisor again takes a firm stand on data. The supervisor philosophizes a bit by asking rhetorically, "What would you gain? What would I gain?" Chris takes this opportunity to channel the conference into the future by seeking another opportunity to observe Pat, with an implied confidence that things will change by then. Chris even says that a comparison will be in order next time. Pat accepts it all.

The supervisor takes this opportunity to praise the teacher. Chris praises Pat for being open-minded and for accepting what are striking data. The compliment is to the point and sincere. The supervisor would indeed have it easier if everyone did not fight the data, but it does not happen that way. Many teachers refuse for a time to realize what the facts are about their performance. This refusal only impedes their improvement.

To signal that the conference has gone as far as it needs to go, the supervisor stands and prepares to leave. It is at this point that Pat takes one last opportunity to express recognition of the need for change. The teacher directly asks for the supervisor to prescribe what to do. The supervisor offers to help, but does it in a way that suggests to the teacher that there really is no need for external help at this point. The supervisor's message is, "I trust you; I know you can do it; since you know what to do, go do it; I'll help if you need me." It is a reassuring message and the teacher responds accordingly by agreeing to work alone on the task for the first time being.

As a way of concluding the conference, the supervisor shifts the topic to a personal matter. The return to the personal topic of Pat's shoes allows Chris another chance to praise Pat. The response is a warm one, and then Chris leaves to see a parent. The supervisor takes a decisive step to end the conference since it had accomplished its goal: the teacher is aware.

Correction Strategy

The correction strategy (see Figure 6-3) helps you to guide the teacher *to correct* what he is doing unsatisfactorily. Your initial purpose is to make the teacher aware of what is occurring so he can have the basis for changing. With this purpose accomplished, you then move to leading the teacher to accept that a problem exists which must be solved. The high point of the strategy is the determination of some possible solutions to the identified problem. The proposed solutions offer the teacher alternative actions to take since it is insufficient to indicate that change is needed. The teacher cannot simply stop doing what he's doing. He needs to replace what he's doing with new actions that will be acceptable.

The difference between the awareness strategy and the correction strategy lies in steps 6 and 8 of the latter. That is, in the correction strategy the supervisor in step 6 elicits or gives an explicit recognition that a problem exists which needs a solution. Then the supervisor in step 8 elicits or gives his own possible solutions to the problem. If the teacher recognizes the problem and offers possible solutions, the supervisor need not do so.

Supervisor	Teacher
1. Establishes positive climate by verbal and nonverbal action*	1. Feels comfortable enough to talk openly about his teaching**
2. Presents data to the teacher	2. Learns what occurred along specific dimensions as observed
3. Waits for teacher's comments	3. Thinks about meaning of data
4. Asks awareness questions, if feels it necessary, to elicit teacher's recognition of existing problem	4. Talks about observational data and possibly what they mean to him
5. Asks, "What do these data indicate to you?"	5. Tells what these data mean to him; that something is wrong; that a problem exists
6. Explores meaning of data with teacher; gives own indication or agreement that a problem exists	6. Explores the nature of the problem and possibly suggests some solutions to it
7. If necessary, asks, 'What are some possible solutions to this problem?"	7. Offers alternative actions which probably will rectify the situation
8. Gives own possible solutions and/or agrees with teacher's suggested solutions	8. Explores and agrees with possible solutions
9. Sets follow-up observation and conference time	9. Proposes or agrees to follow-up steps, including observation and conference checkup
10. Ends conference	10. Ends conference
*Praises and encourages; maintains good climate, as appropriate, in Steps 2-10	**Feels hopeful and good about some behavior; continues to be willing to talk about and change his teaching

FIGURE 6-3. Correction strategy.

It is preferable for you to allow the teacher *to "own" the problem and the solution* since there is more commitment, more independence, and less threat involved this way. Hence, there is a high probability that the teacher will act accordingly and without the feeling that he is being forced to do so. Obviously, it is not always possible for you to lead the teacher to the desired actions within the time constraints you have to work. When this occurs, then you should in step 6 add your own indication of the problem and in step 8 add your own possible solutions.

A dialogue utilizing this correction strategy for a conference between a junior high school supervisor and teacher is below.

SUPERVISOR: Good morning, Joe. Come in, sit down. Do you want some coffee or tea?

TEACHER: No thanks. I'll just have some of this candy, if you don't mind.

SUPERVISOR: Sure, and I'll have a cup of tea so I can get going in my usual way. There's something about a hot cup of tea. Maybe it dates back to my childhood during those cold winter days we had. (*Pause*) Anyhow, thanks for agreeing to come in for us to talk first thing this morning. I appreciate that since I myself have a meeting right after this with Claire Durnham at the central office to finalize our plans for graduation. Do you have any last minute thoughts on graduation that I can take with me?

TEACHER: No, other than let's make it short and sweet. It gets hot in the auditorium.

SUPERVISOR: Good reminder, thanks. I'll remind Claire of that. Anyhow, Joe, I was glad that I visited your class yesterday afternoon. I haven't been in to see you in two months. I concentrated on looking at you and took some notes. Here's what I wrote down. (*Gives Joe a photocopy of the notes.*)

Joe Trannert   6th period   January 19   8th Alg.

    At desk in front of room when bell rings. Stays at desk to take roll and call to order. Reviews homework, stays at desk. Calls on pupils to explain problems for the homework. Answers questions—at least 3 questions on each problem. Still at desk. Explains new lesson on p. 96 at the board to right of desk. Answers questions. Gives two practice problems. Kids who have trouble come to desk: 4 boys, 10 girls. Makes homework assignment and reminds everyone to watch + and − signs before the numbers. Stays at desk as kids leave, talks with 2 boys about basketball team.

(Silence as teacher reads)

TEACHER: I guess that's true—you did leave out some details, like answering a phone call from the nurse to send Sue McGowan down to her. That phone rings every period at least once.

SUPERVISOR: You're right. Thanks. I'll look into it. Thanks, again. Are you aware that you never moved more than 2 to 3 feet from your desk the entire period?

TEACHER: Yes, I'm very comfortable there.

SUPERVISOR: And are you aware that more girls than boys by far asked you for help?

TEACHER: I really don't consider whether it's a boy or a girl asking a question. I focus on the question and answer it. It's the question not the sex of the student that counts.

SUPERVISOR: I'm wondering if you see a connection between staying so close to your desk and having many questions about the work from the students.

TEACHER: There weren't so many; just the normal amount.

SUPERVISOR: About two-thirds of the class and mostly girls. By the way, did you plan to talk with Rob and Mike after class or did they just stop by to chat?

TEACHER: Well, I'd been talking with them in the lunch room, so I guess they just wanted to get in a few last words after class so they stopped to talk. Nothing special; I didn't ask them to talk to me.

SUPERVISOR: Any other thoughts about what happened yesterday—about a connection between your staying at your desk and the number of questions asked?

TEACHER: No—it was just a normal day with the normal stuff going on; review of homework, a new lesson in the text—that idea of parentheses and brackets is always confusing to the kids—and time to try a problem in class.

SUPERVISOR: I see these things differently. It seems to me that there is something wrong with your attachment to your desk. It reminds me of Eeyore, the donkey in Winnie-the-Pooh, who was attached to his tail. You seemed attached to your desk yesterday. And being attached to the desk, you weren't close to the kids. And that's a problem, I think. (*Pauses*)

TEACHER: Well, I still don't see one. The question isn't where I stand, the question is what I do and the students do in algebra.

SUPERVISOR: That's just it. I think that there is a connection between your standing at the desk and questions you received from the students. Would you entertain the idea that girls have more questions because they're confused while boys have fewer questions because they're less involved and because they feel you're distant from them?

TEACHER: It seems a bit far-fetched.

SUPERVISOR: Not to me. We know there's a positive relation betweeen teacher movement among students and classroom climate, and we also know that a better climate yields high achievement. Check it out in this article by Tuckman.[2]

TEACHER: I'll read it.

SUPERVISOR: Good! I think it's a good sign that you're willing to read and consider it. I'd like you to consider also how you can detach yourself from your desk a bit. You might try moving away and among the students when reviewing the homework—stand on the opposite side of the room from the student who's answering. You can also check with the students when they do the practice problems. Try going to their desks instead of vice versa. These are two fairly simple items that won't require you to alter your style much. I'm sure you can come up with other suggestions for moving around, too, and some ideas for getting the girls to do better. I'll be eager to hear from you when you've read the article.

TEACHER: Well, I won't be able to get to it today since I have my class at the college after school. So, I'll read it tomorrow.

SUPERVISOR: Okay. Then will you stop in on Thursday or Friday for a short while so we can talk about that article?

TEACHER: Okay. Thursday or Friday.

SUPERVISOR: I'll see you then. What class are you going to now?

TEACHER: Pre-algebra for the regular eighth graders.

SUPERVISOR: Good luck with them. You've got a nice group there.

In this dialogue, the supervisor starts off appropriately with warm, friendly actions. It appears that the teacher reacts well. He comments on the jelly beans in a friendly way. However, once his supervisor starts talking directly about the math lesson, his remarks become brief and somewhat contrary. He appears to resist exploring the connection in the data suggested by the supervisor.

The supervisor tries to follow the strategy ideally but finds it difficult to get the teacher to talk. Therefore, the supervisor probes with "Any other thoughts...?" When this probe doesn't prove fruitful, the supervisor moves directly to offering a personal analysis, as indicated by the statement "I see things differently." The supervisor does not want to engage in a tug of war with Joe. Rather than string things out over several conferences, the supervisor proceeds to offer a contrary point of view. There is no fear of tackling the issue.

Obviously, the supervisor was prepared for the conference as shown by two statements. First, there is the reference article about teacher movement and classroom climate. Second, there are two possible solutions that the supervisor offers. However, the supervisor requests that Joe read the article and then try to find still other possible solutions. This is an excellent tactic since there is a show of faith in the teacher's ability to confront the issue on his own once he is aware of further ideas. This is consistent with the suggestion given in the section on giving feedback in Chapter 2.

Reinforcement Strategy

The reinforcement strategy (see Figure 6-4) helps you to guide the teacher to continue in the good ways he is teaching. Your purpose is to reinforce the teacher's satisfactory behavior. It is important to urge you to present data here—perhaps more so than when talking about a correction strategy. This is not strange at all because you are much more likely to give data to a teacher who needs to change but may not initially want to change than to a teacher whom you wish to praise and reinforce. The teacher who needs correction may well challenge you, demanding that you back up your position with data. You recognize this and come prepared to the conference to answer the teacher.

On the other hand, the teacher whom you reinforce is hardly likely to challenge you. He is not likely to ask you for data to justify your statements. He is happy to receive your good words and not inclined to demand more from you lest he embarrass or anger you. When receiving reinforcement, it would be tactless to embarrass you. Nevertheless, the teacher needs data. You must also recognize that research shows that teachers are not good self-observers. Hence, they may not know what they are doing even though they are doing well in their classroom.

The difference between this reinforcement strategy and the correction strategy is obvious. Here you have the pleasant task of reinforcing satisfactory or excellent teaching behavior. You even have the opportunity to direct the teacher into new areas professionally either by generating alternatives so as not to get into a rut or by exploring ways in which the teacher can share his talents with others for mutual benefit. A potential difficulty may lie in leading the teacher beyond himself, to find directions and to undertake new activities that may complicate his life yet enrich his career.

A dialogue following this reinforcement strategy follows.

SUPERVISOR: If you have a few minutes, perhaps we can talk now rather than wait until Monday since we have a long Thanksgiving weekend coming up. Do you have some time?

TEACHER: Yes, that's a good idea. No point for me to be thinking about your observation all weekend long. Give me two minutes to clean up after this bunch and wash my hands.

Supervisor	Teacher
1. Establishes positive climate by verbal and nonverbal action*	1. Feels comfortable enough to talk openly about his teaching**
2. Presents data to the teacher	2. Learns what occurred along specific dimensions as observed
3. Waits for teacher's comments	3. Thinks about meaning of data
4. Asks awareness questions, if feels it necessary, to elicit teacher's recognition of existing problem	4. Talks about observational data and possibly what they mean to him
5. Asks, "What do these data indicate to you?"	5. Tells what these data mean to him and possibly that he is doing well; that he teaches as he believes he should; that alternatives are available, too
6. Explores meaning of data with teacher; gives own indication or agreement that congruence between beliefs and practice exists	6. Explores the nature of his teaching and in what aspects he does well; possibly suggests alternate directions and avenues for further development
7. If necessary, asks, "What are some alternatives open to you in your teaching?" Or, "What are some avenues for further professional development?"	7. Offers suggestions for alternative ways to teach and areas that challenge him to develop further professionally
8. Gives own suggestions and/or agrees with teacher's suggestions	8. Explores and agrees with suggested alternatives and new directions
9. Sets follow-up procedures and conference time	9. Proposes or agrees to follow-up steps, including next conference
10. Ends conference	10. Ends conference
*Praises and encourages; maintains good climate, as appropriate, in Steps 2-10	**Feels hopeful and good about his behavior, continues to be willing to talk about and develop his professional activity

FIGURE 6-4. Reinforcement strategy.

SUPERVISOR: Go ahead. I'll just walk around the room and look at all the displays.

TEACHER: Okay. Be right with you. (*Pause*)

SUPERVISOR: Would you like a mint?

TEACHER: Thanks, this will help get rid of the taste of our cafeteria food. I need it.

SUPERVISOR: When I came in today to your class, Leslie, you were already underway. So, I parked myself in the corner and immediately began to look, listen, and touch—even smell—everything that was going on. I jotted down a crude map of the room, marked where the students were working, and started following you around the room with my pencil and my eye and ear. Sometimes I even moved about too, so I could hear better. Here's the map. [See Figure 6-5.] The words on the bottom are to pick out "art" words—it's a hard distinction to make between an art word and a non-art word, but I thought it might give a flavor of what you were talking about to the students as you stopped in your rounds. The words are only the first few minutes since I couldn't keep up anymore. So I just mapped after that.

TEACHER: That's nice. What a great idea! Where did you get this idea for observing?

SUPERVISOR: At a workshop this past summer. After all I have to try new things out, too. Well, what do you think?

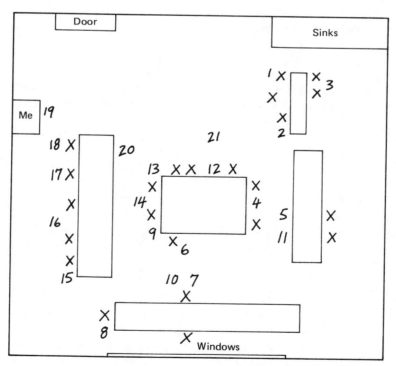

FIGURE 6-5. Mapping an observation.

TEACHER: I think it's great. It shows that I did just what I want to. I believe that the kids need contact with me—some more, some less. But they all need me to talk to—to guide them in their work. So, I try to keep moving and give each some contact, several times each period. Your map shows it. But I didn't realize I was using "perspective" so much today. But it doesn't surprise me since yesterday we devoted the whole period to talking about perspective. They're just learning about it and find the whole thing fascinating and so do I. Maybe it's cause and effect. But which is the cause and which is the effect?

SUPERVISOR: Yes, this is what we talked about in our last conference, and it's great, as you say, to see it in action. You did what you say you believe in and what you believe in makes great sense for an art teacher—or any other teacher, for that matter. I particularly like what you said about guiding them—making contact so you can guide them—that you let them decide for themselves where they want to go and you guide them there. That's great to see in art.

TEACHER: Thanks, it's nice to hear that from you. Thanks.

SUPERVISOR: Look, I'm going to be reporting to the administrator's council for the district next week about the workshop I told you about. I'm wondering if I can get you to come with me. I figure that I can talk in general about this mapping method and then show everyone this map I just made. Maybe then you could talk about how it serves you, why you want to make contact with the students, and how you feel about it all from the teacher's point of view. What do you say, next week on Thursday afternoon? I can arrange for someone to cover your class for an hour or so. What do you say?

TEACHER: Well—uh, well…

SUPERVISOR: Now don't be bashful. You surely can help me out and help out the other administrators. Maybe they'll begin to use something like this with their teachers. What do you say?

TEACHER: Well, okay.

SUPERVISOR: Great. Think about what you'd like to say and I'll do the same. I'll speak to you on Monday afternoon so we can compare notes and get our act together for next Thursday.

TEACHER: Okay.

SUPERVISOR: Have a nice Thanksgiving. Thanks for an opportunity to see theory in practice. Thanks for agreeing to help out next Thursday. Have a good weekend.

TEACHER: You too, so long.

The supervisor in the dialogue above has the pleasant task of holding a conference to reinforce the art teacher's congruent behavior. The teacher's espoused theory of teaching is congruent with the theory of teaching in use. The supervisor notes that and commends the teacher for it. The teacher is grateful and reacts positively to the praise.

With an excellent opportunity to show off a new observation method and a teacher who is congruent in regard to making contact with the students, the supervisor extends a collegial invitation. Appearing before the administrator's council will serve a double purpose. First, the appearance is a feather in the teacher's cap because the entire school district will know what just two people now know. Second, the appearance will serve to give the teacher a new area in which to work. That is, the teacher will be able to share the idea with other people.

The supervisor will now be in a position to utilize the teacher with other teachers. Peer teaching through workshops is one good way to help the entire faculty. It benefits the teacher conducting the workshop by leading him to grow as he prepares to help his peers. It simultaneously benefits the other teachers who learn from a colleague whom they can relate to and talk to afterwards.

In recognition of the value of having the teacher appear before the district administrators, the supervisor switches emphasis, praising the teacher for being congruent and then leading the teacher into self-development by helping others. There is just a very brief time in which the teacher hesitates to move into the new area. The extra push by the supervisor is worth it.

Notice also two small and related factors. The supervisor meets with the teacher in the teacher's art room for convenience sake as well as making it comfortable for the teacher. Also, the short meeting takes place immediately following the observation period. The supervisor offered this time to meet rather than wait several days over the long Thanksgiving Day weekend. The decisions show consideration of the teacher who is eager to hear the supervisor's reaction to the observation session.

Evaluation Strategy

The evaluation strategy (see Figure 6-6) guides you in conducting an evaluation conference in which you *review* several observation sessions together *to give a judgment* about the teacher. You can hold such a conference after an observation session or in addition to the regular individual postobservation session. That is, after your second, third, or fourth observation session of the year you could hold a regular postobservation conference and later schedule an evaluation conference.

This strategy leads you to review several sets of data and to offer an evaluation of the teacher. For this reason, you need to be clear in your own mind when you are reporting, reviewing, or comparing data, and when you are evaluating the teacher based on the data. What is more, you must make these distinctions clear to the teacher.

There are two differences between this evaluation strategy and the awareness, correction, and reinforcement strategies. First, this strategy is to be used after *several* individual conferences have been held. This strategy requires that data be examined over a span of time. Second, whereas the main purpose in the other three strategies is the development of the teacher with evaluation deemphasized, the explicit aim of this strategy is to lead the supervisor to a reasoned and reasonable evaluation.

Here is a dialogue following the evaluation strategy for a conference between a supervisor and a primary teacher (students ages 6–7).

SUPERVISOR: If it's okay with you, Jan, I thought today we would begin with a review of the lesson I observed yesterday and then maybe move to a summary look at all three observations this year so we can talk in some broad strokes. If you have any questions when we're done, you can always raise them since there are a few days before I plan to file a report in any case. There's always time to sit down to talk further. Is this okay with you?

TEACHER: Yes, I guess it'll save us meeting again. I guess it's okay. Let's see how it goes. We tried it last year, if I remember, and it worked out okay. Let's try it again and see what happens.

SUPERVISOR: Fine, let's try it then. You're right, we did do it last year. Thanks for reminding me. You've got a good memory—much better than I. Well, let's get started. Have some munchies if you want. Jan, I made some notes yesterday as I

Supervisor	**Teacher**
1. Establishes positive climate by verbal and nonverbal action*	1. Feels comfortable enough to talk openly about his teaching**
2. Presents data to the teacher	2. Learns what forms the basis of the evaluation
3. Waits for teacher's comments	3. Thinks about meaning of data; comments on data
4. Asks whether additional data are available and should be included	4. Offers additional data or accepts data presented
5. Explains criteria used in evaluation	5. Clarifies ideas on what constitutes the points on the continuum from poor to good teaching
6. Gives evaluation and justifies it by referring to data and criteria	6. Learns supervisor's judgment and reasons supporting it
7. Explores teacher's reaction to the evaluation	7. Comments on supervisor's evaluation
8. Offers implications of the evaluation; sets follow-up steps	8. Talks about implications and adds own implications
9. Ends conference	9. Ends conference
*Praises and encourages; maintains good climate, as appropriate, in steps 2-9	**Feels hopeful and good about some behavior; continues to be willing to talk about and change his teaching

FIGURE 6-6. Evaluation strategy.

observed you teaching reading. You asked only one question in the twenty minutes but got six responses from five different pupils. The pupils—Alice, and Stephen—asked you two questions about or related to the story. You answered none. I...uh...here's a copy of my notes. [See Figure 6-7.]

TEACHER: Thanks—it's easier to understand it all when I see it in front of me. Well, I've changed in one respect. I'm asking fewer questions and getting more answers to each question.

SUPERVISOR: That's not *one* respect; that's a double change.

TEACHER: That's right. Isn't it?

SUPERVISOR: Yes and that's good. Now, let me ask you, did you intend ahead of time not to answer the two questions asked or did that just happen that way?

TEACHER: I don't know. I didn't realize until this moment that I didn't answer the two questions. What did I do if I didn't answer them?

Jan Grayson

Reading   **10:15-10:35**   **Primary Ungraded**   **April 29**

You assembled reading group at side near her reading carpet. 8 pupils. Reviewed yesterday's story by retelling. Stressed new words (get them ready for today's lesson?). Pupils read new story silently first and then each read aloud. Mark had trouble with one word: prepare (it was read "prep are"). Jan corrected: "It's divided differently, Mark. It's not P-R-E-P- and then A-R-E. It's P-R-E and then P-A-R-E. I can understand why you did that. Sorry. Try again now."

Teacher Questions: | **Pupil Res:** ꓘꓕꓕꓒ |

Pupil Questions: || (Alice, Stephen)

Teacher question: In what ways did Sara show that she was concerned about her dog?

Responses: Mark, Tommy, Alice, Marilyn, Alice, Jennifer.

Didn't answer one question (See TIP article).

Never once disturbed by pupils not in reading group. Kept eye on them, however.

FIGURE 6-7. Observation notes.

SUPERVISOR: You first asked each one to repeat the question, and after they did that you asked if someone in the group knew the answer to the question.

TEACHER: What do you think of that?

SUPERVISOR: We're back now to our first conference because there, too, we talked about your not answering questions. Let's look at the last twelve months since it's about a year since we had that combined conference. In our first conference we talked about student questions and how you field them. I said then that I don't believe that there is a hard and fast rule about answers to pupils' questions. I suggested that you should read the article in *Theory Into Practice* magazine[3] on the topic because we agreed that to be knowledgeable and aware is better than being unaware of what you're doing. You teach the students to read in a way where most of them read on grade level. You have changed from asking about fifteen questions in a short lesson—that is, during the talk-time when the pupils aren't reading silently or aloud—to one, as you did yesterday. And I think that's good since you've also changed the type of question you ask and the number of responses you receive for each question. We focused on this in our second conference. That's good improvement because it leads to more participation by the pupils and thus more involvement in reading. So there's been change here on the positive side. On the other hand, you're still not answering student questions, and *I* think that the result is the holding back by the boys and girls. They don't ask because they know you won't answer. So why should they bother? And I think that's not so good since interest in reading doesn't really get going with the children. And I think that one of your aims is and should be the increased interest of the pupils in reading. Here you haven't changed much. I think that you can change here, too, and will change once you're aware of the consequences of your behavior in the pupil question-teacher answer game. This is what you need to work on during the coming months, especially in the summer. I think that you can do it since this aspect of enthusiasm on your part and the pupils' part is the missing element in your becoming an excellent reading teacher rather than an average, satisfactory reading teacher. Your work as a faculty person on committees and all of that kind of thing is certainly good. I have no problems there with your sincerity and professionalism. Any comments on all of this?

TEACHER: What you say is sensible. I guess I've been so concerned with my questioning that I forgot to work on my answering. I guess it's time for me to face up to it. It's not news to me what you're saying, but it's still hard to hear it.

SUPERVISOR: Let's set this, then, as your target to hit in the next few months. Let me know in the next day or so how you plan to work on this and I can incorporate it into the report I have to file. In the meantime, would you review your copies of the previous observation reports and review the new report I'll put in your mail box late today or tormorrow?

TEACHER: Okay, I can do that.

SUPERVISOR: Please give me your written or oral reactions. Okay?

TEACHER: Okay.

SUPERVISOR: Thanks for your time. Are you aware that you ate every tiny chocolate bar in the bowl?

TEACHER: My goodness, not that too! Oh well, a chocaholic is always noticed—thanks for the candy bars—all fifteen!

In this dialogue, the supervisor at an opportune moment shifts from the data referring to just one observation to the larger picture. The supervisor shows the movement made over time. In this way, the teacher can also see what is happening as a result of the observation-conference process. The supervisor shows that the changes taking place are not secret, but are noticed and approved.

Notice also that the supervisor gives an evaluation and justifies both the negative and positive aspects, telling why the shift in type of question is good and why the lack of answers to pupil questions needs correction. The giving of reasons for positive as well as negative is most important. Since the judgment of the teacher grows out of the previous observations and conferences, it does not come as a surprise to the teacher.

Another important part of the dialogue is the supervisor's comment about the teacher's potential for further change. The supervisor notes and recommends what the teacher should change and then points out in a positive way that the teacher can do it. There is direction and a show of confidence to the teacher. There is commendation for the teacher's general display of professionalism as a faculty member in order to show a demonstration of faith that the teacher can improve further and become an excellent teacher.

CONFERENCE TACTICS

Once you have made your preparations, including the choice and modification of a conference strategy as previously indicated, you need to begin your implementation.

Here is where you need tactics, specific points for conducting the conference, rather than broad directives for setting your goals. To guide you in the conference, two lists follow, one a set of positive tactics and the other a set of negative tactics. The emphasis is on the positive because in every learning situation where people seek to develop further there needs to be an emphasis on what to do. On the other hand, there is always need for recognizing what *not* to do. However, keep in mind that your eye must be focused on the positive because no list of negatives, no matter how long, can tell you what to do. A list of negative tactics tells you only what not to do, but in a conference you need to "do," to act. You cannot just sit there following a list of "don't" rules.

Positive Tactics

- Set the physical environment to convey an open, cooperative tone. Remove communication barriers. You might: face the teacher; sit close to the teacher so that you can talk in a soft voice; sit around a low coffee table so that no large desk becomes a barrier between the two of you; sit at a conference table at a corner so you can share notes and examine forms together (*cross-corner* seating rather than cross-table seating promotes communication and removes the nonverbal message that you two are opposites); and offer the teacher candy, or coffee and cookies, or some other snack as a symbol of cooperation.

- Make it clear to the teacher that your intention is to help him grow professionally. Make it clear that you do not intend to humiliate, attack, or play one-up-manship. Once you have clarified your intention, take care that your subsequent actions and words are congruent. The teacher must know and feel that you are not an adversary but a leader interested in his development.

- Speak about and emphasize positive concrete actions for the teacher to do or for the two of you to do together. This emphasis will indicate that you are guide, leader, helper. Use words and terms that indicate that you are cooperating with your teacher and facilitating his development. Seek alternative actions for the teacher to take. For example, speak about planning a lesson together or viewing a tape recording together. Suggest that the teacher can alter homework assignments, use a simulation activity, move the furniture to facilitate student–student talk when small group work is in progress, or explicitly teach students how to take notes. In general, teachers are practitioners who spend their time doing things; they are active people. Hence, they need and respond to suggestions on what to do in concrete terms given from the perspective of guidance toward further development.

- Concentrate your remarks on the teacher's performance rather than his personality or attitudes. A focus on performance is a focus on the observable and objective aspects of teaching. Such a focus is much more acceptable to the teacher because it is less threatening to his person. It is also more readily changed than the personality and attitudinal aspects of the teacher's professional and personal life.

- Look for and set one or two behavioral changes for the teacher to make within a reasonable, agreed-upon time. It is better to make the changes you set simple, "low risk," achievable, and thus reinforceable ones rather than to set many and complex changes that may only overwhelm the teacher. If the teacher becomes over-whelmed, the changes you set may turn out to be counterproductive, actually inhibiting change because the teacher feels helpless in the face of so many things to do at one time. By keeping your eye focused on change and remembering that you do not want to destroy a teacher's sense of self, you should look for what the teacher can do to grow. This is especially true if the conference is focusing on correction of unsatisfactory teacher behavior. No teacher is all bad and totally hopeless. Offer a specific change that will help the teacher. Help the teacher move into the future rather than fear the future.

- Indicate that the changes in behavior that are being suggested either by your teacher or by you involve low risk. Point out that the changes are achievable and within his capabilities. If the teacher feels that the changes involve high-risk, he may shy away from an attempt to change. With too much at stake, he may fear to act, become overwhelmed, and freeze in the status quo.

- Praise the teacher for his achievements even if they are small. Specify the particulars of what you are praising so the teacher knows clearly what he has done well. With such praise, which is effective praise, you can lead the teacher to a precise understanding of what he is doing with the potential that he can and will emphasize those behaviors in the future.

- Once there is movement toward change or even agreement by the teacher about the direction for him to take in order to effect change, accept it. Praise the change and encourage it so it can develop further. Be patient with it so that the bud you see can blossom beautifully. Reinforce it.

- Be brief in your remarks, especially at the beginning of the conference. By speaking briefly you indicate that you intend the teacher to join you in talking during the conference. By being long-winded, you silence the teacher, and this prevents you from learning the teacher's reactions to the collected data and your remarks.

- After you ask a question, wait for the response. Allow the teacher time—at least five seconds—to respond to your question. If you give too short a response time by asking another question, rephrasing your question, or answering the question yourself, you will be silencing the teacher. In short, ask one question at a time and, by waiting, express your expectation of receiving a response and your willingness to listen to it.

- Listen carefully to the teacher. The act of careful, attentive listening is perhaps the most powerful nonverbal act you can perform. By listening, you demonstrate clearly that you care about the teacher. By listening, you have the opportunity to hear what is on your teacher's mind. You will hear explanations for his actions, which will influence what avenues you can suggest to him to take toward further growth. When you listen, you increase the probability that he will listen to you.

- Put your notes and documents where the teacher can see that you have them and where you can refer to them easily. Let the teacher know that you are prepared. The teacher will know from this nonverbal message that you take the matter of conferring seriously. Your notes and documents are a concrete sign that you care. This open display does not mean that you must allow the teacher to read your notes and documents. It only means that you should not be afraid to show that you have notes, a prepared strategy, and supporting documents to use during the conference. Refer to your materials as you need them. The impact on the teacher will be positive.

Negative Tactics

- Don't talk in generalities. Avoid such general phrases as, "You're doing fine," "Things seem to be going well," and "We all know that it'll turn out okay." If you do use such a general expression, follow it with another which gives specifics. For example, "You're doing fine. By that, I mean you're improving in your questioning, your lesson plan shows more organization, and the time between shifts in topics or subjects during the course of the day does not develop into chaos time for the students." Generalities are okay only when backed up with specifics. Otherwise, avoid them.

- Don't flaunt your power. There is little need to wave your "power flag," so to speak, before the teacher to announce that you as supervisor have the power over the teacher. The teacher and you both know and recognize that you have power. By flaunting your power, you will only antagonize the teacher and possibly cause negative behavior.

- Don't lapse into monologues, or lectures, or sermons. Long episodes of talking on your part will serve to silence the teacher and prevent you from learning what the teacher thinks about the topic you are discussing. Thus, you will not fully understand the teacher's motivation or understanding and be able to personalize the actions needed to be taken in the future. A "sermon" or "lecture" may allow you to get something off your chest, but it may strike the teacher as unnecessary and condescending. Avoid long-winded talk and stay on course by focusing on behavior that will help the teacher develop further.

- Don't hide your inexperience if you are inexperienced. Don't pretend that you have years of experience if you are a first- or second-year supervisor. The teacher no doubt knows about you from the grapevine and will consider it offensive if you pretend to be what you are not. Furthermore, you can ask the teacher to help you learn and develop, too, since every educator, teacher, and supervisor alike needs to develop continually. Don't be afraid to acknowledge that you are learning and developing your skills as a supervisor.

- Don't make vindictive remarks. If you play the "gottcha" game with the teacher and mete out punishment because of a previous event, surely the teacher will play the game also. The teacher will no doubt be able to catch you in some slip or error in order to get even with you. He, too, will soon say, "Gottcha on that one." This getting even interplay will only decrease the potential for having a successful conference focused on further development.

- Don't push the teacher into a corner where there is no way leading to development and change. Don't make the situation appear so grim and terrible that the teacher believes there is no change possible. Such a situation leads to a sense of hopelessness and helplessness, neither of which is positive.

TEACHING YOUR TEACHER TO CONFER

The previous sections deal with how you should act at the conference. They offer strategies and tactics for conferring that will aid you in sending positive and correct messages. In other words, they guide you in giving helpful and meaningful feedback.

Although such strategies and tactics are necessary, they are not enough. You need to do one more thing.

To help your teacher and yourself, you should teach him how to confer. You should not expect him to know or to realize that there are ways that will promote a fruitful conference for the both of you. He may be so apprehensive about the conference or so accustomed to acting negatively that he cannot figure out by himself what behavior would be mutually helpful. As leader of the conference, it is your responsibility to help the teacher to learn new skills. This will not only make your job easier in the long run, but make his job and relationship with you more fruitful.

You can talk with your teacher about such topics as motivation, awareness, correction, reinforcement, evaluation, and dissonance. You might, if you feel you have a strong relationship with the teacher, even raise the topic of resistance to data and suggestions by you. But, perhaps the easiest and least threatening way is to review Figure 6-8 with the teacher. It presents a short list of nine things that the teacher should do during the conference. They are guidelines for receiving feedback in a helpful, meaningful way. They will help the teacher to benefit from the conference even though you do not perform 100 percent correctly.

---

1. Focus on what is being said rather than on how it is said.

2. Focus on feedback as a learning tool rather than as criticism.

3. Focus on accepting the information and suggestions offered rather than on defending what you did.

4. Focus on developing further rather than maintaining the status quo.

5. Focus on seeking specific, concrete suggestions regarding your performance rather than abstractions about your approach or attitude.

6. Focus on clarifying what's been said to you rather than passively absorbing a lecture from someone.

7. Focus on understanding the sender's vantage point rather than on indicating your own vantage point.

8. Focus on allowing the person to give you feedback in a personally comfortable way rather than in a structured way predetermined by you.

9. Check the feedback you receive from a person by summarizing the main points for both of you.

FIGURE 6-8. Guidelines for receiving feedback in a helpful, meaningful way.

CHAPTER 6 ENDNOTES

1. Leon Festinger, *A Theory of Cognitive Dissonance* (Stanford, Calif.: Stanford University Press, 1962).

2. Bruce W. Tuckman, D. W. Cochran, and E. J. Travers, "Evaluating Open Classrooms," *Journal of Research and Development in Education,* Vol. 8, No. 1 (Fall 1974): 14–19.

3. Ronald T. Hyman, "Fielding Student Questions," *Theory into Practice,* Vol. 19, No. 1 (Winter 1980): 38–44.

7

QUESTIONING

IN

SUPERVISION

There is no denying that questioning is very important in supervision. Yet, for some unknown reason, questioning frequently is not discussed. Perhaps some people assume that because supervisors are former teachers there is no need to discuss what is so basic to teaching. Although there are many similarities between supervising and teaching, there are still enough differences to make the topic of questioning an important one for supervisors to consider.

Chapter 7 treats the topic of questioning from the supervisor's perspective. It will look at the role of questioning in supervision, the types of questions to ask, and the techniques for asking those questions. The related skills of fielding responses, fielding questions, and helping teachers with their questioning skills also will be discussed.

After reading this chapter, you should be able to:

- Understand the role and types of questioning in supervision as well as the tactics needed for asking questions effectively.
- Describe the role of questioning in supervision.
- Define five general types of questions.
- Offer examples of different types of questions and their uses in supervision.
- List at least ten tactics for asking questions, fielding responses, and fielding questions.
- Describe two ways of helping teachers with their questioning skills.

THE ROLE OF QUESTIONING IN SUPERVISION

There is no other single act so pervasive in education as the act of questioning. Educators are constantly asking questions. They begin as teachers asking their students several hundred questions per day. Teachers ask questions on the average at the rate of about three a minute. They are generally unaware of the number of questions they ask, underestimating the number they ask by a factor of about five. After several years of such experience, asking questions appears to get into the teacher's bones. It is, therefore, not surprising that supervisors also ask questions because they are former teachers. Some still teach part of the day.

Reasons for and Consequences of Asking Questions

Question asking is a normal everyday activity performed in just about every area of life. Parents ask their children questions, doctors ask their patients questions, patients ask their doctors questions, drivers ask police officers questions, and so on. Perhaps the primary reason we think of for asking a question is to seek information. That is, the motive for the doctor asking the patient, "Where does your arm hurt you?" and "When does it hurt you?" is that the doctor's diagnosis depends on knowing about the patient's pain. The subsequently prescribed treatment is based on the information gained from asking questions in addition to examining the patient.

Seeking information, however, is not the only motive for asking questions. For example, we ask questions in order to obtain permission to do something: "May I park here after 6 P.M.?" or, "May I use your telephone?" We also ask questions in order to receive advice ("Should I take aspirin?"), to stimulate thinking on a given topic ("How would *you* decrease the use and abuse of cocaine in our society today?"), to test a person's knowledge of our government ("What functions does the Senate perform in our government?"), and to criticize or chastise someone for actions we disapprove of ("Why in the world didn't you take the shortcut home from the bus station?"). There are other motives, too.

In addition to the explicit motives for asking questions, there also are hidden motives. For example, as a doctor's patient you may ask a secretary, "What time is it?" and thus seek information. However, the hidden motive is to gain the secretary's attention so you will be taken care of sooner. You may not be aware of the hidden motive of your question. You may not intend to call attention to yourself.

Other possible hidden motives for asking questions are also well known. For example, your questions can serve the function of asserting your superior position, of putting someone on the defensive, and of involving your faculty in decisions affecting the policy of your school program. If you are aware of these intentions, they are no longer hidden. Indeed, you may well admit to yourself that the motive for asking the secretary "What time is it?" is to call attention to yourself and to be taken care of promptly. In this case, the motive becomes an explicit one. Thus, you have two simultaneous motives, the first (seeking information) being actually only a means to the expression of the second (gaining attention in order to get prompt treatment). The secretary, however, may or may not recognize your "real" motive and may react only to your explicit motive of finding out what time it is. You may in this way succeed and fail simultaneously—succeed in gaining information from your surface motive and fail in gaining attention from your hidden motive.

Whatever your intended explicit motive and your recognized or unrecognized "real" motive are (see Figure 7-1), there also are unintended consequences arising from your questions. For example, you may ask a question to seek information ("What time is it?") and the unrecognized "real" motive may be to gain the attention of the secretary. At the same time, however, it also may be true that you do not intend and do not even realize that you have annoyed the secretary, causing that person to avoid doing you a subsequent favor. Thus, in general, through questions you can unintentionally and

1. Seek information

2. Request permission

3. Test respondent's knowledge

4. Criticize/correct respondent's behavior

5. Gain respondent's attention

6. Assert your superior position

7. Put respondent on defensive

8. Involve respondent in decision making

9. Seek advice

10. Stimulate respondent's thinking on an issue

11. Cause awareness of data about behavior of respondent

12. Initiate a conversation or conference

(These are not necessarily positive reasons. Rather, these are descriptive of why people ask questions.)

FIGURE 7-1. *Some reasons for asking questions.*

unknowingly attack, anger, silence, or humiliate your respondent. You also can please, satisfy, motivate, or compliment the respondent unintentionally. Naturally, it is never possible to know all the motives and consequences that are associated with your question asking. Nevertheless, you can and should be aware that unintended consequences can result, especially negative ones (for example, the faculty feels attacked by your many questions and feels that you are spying on them).

When you are aware of the unintended consequences, you can act accordingly, building on the positive ones and eliminating the negative ones. You can and should be on the lookout for the consequences of your questions, for knowledge of them can help you understand your relationships with your teachers and preserve your autonomy by not allowing you to become a victim of unknown circumstances.

The Need to Know About and Use Questions

As a supervisor, you need to know about questions and be sensitive to them for two important reasons. First, you will be asking questions in the postobservation conference. You need to know the types of questions available to you and the likely consequences of asking them. Second, your question asking will serve as a model for the teacher to use with his or her students. This occurs because the supervisor-teacher relationship essentially involves teaching.

When you confer with teachers, you will ask questions partly because conferring is but one of life's activities in which there is verbal interaction between two people. As such, to ask questions is normal. In addition, you will be asking questions because questions will serve your supervisory goals better than declarative statements or evaluative pronouncements. That is, a question whose purpose is to arouse awareness in the teacher so that the teacher can deal with the matter at hand is better than an evaluation of the teacher on your part. It is better in the sense that an awareness question strategically and tactically asked will promote your supervisory goal of teacher development and self-growth.

Obviously, it is not the question itself—its type and form—but the use of the question—in time, context, and manner—that will help you. A particular type of question at a given point in your conference (strategic placement) will help you. Furthermore, you need to ask that question in a way that is congruent with your goal.

As shown in Chapter 6, questions are at the core of the four conference strategies of awareness, correction, reinforcement, and evaluation. This does not mean that you should ask many questions or that you should only ask questions, as opposed to making statements and offering judgments. Certainly, a barrage of questions aimed at the teacher will have its negative effects, probably causing your questions to prevent you from achieving your goal in the conference. While two or three well-chosen, well-placed, and well-asked questions may be effective, it is by no means true that twelve or eighteen questions will be six times as effective.

Although it is possible to reduce the number of questions you use in the future if you decide that you currently ask too many, it is pointless to try to eliminate questions from your conferences. Rather than try to avoid or eliminate totally a perfectly useful and normal technique for promoting your interaction, it is more sensible and reasonable to concentrate on utilizing questions as best you can. The physician or dentist who is concerned with X-rays and their potential for harm does not ban the X-ray as a medical tool but seeks ways to use it reasonably. The same is true with questions in supervision and teaching.

TYPES OF QUESTIONS AND THEIR USE IN SUPERVISORY CONFERENCES

Let us concentrate on asking questions during a supervisory postobservation conference. What holds for that situation applies to others as well, such as the preobservation conference and an informal conference in the hall or parking lot. If you generally conduct a preobservation conference with the teacher, you can begin thinking about the observation and postobservation conference as you review the points the two of you have discussed. If you generally do not hold a preobservation conference but arrange for your observation and postobservation conference some other way, you can plan ahead based on your previous arrangement. In any case, you will need to plan some key questions prior to your encounter with your teacher. (*Note:* To explain the five types of supervisory questions, let's refer to an observation session that focused on teacher questions.)

Assume that based on previous agreement with the teacher you have decided to observe the teacher's questioning activity, a justifiable and common focus for observation. Your observation notes appear in Figure 7-2 and are formally written on the "Observation Report" in Figure 7-3. You have tallied each time the teacher asked a cognitive-memory, convergent, divergent, evaluative, or classroom routine question. (See Chapter 3 for details.) Brief definitions are as follows: Cognitive-memory questions elicit recall of remembered content; convergent questions elicit responses that are more than mere recall and require the merging of diverse data productively; divergent questions encourage the elaboration of previous ideas and the generation of new data and ideas in an original and flexible way; evaluative questions elicit the expression of a person's opinion, interpretation, or judgment based on a previous statement; and classroom routine questions elicit responses about teaching and personal matters.) Also,

Oct. 16   Pat Jones—English, Soph.

10:15-10:50   (short period)

Based on story by Brenda Brickford, "Home at Last."

(T = teacher   S = student)

T questions

1. Cognitive Memory	︙	= 41
2. Convergent	︙	= 6
3. Divergent	︙	= 1
4. Evaluative	︙	= 1
5. Routine	︙	= 8

Who speaks?

T after boy	︙	= 26
T after girl	︙	= 15
S after boy	︙	= 3
S after girl	︙	= 22

FIGURE 7-2. Observation notes.

Date ____October 16____   Subject or Grade Level ____10th grade English____

Teacher's Name/School ____Pat Jones, Hamilton H.S. (nontenured)____

Observed by __C. Johnson, Principal__ Time __3rd period (35 min., short)__

Date and Time of Conference ____October 20   2:30 p.m.____

Reason for Observation ____first of three required for this year____

COMMENTS:

During the lesson (10:15 to 10:50 a.m.) Pat and the students discussed a story by Brenda Brickford, "Home at Last." They talked about the story and the motives Nancy, the main character, had for running away from home and then returning on her own after six hours. The focus of the observation was the type of teacher questions and who spoke after whom:

A. Teacher Questions

1. Cognitive-Memory = 41

2. Convergent = 6

3. Divergent = 1

4. Evaluative = 1

5. Routine = 8

B. Who Speaks After Whom

1. Teacher after boy = 26

2. Teacher after girl = 15

3. Student after boy = 3

4. Student after girl = 22

5. Other = 0

Homework assignment: Students are to ask their parents if they ever ran away from home as children.

Teacher's Signature _____ Date _____

☐ Check if you wish to comment. Submit comments with three copies to be attached.

FIGURE 7-3. Observation report.

you have tallied who speaks after whom because it struck you as you sat in the room that a pattern was developing in the interaction.

Awareness Questions

Awareness questions have as their purpose the alerting of the teacher to what occurred. With an awareness question, your aim is not to challenge, attack, test, or criticize the teacher but simply to ask her to think about what she did or what happened in the classroom. It is wise to jot down some awareness questions because you may not be as familiar with them as with other types, and you want to be sure to ask them as you have planned.

Two awareness questions based on Figures 7-2 and 7-3 are:

> A. Did you plan to ask more or fewer than 57 questions on the story by Brickford?
> B. Did you plan to ask more, or fewer, or the same amount of cognitive memory questions about the story?

Acceptable awareness questions share some common characteristics: (1) their purpose is to bring about awareness; (2) they refer to what happened in the past in a specific class session; (3) they do not require the teacher to generalize, interpret, or evaluate her actions; (4) they have one of two formats, either a "select-the-option" format as the two above or a "yes-no" format.

It is good, although a bit hard, to phrase awareness questions in a "select-the-option" format since such a format gives a clue to the teacher as to what terminology he should use in talking about the observation data. If you find it difficult to formulate awareness questions in this "select-the-option" way, you can use a "yes-no" format. You might, for example, add to Figure 7-3:

> C. Did you plan to ask about 57 questions on the Brickford story?

The following are six more acceptable awareness questions based on Figures 7-2 and 7-3:

> D. Did you deliberately speak immediately after the boys?
> E. Did you intentionally speak after the boys about twice as much as after the girls?
> F. Do you think that the parents will approve or object to the assignment you gave—that the students should ask their parents about their own childhoods?
> G. Is the ratio of about 50 substantive questions to about 8 routine questions what you sought—that is, about 16 percent routine questions?
> H. Did you plan to speak after a student about twice as often as another student did—41 to 25?
> I. Do you know that most of your questions today were cognitive-memory ones?

As a further measure for clarifying the characteristics of awareness questions, *negative examples* of awareness questions follow:

A. Do you always ask mostly cognitive-memory questions?
B. What do you think is the significance of the fact that you spoke after the boys more than after the girls?
C. Is this a good balance of questions?

Such questions as these last three are not acceptable as awareness questions because they have the potential to put the teacher on the defensive and to give the distinct impression that you are attacking him. Question A deals with a generality and not the specific lesson observed. Question B asks for interpretation, not awareness. Question C requests a judgment, not awareness. As such, these questions negate the approach to supervisory conferences that aims to guide the teacher to self-awareness as the basis for the implementation of change.

In short, you must take care when asking awareness questions because the teacher may take a question to be an attack even though you do not intend it to be one at all. Try to ask awareness questions similar to the acceptable ones given above, and try to ask them in a tone that seeks clarification and awareness rather than one that tests, challenges, or attacks. Have faith and patience that the positive awareness questions work—that there is no need for negative questions.

Information-Seeking Questions

The purpose of information-seeking questions is to elicit new data in order to provide a strong foundation to support subsequent interpretation and evaluation. When you ask such questions, you want to learn more about the teaching situation, the students, and the teacher so you can better understand the context of the lesson you have observed.

Two information-seeking questions based on Figures 7-2 and 7-3 are:

A. What did you say about this story when you asked the students to read it for homework?
B. How do you plan to deal with the homework assignments when they come in?

Acceptable information-seeking questions elicit data that are helpful in understanding what the teacher's purposes and actions were. These questions yield information to help you fill in the gaps. They seek information about the past and the future (plans and predictions). They do not seek opinion, generalization, interpretation, or evaluation but seek information that goes beyond what you learned or could have learned during the observation period.

Three more acceptable information-seeking questions based on Figures 7-2 and 7-3 are:

C. What reason did Steve and Harold give you for not having read the story last night at home?
D. Which other short stories about children and teenagers have you discussed so far this year?
E. Are you reading the same story and making the same homework assignment with your other English 10 class?

Delving Questions

Delving questions supply follow-up data to what is already available. When you ask a teacher to delve by supplying specifics, for example, you are requesting further data to help both of you clarify the situation. Your question asking for specifics says implicitly that the previous information offered was too general to be helpful to you at this point. Hence, you would appreciate some details.

Two delving questions based on the foregoing information-seeking questions are given here. (Note that the delving questions are second and marked with an asterisk; the information-seeking questions come first.)

A. Supervisor: Are you reading the same story and making the same homework assignment with your other English class?

Teacher: Well, the same story but a different assignment.

*Supervisor: What's the assignment for *them?*

B. Supervisor: How do you plan to deal with the homework assignments when they come in?

Teacher: :We'll do what we generally do—we'll read a few in class.

*Supervisor: Which method will you use to select the ones you'll read—volunteers, rotation, random, or whatever—in light of potential parental resistance to the assignment?

There are many ways to delve as you seek further information. The most common follow-up question asked by people upon receiving information is "Why?" The why question has several distinct disadvantages in supervision: (1) it seeks an explanation or a justification rather than further information; (2) it is so widely used that it borders on the routine—on being overworked; and (3) when used with interpersonal and policy issues, it is a threatening question that calls for the teacher to justify herself. Such a question challenges personal beliefs and actions by requesting a reason for them. With such a why question, the respondent is in a defensive position, and this situation does not encourage or foster open communication.

A request for a reason concerning a natural event, for example, which is external to the teacher does not have a threat attached. That is, the question "Why did it rain yesterday?" does not carry a threat in the way that "Why did you make that particular homework assignment?" does. Since in supervision you will be dealing mainly with private matters and interpersonal affairs rather than with external events, it is advisable to call a moratorium on the why question. This is easier than trying to monitor the use of the why question. On the spur of the moment, you may find it difficult to differentiate between a why question seeking a reason (explanation) for an event external to the teacher and a reason (justification) for a personal decision internally made.

Five types of delving questions are consistent with and appropriate for the approach to supervision being presented in this book. These five types allow you to delve but to keep threat at a minimum and thus promote open communication between the teacher and you. These five types are:

- Clarifying terms (or expressions) used
- Specifics

- Consequences
- Implementation
- Role switch

Let us look at these five types of delving questions individually and give an example as a way of showing what questions you can use to delve in a low-threat manner. (*Note:* As before, the delving questions are second and marked with an asterisk; the information-seeking questions come first.)

CLARIFYING TERMS (OR EXPRESSIONS) USED

SUPERVISOR: What reason did Steve and Harold give you for not having read the story last night at home?
TEACHER: They gave me some bushwhacker malarkey.
*SUPERVISOR: What do you mean by that— "Bushwhacker malarkey?"

The general rule with this type of delving question is to ask for the *meaning* of a term already used by the teacher. The format is "What do you mean by the term _____?" You are focusing on the meaning of a term rather than asking for details or examples, as with the second type. This type has the lowest threat of the five delving types by referring exactly to a term that the teacher has already used.

SPECIFICS

SUPERVISOR: Are you reading the same story and making the same homework assignment with your other English 10 class?
TEACHER: Well, the same story but a different assignment.
*SUPERVISOR: What's the assignment for *them?*

Notice that the question here does not explicitly call for specifics or use the word. Nevertheless, the question calls for specifics because you are asking for details. Just to know that the assignment is different is not enough. You want to know what specifically is different from the other class. This type of question is different from the first delving type in that it requests details rather than focusing on the meaning of a term. (If the difference is not signficant for you and you wish to think of these two types as being the same, feel free to do so as long as you refer back to the need to elucidate what the teacher said.)

CONSEQUENCES

SUPERVISOR: How do you plan to deal with the homework assignments when they come in?
TEACHER: We'll do what we generally do—we'll read a few in class and get a variety of answers.
*SUPERVISOR: What do you think will happen when someone reports that her parents refused to answer the student's question?

Here, too, the question does not explicitly call for what it seeks, consequences of a particular action. It need not do so in order to fulfill its purpose. The question asks the teacher to consider what will be the consequences of getting a variety of answers when the students read their homework.

IMPLEMENTATION

> SUPERVISOR: Are you reading the same story and making the same homework assignment with your other English 10 class?
> TEACHER: No. But now that I realize it, I could do it.
> *SUPERVISOR: What will you do to bring the two classes in line together at this point?

Here the question asks the teacher to state what steps he will take to implement his decision to bring the two classes together, reading the same story and doing the same homework assignment. It asks the respondent to state what he will do in order to carry through a decision. The focus is on the action she will take in order to implement her announced decision or plan.

ROLE SWITCH

> SUPERVISOR: How do you plan to deal with the homework assignments when they come in?
> TEACHER: We'll do what we generally do—we'll read a few in class.
> *SUPERVISOR: If you were John Benson or Stu Chandler, what would you do with homework papers?

With this question, you ask the teacher to pretend to be someone else and to respond again as if she were that person. You can ask the teacher to switch roles by naming a specific person or by giving a general category to assume when responding. For example, you could substitute the following role switch question, "What would you do with the homework assignment if you were one of the delinquent kids in your homeroom?" Here the *general* term "delinquent kids" is used whereas in the foregoing examples two *specific* students are mentioned.

With these examples of delving questions before you, try your hand at writing some yourself based on Figures 7-2 and 7-3. The following are two teacher responses to information-seeking questions. Try to write several delving questions of various types for each response:

A. Supervisor: Have you ever used this homework assignment before?

  Teacher: No, this is the first time with this one, but I've used a similar one last semester.

Supervisor:

B. Supervisor: What did you say about this story when you asked the students to read it for homework?

  Teacher: I just said that this story would raise issues for them to think about.
Supervisor:

Some delving questions to the teacher responses follow:

> A. Supervisor: What do you think will happen when the parents have to answer the kids?
>
> Supervisor: What was that assignment?
>
> B. Supervisor: If you were the author, Brenda Brickford, what would you say as you asked the students to read your story?
>
> Supervisor: What specific issues did you have in mind?
>
> Supervisor: What do you think will happen now that you told them that there will be issues raised?

Divergent Questions

The purpose of divergent questions is to elicit creative thinking about teaching. They encourage the elaboration of previous ideas; they encourage the generation of new data in an original and flexible way; and they seek alternatives to what is current practice. Divergent questions deal with the unknown future by asking the teacher to use her imagination to create a possible scenario. They also ask the respondent to deal with a contrary-to-fact situation. For example, you might ask the teacher the following question regarding homework: "What assignments would you make if we didn't bus our students home at 2:45 each day?"

Two divergent questions based on Figures 7-2 and 7-3 are:

> A. If you were the father of Tommy Kempert what would be your reaction to this homework assignment?
>
> B. Now that you have this information, what will you change in your lesson plan when you teach this story next time?

Divergent questions ask the teacher to stretch a bit. They give an opening and ask the teacher to move in a different direction. They do not lock the teacher in. On the contrary, they free the teacher and encourage her to be creative as she uses the available data and herself. Divergent questions try to fill gaps in our thinking. They acknowledge the fact that all the desired information may not be at hand. They admit (1) that we often must act on partial information, and (2) that the way to help cope with acting on the basis of partial information is to think divergently—that we need to be creative and flexible as we deal with the complex situations arising in education.

Four more divergent questions based on Figures 7-2 and 7-3 follow:

> C. If you were the author, Brenda Brickford, what would you say is the one question teenagers would ask the main character, Nancy?
>
> D. What are two ways that you can think of to get the girls to talk after the boys?
>
> E. What is one alternative approach for you to use in order to deemphasize the cognitive-memory questions in class and yet feel comfortable that the students know what happened in the story?
>
> F. If you were a delinquent teenager, what would you advise a high school teacher?

Some of these illustrative divergent questions are quite similar to several delving questions. One of the ways to delve in addition to asking for future plans or solutions is to ask the teacher to switch roles. This switch in roles requires the teacher to react to a contrary-to-fact situation. This contrary-to-fact situation elicits divergent thinking. Thus, there is a natural overlapping stemming from the complex nature of your interaction with the teacher.

Interpretation/Evaluation

The purpose of interpretation/evaluation questions is to elicit the meaning of available information and judgments about them. These questions deal with matters of interpretation, judgment, value, and choice. They ask the teacher to speak about right and wrong, good and bad, beautiful and ugly, and other dimensions that indicate that a judgment is being made about the value or worth of something. They direct the teacher's attention to matters of personal preference, moral values, and esthetics.

Two interpretation/evaluation questions based on Figures 7-2 and 7-3 are:

> A. On a scale from 1 to 10, with 10 as high, what would be your self-rating regarding your interaction pattern today?
> B. What do you think it means that you spoke more after the boys than after the girls?

Try your hand at forming some interpretation/evaluation questions based on Figures 7-2 and 7-3.

Three more interpretation/evaluation questions follow for you to see and compare with your own examples.

> C. What do you think is the flaw in Brickford's story as far as how our high school students generally behave?
> D. Suppose a parent challenges you on the assignment. What will you say is accomplished—is the worth of it all—for kids to talk to their parents about the parents' childhood experiences?
> E. Are your students honest enough with you and you honest enough with them to talk about the values of family and commitment?

Interpretation/evaluation questions are a source of potential danger in supervision. These questions may easily put the teacher in an uncomfortable position—especially one that requests a self-rating, such as example A. The teacher may not be willing to respond sincerely and to commit herself publicly to a self-rating or another value judgment. Therefore, the use of these questions must be with teachers who are secure in their relationship with you. Otherwise, you may well get forced, insincere responses coupled with a defensive, uncomfortable posture on the part of the teacher. In short, you should use the interpretation/evaluation question judiciously.

QUESTIONING TACTICS

It is obviously not enough to know the various types of question to ask in conferring with your teacher. You need to use these various types within a strategy formed to achieve the purpose of your conference. Four such conference strategies with dialogues are presented in Chapter 6. Conference tactics to help implement them are also presented in that chapter. It will be helpful to combine your reading of the material in this chapter, especially this section, with your reading of the material on conference strategies and tactics.

In this section, we will look first at some tactics for asking questions effectively. Then we will look at how to field the teacher's responses. Finally, we shall offer some suggestions for fielding the teacher's questions.

How to Ask Questions

- Ask your question in a helpful, positive tone. We begin with the basic idea that the manner of asking a question is critical to the use and effectiveness of the question. An awareness question asked with a harsh tone and a loud voice will cause much more than awareness. It will create fear and defensiveness. It will lead the teacher to feel attacked and scolded, thus destroying its primary purpose of alerting her to what has occurred so she can proceed to correct the necessary situations willingly. Similarly, any type of question may fail to elicit correct or full responses if the teacher feels that you ask your questions in an attacking manner. In short, remember to ask questions so that they achieve their primary purpose. Use a tone that communicates a positive approach to foster sincerity and openness.

- After asking a question, wait for a response. Do not answer the question yourself, repeat it, rephrase it, or replace it with another question until you have waited at least three to five seconds. A teacher needs time to think about the question and to prepare a response. The research results on wait-time in teaching apply to conferring as well. When teachers have waited three to five seconds, as opposed to less than that amount of time as they had been doing, students responded more, increased the length and number of their responses, used complex cognitive processes, and began to ask more questions themselves. If you do reword your question because you feel that your initial question is unclear, you may create greater confusion. The teacher may become uncertain as to which question to answer. Therefore, be patient. Ask your question, wait, and thereby express your expectation of receiving a response and your willingness to listen to it.

- Ask only one question at a time. Do not ask a string of questions in the same utterance. For example, ask, "Did you plan to ask more or fewer classroom routine questions?" Do not ask, "Did you plan to ask more or fewer classroom routine questions? If more, which ones did you omit and why? If fewer, what caused you to ask the ones you did at the beginning and the end of the lesson?"

 A series of questions tends to confuse the respondent. She may not be able to determine just what you are requesting from her. In a study of videotapes of classroom teaching, one researcher found a pattern that occurs when the teacher asks a series of questions. Students raise their hands as the teacher asks the first question. During the second question, some hands go down. As the questioning continues, more and more hands go down. This pattern appears to reveal that as the questions continue students are less and less able to respond—or willing to respond. The point applies to your conference with the teacher as well.

 In brief, even if you believe that your question is unclear, wait for a response. You may find that the teacher does indeed understand your question. By attempting to clarify, you may change the meaning of your question and cause confusion.

- When you want questions from the teacher but are not getting them, request them explicitly and then acknowledge their positive contribution to the conference. For example, you might say, "Do you have any questions in order to clarify the criteria I used in evaluating you?" Or, "This is a new system for gathering data so you might have some questions about it. Please ask them so we'll both know what's what." By requesting questions and acknowledging them, you indicate your belief that questions are not a sign of stupidity. Rather, they are a manifestation of concern and thought about what you are discussing with the teacher. Be careful not to convey the message subtly or even jokingly that the teacher is inattentive or dumb when she asks for a clarification or restatement of an idea you have already raised in the conference.

- Ask a variety of questions. In most conferences, you will find that it is impossible—as well as undesirable—to follow your conference strategy 100 percent. There always is something that occurs in the conference to lead you to improvise somewhat. Your strategy, whichever one you use from among the four models presented in Chapter 6, is your fundamental plan. You will always need to modify it somewhat, however. As you do, you probably will be asking questions. When you ask your planned and additional questions, use different types.

You often will begin with awareness questions. From that point, you may find that a contrary-to-fact or future solution divergent question is appropriate. Rather than stay only with awareness questions, you will find it more interesting—and so will the teacher—if you seek new information, use a variety of delving questions (not just for "specifics" or "consequences"), ask the teacher to diverge via contrary-to-fact situations and requests for future solutions, and ask for some interpretations. Such a variety of questions will stimulate the teacher to perform many cognitive processes, and the responses will enliven the conference.

How to Field Responses

How you field the teacher's response is as critical as how you ask your question. This point is virtually forgotten when people begin to consider planning for a conference—or just about any other activity that involves interaction. The ways in which you field teacher responses will influence future responses.

There are many options open to you after the teacher responds to one of your questions. Yet there are no absolute rules mandating a particular behavior on your part. Nevertheless, you need not be a psychologist to realize that a helpful guideline to follow is to reinforce the teacher's responses when they are on target and appropriate. The teacher looks to you for guidance and support. If you ignore the teacher's responses or show indifference to them, the teacher may feel reluctant to respond in the future even if previous responses have been appropriate. Another guideline states the same idea in the negative: Do not humiliate the teacher for responding. The teacher may become so angry or fearful that she may refuse to respond in the future.

The overall guideline, then, is for you to field responses in such a way that the quantity and quality of future responses are enhanced. The following tactics are designed to help you follow this overall guideline. Keep in mind that these tactics do not indicate how to field all teacher responses under all conditions.

- Praise the teacher with strong, positive words for an excellent response. Use such terms as "excellent solution" and "imaginative alternative." These terms are quite different from such common mild phrases as "Okay," "hm-hm," and "all right." When the response is a lengthy one after you have asked an implementation delving question, for example, make a special effort to find the key point and give it the praise it deserves. Teachers, like students and like you, need praise.

- Make comments pertinent to the specific teacher response. For example, suppose you have asked, "If you were one of your student's parents, how would you react to that homework assignment?" Suppose also that the teacher offers an illuminating and insightful response. You might say, "That's insightful, Pat. You really have a handle on your students and their parents. The point about revealing themselves to their kids is a good one." Your comment gives an excellent rating and makes it pertinent to the teacher's ideas in an explicit way. It shows the teacher that you have listened attentively to the response.

- Make no rating comment at all after each specific response within a series of responses to a single question; make a general comment after the series of responses is complete. Suppose that you have asked, "Give me two or three possibilities of things you can do to change your pattern of talking after the boys talk." After the teacher gives the first one, you can remain silent, nod, or simply make an *acknowledging* remark, not a *rating* one, so as to show that you are listening and encouraging the teacher to continue to respond. For example, you could say, "That's one out of two."

There are two good reasons for using this tactic to field multiple responses to a single question. First, when you talk, there is the tendency for the focus of the conference to shift back to you. By being silent, nodding, or only acknowledging briefly, you keep the focus on the teacher. Second, and more important, if you praise the first response, the teacher likely will pick up the message that you expect a second response similar to the first one. The teacher may hesitate to go off on another track even though it may be a better one.

You must keep track of the responses in a series so that you can reinforce them at the end. You can make a general comment to include them all to show that the teacher has responded to the question well. For example, you could say, "Great, you gave three alternatives that make sense in just one minute."

- Avoid the "Yes but..." reaction. Many people say, "Yes but..." or the equivalent when a response is wrong, partly wrong, or inappropriate. The overall impact of these phrases used to field a response is negative and deceptive. Furthermore, they tend to set you in opposition to the teacher. The "Yes, but" fielding reaction says that the response is appropriate with one breath and then takes away the praise with the next breath.

The "Yes, but" reaction is particularly bad when used after a question seeking alternative solutions. Suppose you ask the teacher for a way to break her pattern of following up boys' responses rather than girls'. If you get a response and follow with a "Yes, but" reaction, you are sending a negative message. The message is, "That alternative is no good; it won't work; don't try it." A few such reactions, and the teacher will stop seeking ways to change. She will consider the situation hopeless and be unable to imagine a different way to act.

Some straightforward alternatives are:

1. Wait to a count of five with the expectation that the teacher will offer another response or even comment on the first one. Then you can talk about the teacher's further comments.

2. Ask a delving question, "How did you arrive at that response?" (Be careful, however, not to ask this delving question only when you receive an inappropriate or strange response. Ask it also at times when you receive a perfectly appropriate response.)

3. Say, "You're on target regarding part X and that's great. I personally have trouble with part Y. Please elaborate on Y so we can discuss it further."

These three alternatives are obviously not adequate to fit all cases. However, with these three examples you will probably be able to generate your own when necessary so that you can be straightforward—praising, objecting, discussing specifically what the teacher says. The main point is for you to remain encouraging, not to cut off further responses with your own reactions.

- Build on the teacher's response. In your subsequent comments, try to incorporate the key elements of the response to your question into the points you make during the conference. By using the teacher's response, you show that you value what the teacher says. The message you send to the teacher is positive and supportive.

How to Field Questions

One of the most neglected areas concerned with interpersonal interaction—supervisor-teacher as well as teacher-student—is the area dealing with questions coming from the person who generally does not question. Here, this area deals with fielding questions from the teacher. Fielding is a broader concept than responding; responding to a question is but one fielding option. The skill of fielding teacher questions is vital for conducting effective conferences.

Teachers in a conference may not ask questions for several reasons. First, your teacher may be afraid to ask questions because she thinks that a question is a sign of ignorance and she does not want to appear ignorant before you. You may not hold this view but consider it wise for her to ask questions as a way of clarifying confusing procedures and regulations. Nevertheless, the teacher may hold this view of not questioning you in this situation because you are the person to direct, advise, and evaluate her.

Second, the teacher may not wish to challenge your role. In many interactive situations, the person in authority or power is the one who asks the questions. The extreme example is the case of the spy who is questioned by his captors. The captor asks the questions, the spy answers. The teacher may somehow feel that she is usurping your role by asking questions and thus is challenging your authority also.

Third, you may be unwittingly discouraging the teacher from asking questions. You may feel that control of the conference and teacher questioning are related. That is, you need to accomplish your conference goal and the teacher's asking questions tends to lead you astray. You may feel that the teacher's questions block you from achieving your goal because they consume precious time, sometimes on matters of minor importance in your estimation. If you hold this view, you probably are sending nonverbal messages, if not explicit verbal ones, to tell the teacher not to ask questions.

While it is true that teacher questions may pose the threat of a loss of control for you, you must still weigh the advantages of teacher questions against the disadvantages. The advantages of teacher questions and the involvement they create far outweigh any of the disadvantages, including a possible loss of control, which is minimal at most. With the conviction in mind that teacher participation and openness are desirable, some tactics for fielding teacher questions in a positive way are in order. Again, these tactics do not fit all situations but are simply examples of the options available to you.

- Praise the teacher for asking a question. For example, say, "That's a good question," or, "That's pertinent here and I'm glad you asked so we can both be clear about that." These are simple reactions, and yet they reinforce the teacher effectively. They will help the teacher to overcome being afraid to question if she is somewhat hesitant.
- Answer the teacher's question directly as often as possible. The teacher, by and large, does not ask questions to be cute or disruptive of your plans. When she asks a question, she wants a response. Don't play games with her—answer her without asking a question in return or without stalling her. By responding directly, you give an indication that the question is worthwhile.
- Let the teacher know when a question leads into a new topic. If the teacher's question prompts you to launch into a new area of the conference, indicate that to her as you shift to that area. For example, say, "That's an excellent question and it deserves further exploration. Let's switch over to our criteria for evaluation. I think you'll see my response to your question evolve. If not, please ask again." While this fielding move may not satisfy the teacher immediately, it does give an indication that the question is appropriate and valued. It sends a positive message to the teacher.

In summary, these three groups of tactics offer you ways of using questions during the conference to help you achieve your overall goals. If you use these tactics together with the conference strategies and other conference actions that are described elsewhere, you will have many resources for conducting an effective conference. Of course, you can use these tactics outside of the conference, too, as you talk with your teacher in the faculty room and in the halls. With continued practice, you can develop your skill in dealing with questioning in supervision.

HELPING TEACHERS WITH CLASSROOM QUESTIONING

There are two essential ways that you can help your teachers with classroom questioning—a critical area of teaching in which most teachers need further help. The first way is modeling. You can be a good model of questioning for your teacher to emulate. By following the suggestions offered in this and other chapters, you can demonstrate how to use and deal with questions and responses. This form of help to the teacher is important because the impact of a model is great. A model shows the teacher that appropriate and effective ways to question and to field are possible. After all, if you can do it, so can she. Also, by being a model you have the accepted credentials to talk to the teacher explicitly about her questioning.

The second way for you to help is to focus your classroom observations of the teacher on her questioning behavior. Just as you can focus on classroom climate, cognitive processes, content taught, or student groupings, you can focus on the questions the teacher asks, the way she fields student responses, and the way she fields student questions. Indeed, if you are concerned about classroom interaction and the paucity of student questions, you may be able to find the key in how the teacher fields student questions. It might well be that the teacher fields questions in such a way as to send the message, "Don't ask any more questions."

Perhaps the best way to facilitate a conference focusing on your teacher's questioning skill is to listen to a tape recording of a classroom session together. As you listen, you can focus during the initial replay on the questioning tactics only, talking together about what is happening on the tape. During another replay you can key in on the teacher's fielding of responses or fielding of student questions. With a tape recording, you can observe the lesson repeatedly, focusing on any given aspect at a time. This simplifies the observation and the conference. The many points about questioning made in this chapter and the others can surely be adjusted to apply to the classroom. Supervision, which is a form of teaching, is not all that different from classroom teaching.

An audio cassette tape recording is adequate and is easy to make. Just about everyone and every school has a small, unobtrusive recorder available. You do not need a videotape recording for the purpose of conferring about the teacher's questioning skill. It is a bit cumbersome to make a videotape recording, and the extra equipment in the room might inhibit a self-conscious teacher in need of your help. On the other hand, if the teacher is willing to be videotaped, you will have a rich source of data available to you because of the nonverbal behavior both you and the teacher can observe during each replay.

8

WRITING SUPERVISORY REPORTS

Just as you must confer with your staff as part of your supervisory responsibilities, so, too, must you write reports. These written papers are crucial to the operation of any school or other institution with an overseeing board responsible for its long-term management.

Chapter 8 deals with the reasons for writing reports, the explicit and hidden functions of written reports, advantages and disadvantages of checklist reports and open narrative reports, reports of classroom observations, annual evaluation reports, and suggestions on writing style.

After reading this chapter, you should be able to:

- Understand the functions of reports and know how to write them effectively.
- List at least four reasons for writing reports.
- Know the explicit and hidden functions of written reports.
- Describe advantages and disadvantages of the checklist and open narrative reports.
- Distinguish between observation and evaluation reports.
- List the features to be included in observation and evaluation reports.
- Implement recommendations on writing style and approach as a way to achieve effective reports.

THE NECESSITY OF WRITTEN REPORTS

It is human to want to record events for future eyes to see. The ancient cave dwellers recorded important events on their walls pictorially, the Sumerians inscribed clay tablets in cuneiform, the Egyptians chiseled hieroglyphics into stone, and the Hebrews wrote on parchment scrolls to report their experiences with surrounding nations. With the growth of population and the rise of our technological and bureaucratic institutions, the need for writing about events and people has developed to the point where reports are a necessity. The writing of reports has become a major task in the lives of many workers because contact with the people making decisions and with the people analyzing a situation is no longer a personal matter. Indeed, the writing of reports, a significant part of what is called "paper work" in our society, consumes much time and effort. Although you may complain about it and sometimes bemoan it, the structural organization of our society today requires reports. Report-writing is here to stay, and any wishes to the contrary will not alter the situation.

A State-Level Requirement

Requirements for writing reports start not at the local level but at the state level. The state, which is legally responsible for public education, considers teachers as public employees and thus requires reports about teachers as one way of monitoring the quality of tax-supported education. For example, the New Jersey State Board of Education in 1978 (Administrative Code 6:3-1.21) established a requirement that supervisors must write an annual report for each tenured teacher in their charge. While some local school systems had already established this requirement for tenured teachers and the state had already required reports for nontenured teachers, this new decision significantly increased the number of written reports required, because approximately 75 percent of New Jersey teachers are tenured.

It doesn't much matter where the requirement for your writing of reports comes from—the state, your local board of education, or the personal request of your immediate supervisor. The effect is the same: you as supervisor must file written reports. Nor does it matter much if your own superiors don't read every single report with a "magnifying glass," searching for crucial comments. You don't know which ones will be read, and you can't assume that a particular report will not be scrutinized by someone else. Every report must be done well.

Five Reasons for Writing Reports Well

Several good reasons exist for writing reports well. First, even one poorly prepared report among twenty-five is enough to cause your professional or lay superiors dissatisfaction and even trouble. However, it certainly is likely that you will be tempted to do a perfunctory job with some reports. For example, you may have difficulty writing a report because you must say negative things about a teacher who is close to you. To avoid dealing with the task in the way it deserves, you may rush through a poor report. By chance or because the board has its own outside motivation to learn about your particular teacher, this may be the only report you've written that is read carefully by several superiors. Unfortunately, these readers will get a negative impression of your work based on their one-item sample.

Second, even if your superiors don't read your reports, your teachers do. Teachers read your reports because they have an obvious stake in the contents. They are concerned, as well they should be. If a report is well done, it will enhance your ability to work with the teacher productively in the future. If it is done poorly, it may well jeopardize your relationship with the teacher, leading to a less than adequate supervisory program.

Third, you are paid, as part of your supervisory salary, to write reports. Your superiors want and expect carefully prepared reports. They have every right to expect that you will fulfill your responsibility as you expect your teachers to fulfill their responsibilities.

Fourth, a well-prepared report will foster and a poorly prepared report will hinder your supervision program. A poorly prepared report will defeat the report's original purpose—to help you run a better school program.

Fifth, when you write reports well, you get professional and personal satisfaction from your work. You yourself know when you've done a good job. Your own self-esteem increases and is reinforced as you recognize that you operate as you should, as others expect. You have the right to expect of your teachers what you do of yourself—a professional job well done. The net result of all of this is the furthering of the supervisory program you run. There is an interdependency between your increased positive self-esteem and your ability to function properly as a supervisor.

THE FUNCTIONS OF WRITTEN REPORTS

Complex endeavors can and do serve several functions at one time. The inauguration of the President of the United States, for instance, fulfills at least the three functions of legally swearing in the elected person to the office, raising the national spirit of Americans, and allowing the winning political party a time for gala celebration. Similarly, written reports about teachers fulfill at least the following ten functions.

The written report:

Embodies Feedback and Efforts Toward Improvements

In state or local regulations concerning supervision and in contracts between boards of education and the teachers' organizations, the purpose of supervision is stated explicitly as the improvement of teaching. Other purposes are often mentioned, too, including the evaluation of faculty. The New Jersey requirement established in 1978, for example, states three clear purposes for the annual evaluation of teachers:

1. Promote professional excellence and improve the skills of teaching staff members.
2. Improve student learning and growth.
3. Provide a basis for the review of performance of tenured teaching staff members.

In other words, supervisors are to work toward improvement through observations, conferences, and reports. The report becomes the culminating embodiment of the supervisor's efforts. The acts of observing and conferring are not recorded and stored, but the report is. The report, not oral but written, becomes the concrete evidence that supervisors are carrying out their responsibility to improve the quality of education.

Serves as Basis of and Gives Direction to the Postobservation Conference

The expectation that a written report will be prepared, signed, and filed gives direction to the postobservation conference. This is the case whether you hold the conference before the writing of the report or after the initial drafting of the report. When the teacher and supervisor know that a report is part of the sequence of requirements, they raise certain issues in the conference in order to clarify points that will appear in the subsequent permanent report. The conference takes direction as an opportunity to influence the contents of the report before it is filed as an archival record of the supervisory efforts that have taken place.

Fulfills Legal Requirement

As mentioned earlier, the requirement that a particular supervisor write reports is a legal requirement passed by a state board of education or state legislature. The administrative code or legislative law states that a written report by the superintendent or principal must be filed annually for each nontenured or tenured teacher.

Allows Others to Know about a Supervisor's Efforts with a Particular Teacher

This fourth function concerns other people active in a school system—other supervisors and members of the board of education. A written report offers board members and other supervisors the opportunity to become familiar with the work of the supervisors and teachers they have in their charge. For example, suppose that you are a principal supervising Mrs. Jones, a classroom teacher of general science in your middle school. On the basis of your statements in the written report on Jones, the assistant superintendent and the superintendent can make recommendations and comments to you regarding the course of action you should take with Jones. The superintendent might, for example, suggest that you spend more time with Mrs. Jones, steer her into additional in-service study in biology at a nearby university, or seek the cooperation of another supervisor who has had previous experience with her. Without a written report head supervisors, even in a small school district, let alone a large one, could not know how their teachers are progressing or take effective action.

Serves as Evidence in a Dispute

The written report serves as evidence, when necessary, during a dispute between a school district and a teacher. If your school district decides to dismiss a tenured teacher or not rehire a nontenured teacher in your charge, both sides in the dispute may wish to refer to your supervisory report. The written report can be presented as evidence that, for example, you as supervisor worked closely with Mr. Smith, the teacher, to identify his deficiencies, to extend assistance, to correct those deficiencies, and to recommend ways to increase his professional competence as a teacher. If you haven't written adequate reports, Smith's lawyer will undoubtedly attempt to show that the school district is acting inappropriately. The lawyer will argue that because you didn't mention deficiencies in your reports, Smith did not know what and how he could improve in order to maintain his job. Thus, your written report could serve as a critical piece of legal evidence in the dispute because it is an official document describing your interaction with Smith.

Emphasizes the Significance of Supervision

The written report, because it is an official document filed in the school district's offices, serves the function of emphasizing the importance of supervision. As a result, the activities of observing and conferring that precede the filing of a written report take on added meaning. First, the act of writing the report requires you as supervisor to give more than casual consideration to the information about the teacher to be conveyed to the teacher, other supervisors, and the board of education. Because you know that the supervisory relationship is not limited to two people, you give greater thought to what will become official and permanent. Second, the teacher receives the report in a serious and attentive frame of mind because it is official, permanent, and not for your eyes alone. Because the report is written and therefore a document that can be used to give evidence and to communicate with other supervisors as well as with the board of eduation, your teacher will pay greater heed to it than to private and casual comments you make in the faculty room.

Facilitates Reconsideration of Supervisor's Points

The written report allows the teacher to consider the supervisor's comments, reconsider them, and reconsider them again. Unlike an oral conference, a written report has a permanency that allows and encourages the recipient to ponder the contents—to return to specific sentences, phrases, or words again and again in order fully to understand their meaning. It allows your teacher to study your exact words and the points you made to promote improvement.

Serves as a Historical Record

The written report serves as a historical record of how the teacher and supervisor performed at a given point in time. After a month, a year, or any long period of time, a teacher and a supervisor have available the data and comments that will allow them to assess what has transpired. The written report prevents fuzzy memories from distorting the facts and agreements made between teacher and supervisor.

Provides the Basis and Vehicle for Evaluating a Teacher

Most supervisors use their written reports as an opportunity—the basis and the impetus—to evaluate the teachers in their charge. This is the case even when the form of the report doesn't require an evaluation. That is, the report form, whether it sets specifications or is just a blank piece of paper, may not require an evaluation but only a description of an observation or a comparison with previous behavior. Yet the report serves as the vehicle for the supervisor to submit an official, written evaluation of a teacher. Unfortunately, many supervisors believe this is the written report's only function.

Provides an Implicit Report on the Supervisor

Finally, there is another function of the written report that seldom receives attention. Whereas the teacher and members of the board of education legitimately view the written report as a source of commentary on the behavior of the teacher, it is certainly possible to view the report in another way, too. It is equally legitimate for the teacher and members of the board of education who read the written report to think of it as a commentary on you the supervisor. Since the conference between the supervisor and the teacher is most often private, the written report often provides the only, or at least the prime, information about what a supervisor is doing with the teacher to improve teaching. You as supervisor convey in the written report the nonverbal message, "Here is how I do my job; this tells you how I function, what I have observed, what I have conveyed to the teacher in my charge, and what I believe is important regarding teaching; you can come to know me by studying this and other reports." The written report tells as much about you the supervisor as it does about the teacher, taking on an important function as a report on both you and the teacher.

BASIC FORMATS FOR THE WRITTEN REPORT

There are several ways to categorize written reports in order to talk about them and understand them. First we shall look at the formats of the reports and then at the impetus for writing them (that is, you write one because you've observed a teacher or because it's the end of the year). In regard to format there are two extreme poles, the *checklist* and *the blank piece of paper* for writing a free narrative. Obviously, most reports fall in between these two extremes by combining elements of both. Yet, to understand any given report's format it is helpful to look at the characteristics of the two extremes, or pure forms.

The Checklist

Although the checklist format has come under attack, it survives because its advantages are clear.

FOUR ADVANTAGES

The advantages of a checklist are:

- The checklist provides the supervisor, the teacher, and the reader (a member of the board of education or another, higher-level supervisor) with the information that they have decided they want. Each school system decides what it wants to know about its teachers in order to make decisions about granting tenure and awarding salary increments. A completed checklist presents the desired information clearly and makes it obvious—even a cursory glance suffices—when information is missing. You know what you should provide, and you know when you have provided it.
- The checklist indicates what the school system values. For example, suppose that in the overall report under the "Teacher's Personal Qualities," Figure 8-1 appears.

  The teacher and you know immediately not only that you must provide information about the five listed items but also that these five constitute what is valued in a teacher. You know what qualities are valued even though these five are not rank ordered or weighted. You know that how a teacher dresses and is groomed is important, that how a teacher conveys ideas and attitudes to students and colleagues is important, and that how regular a teacher is in coming to school, and in arriving on time, is important. You know that these things are important because they are specifically listed, whereas such items as Fairness, Courteousness, and Modulation of Voice are not listed. Since no information is requested about these latter three qualities, you can infer that they are not considered as important as the five listed qualities.

QUALITY	Outstanding	Good	Needs Improvement
1. Appearance			
2. Poise			
3. Attendance			
4. Communication Skills			
5. Emotional Stability			

FIGURE 8-1. Teacher's personal qualities checklist.

- The checklist is fast. You fill out the name of the teacher and date the form and within a minute or so you can complete the checklist. With the load of paperwork that supervisors face, this feature of the checklist is not easily disregarded.

- The checklist is relatively simple to complete. The checklist indicates what qualities are of value and what information is needed (for example, Is the teacher Outstanding, Good, or Needing Improvement regarding Appearance?). All it requires of you is a check or an X. Since it doesn't require you to give reasons or supporting data, you don't really spend great amounts of time considering each item. The checklist encourages you to give quick responses with a minimum of strain.

FIVE DISADVANTAGES

On the other hand, the checklist format has some distinct disadvantages that lead people to be cautious of it. These are:

- The checklist items are often vague or ambiguous. For example, in regard to the five items listed in Figures 8-1 it is fair to ask, "What is Appearance? What does it mean? Does it include dress? Grooming? Posture? What constitutes Poise? What is Emotional Stability? How is emotional stability measured so that you know when your teacher's stability becomes 'instability'? What skills are the communication skills?" Thus, the meaning or scope of each item may be unclear to you or the teacher or the reader. Or, two of you may agree about an item but the third may have a different perception of, for example, what constitutes Emotional Stability.

- The checklist items may be conceptually fuzzy because of the categories to which they are assigned. The easiest way to clarify this point is to show you a sample of items on a checklist from School District X. On District X's teacher evaluation form, thirteen items appear in two groups labeled "Personal Attributes" and "Professional Attainments." In Figure 8-2, all thirteen are listed together alphabetically so that you can compare your categorizing of these items with District X's. Try categorizing the thirteen items now.

For each item below, write "Personal" or "Professional" on the line to the left of it.

_____ 1. Acceptance of professional criticism.
_____ 2. Alertness to departmental needs, both present and future.
_____ 3. Attention to records and reports.
_____ 4. Command of subject matter.
_____ 5. Contribution to total school operation.
_____ 6. Dependability.
_____ 7. Enthusiasm.
_____ 8. Impression, speech, poise.
_____ 9. Interpersonal relationships with co-workers.
_____ 10. Knowledge of the status and sources of research in subject area.
_____ 11. Observance of school policies and procedures.
_____ 12. Punctuality/attendance.
_____ 13. Understanding the nature of learning.

FIGURE 8-2. Personal attributes and professional attainments.

According to the teacher evaluation form from District X, only items 6, 7, 8, and 9 are considered "Personal Attributes." The other items are categorized and listed under "Professional Attainments."

The point here is that because items appear in a checklist without further clarification their meaning may be different to different people. What you consider a *professional* item may be a *personal* one to your teacher, or vice versa. Therefore, the way you perceive the item influences the importance you assign to it and the way you score it. Indeed, in two districts located near the District X of the example, "Maintains a good attendance record" and "Punctuality and Consistency" are listed as *personal* items. The very category you assign to an item influences the way you will check it.

- The checklist items are not personalized. The checklist doesn't make distinctions among teachers and doesn't encourage you as reporter to make them. The checklist is impersonal, treating all teachers alike when we know that people are not all alike. You must apply the checklist's standards and only these standards to every teacher. I have never seen a checklist on a report form which solicits the reporter to add or subtract items for each individual teacher.

- The checklist doesn't request or demand supporting data. The checklist requires only a check, no data to show your reasons for checking the item as you did. Consequently, the teacher reading the report or any other reader, even yourself at a later date, doesn't know, for example, what led you to check Enthusiasm as "good." Knowledge of supporting data that explain the items checked is always helpful, but the checklist doesn't provide the data to enlighten subsequent readers.

- The checklist often has fuzzy and/or nonparallel rating levels. For instance, recall the five-item example offered in Figure 8-1 to illustrate what a school system values. With such a checklist you must score each of the 5 items on one of the 3 levels. Yet the difference between Outstanding and Good is not clear. What may be "Outstanding" to you may not be so to your teacher or reader. Furthermore, Needs Improvement is not parallel to Outstanding and Good. If you have high standards, for instance, you may find it reasonable to believe that even a "good" teacher "needs improvement." Every teacher can always improve because teaching is so complex an endeavor. No one is so masterful as to be beyond the point of improvement. Some school districts perhaps use Needs Improvement as a euphemism to mean Unacceptable. If so, then the checklist is unclear and misleading to the people not informed of the "true" meanings of the terms used.

Remember, there are many types of checklists. The examples in Figures 8-3, 8-4, and 8-5 deserve your attention in light of the advantages and disadvantages described.

The Blank Piece of Paper

The opposite of the checklist with its predetermined items, categories, and levels is the blank piece of paper. The blank piece of paper probably was the first—whenever that was—format used. The checklist was no doubt derived from the blank piece of paper as people realized that they wanted similar information about all teachers, that they were using similar terms to describe teachers, and that they wanted a faster, easier way to write a report.

FOUR ADVANTAGES

The blank piece of paper has very clear advantages. They are:

- The blank piece of paper fosters personalized reports. The blank paper encourages you to write about the uniqueness of your teacher. You may write about an event that is indicative of the behavior of the teacher, or you may list the qualities that pertain to the teacher as an individual. In either case, you individualize your report to demonstrate that no two teachers are alike and that you treat your teachers in a personal way. The hidden message is that you know your teacher well. If the blank piece of paper doesn't guarantee personalization, nothing can.
- The blank piece of paper allows and promotes clarification. Since you are not restricted by space or predetermined categories, you have the opportunity to clarify any broad statements made. You can describe events and teacher performances to clarify your points, descriptions, interpretations, conclusions, and evaluations. You can offer supporting data and reasons for your judgments. What is more, the blank piece of paper encourages you to fill it up with words so that the teacher and reader will understand exactly what you mean.
- The blank piece of paper permits the appropriate emphasis. It allows you to zero in on the specific issue(s) that leads you to write your report at this particular time or the specific issue(s) that arises out of your observation of and conference with your

Teacher _____

School _____

Date _____

EVALUATION KEY
S — Satisfactory
N — Needs Improvement
U — Unsatisfactory
NA — Not Applicable

I. INSTRUCTIONAL SKILLS

The instructional process is the focus of the educational enterprise. It involves the behaviors, practices, and techniques directed toward effective teaching and efficient classroom management.

A. Knowledge and Training

1. Demonstrates academic competence in the area of teaching assignment.   S   N   U   NA

2. Demonstrates knowledge of learning theories, child and adolescent psychology, and curriculum development and research.   S   N   U   NA

3. Is aware of and utilizes new knowledge and techniques   S   N   U   NA

B. Classroom Management

1. Keeps classroom safe, comfortable, neat, attractive, and efficient.   S   N   U   NA

2. Teaches good manners and self-discipline by example and by insistence on high standards in this regard.   S   N   U   NA

3. Is fair and consistent in interpreting and applying established standards of behavior.   S   N   U   NA

4. Maintains good order appropriate to the learning activity.   S   N   U   NA

C. Instructional Methods

1. Uses varied methods, materials, and strategies, standard as well as innovative.   S   N   U   NA

2. Arranges classroom activities to meet the needs of the individual student.   S   N   U   NA

3. Affords students active roles in the presentation of the lesson.   S   N   U   NA

4. Stimulates student interest by effective questioning, encouragement, acceptance, and reward, as well as by demonstration of personal enthusiasm.   S   N   U   NA

5. Helps students to develop efficient learning skills and work habits.   S   N   U   NA

6. Provides clear and lucid explanations.   S   N   U   NA

7. Demonstrates flexibility in the pursuit of the stated teaching objectives.   S   N   U   NA

D. Planning

1. Establishes definite instructional objectives with sequential steps for their attainment.   S   N   U   NA

FIGURE 8-3. Professional evaluation.

2. Provides appropriate assignments for work in and out of the classroom.   **S   N   U   NA**

3. Organizes and uses materials and supplies effectively.   **S   N   U   NA**

4. Prepares daily learning experiences for students which achieve the objectives of the program.   **S   N   U   NA**

5. Plans enrichment and remedial work to meet individual student needs.   **S   N   U   NA**

E. Evaluation

1. Uses methods and tools of evaluation that are fair, valid, effective, positive, and supportive for students. **S   N   U   NA**

2. Uses methods and tools of evaluation that are appropriate to the subject area.   **S   N   U   NA**

II. PERSONAL/PROFESSIONAL QUALITIES

The effective teacher recognizes that personal qualities affect teacher performance in the total school program in which he takes an active role; and that such qualities have a direct bearing on the total effectiveness of the individual as a member of the educational staff.

A. Human Understanding

1. Treats others with kindness, compassion, and understanding.   **S   N   U   NA**

2. Shows genuine interest in each individual.   **S   N   U   NA**

B. Judgment

1. Possesses a positive self-concept which is demonstrated by poise, self-control, and self-confidence.   **S   N   U   NA**

2. Evidences ability to adjust to varied situations.   **S   N   U   NA**

3. Is calm and mature in reactions.   **S   N   U   NA**

4. Handles confidential materials in a discreet, professional manner.   **S   N   U   NA**

C. Appearance

1. Practices positive grooming and dress habits which instill attitudes of neatness in students by personal example and atmosphere.   **S   N   U   NA**

D. Speech and Expression

1. Possesses a voice which is well modulated and distinct.   **S   N   U   NA**

2. Written and oral communications for students, parents, or any professional purpose are in good form and good taste, as well as showing correct spelling, appropriate grammatical forms, and legible handwriting.   **S   N   U   NA**

3. Expresses ideas clearly.   **S   N   U   NA**

FIGURE 8-3 (continued)

E. Health

1. Is vigorous, energetic, and alert.   S   N   U   NA
2. Exhibits general good health to meet the daily obligations of school life.   S   N   U   NA

F. Work Habits and Obligations

1. Keeps records and reports up-to-date and accurate, and is generally punctual in submitting all material.   S   N   U   NA
2. Complies with school and district regulations.   S   N   U   NA
3. Exhibits punctuality to school, classes, meetings, and other assigned duties.   S   N   U   NA
4. Accepts and works to implement established policies.   S   N   U   NA

G. Interpersonal Relations

1. Shows tact, courtesy, and a willingness to listen to and understand others' viewpoints.   S   N   U   NA
2. Receives constructive criticism and suggestions in a positive sense.   S   N   U   NA
3. Cooperates and maintains good relations with students, parents, community members, administrators and supervisors, classroom teachers, special subject teachers, and other staff members.   S   N   U   NA
4. Willingly participates in and contributes constructively to committees, faculty meetings, and other school system groups.   S   N   U   NA
5. Demonstrates professional consideration and respect for the problems of other teachers where cooperation is essential and beneficial for the youngsters in our school system.   S   N   U   NA

H. Professionalism

1. Continues professional growth by such means as courses, trips, workshops, reading, writing, and participation in professional associations; and applies this knowledge to improving the instructional program.   S   N   U   NA
2. Keeps abreast of and exhibits a willingness to implement new ideas and developments to improve educational opportunities for children.   S   N   U   NA
3. Adheres to the ethical standards established for the profession by the National Education Association.   S   N   U   NA
4. Promotes respect for the teaching profession and represents the school in the best light to the community.   S   N   U   NA

Property of the Rahway Board of Education, Rahway, New Jersey. Reprinted with permission.

FIGURE 8-3 (continued)

TEACHER _____ DATE _____ TIME: FROM _____ TO _____

SCHOOL _____ GRADE AND/OR SUBJECT _____ ACTIVITY _____

INSTRUCTIONS FOR USE All questions should be checked "yes," "no," or "not applicable." Anecdotal comments which help recall specific incidents may be noted in the space entitled "Indicators." Indicators should be numerically related to the checklist. The entire checklist is intended as a set of notes which will provide some concrete data upon which the performance evaluation report will be based.

PERFORMANCE AREAS/CRITERIA	YES	NO	N.A.	INDICATORS
PLANNING AND ORGANIZING				
1. Is there a perceivable objective for this lesson or assignment?				
2. Does the lesson provide learning opportunities beyond recall and memorization?				
3. Does the lesson include opportunity to deal with and/or involve values, attitudes?				
4. Does the instruction include opportunity for skill development?				
5. Is the level of difficulty appropriate for the students?				
6. Are the instructional resources appropriate to the objectives of the lesson?				
7. Are the instructional methods appropriate to the objective of the lesson?				
8. Does the class climate or social setting (large group, small group, independent study) facilitate achievement of the objective of the lesson?				
9. Do the students have opportunity to experience alternative learning strategies?				

FIGURE 8-4. Teacher observation form.

10. Can students locate needed materials efficiently?				
11. Does the teacher appropriately arrange classroom space, furniture, and equipment?				

IMPLEMENTATION AND INTERACTION

1. Is the purpose of the lesson or activity apparent to most students?			
2. Is the pace of the lesson appropriate for students?			
3. Are students attentive to the subject matter presentation?			
4. Are the students reacting to the instructional strategies (methods, materials and media, social settings) employed?			
5. Does the teacher use questions in such a way as to clarify and enhance communication?			
6. Does the teacher use discussion activities in such a way as to promote communication?			
7. Does the teacher use problem-solving methods?			
8. Do students know and use appropriate classroom standards of conduct?			
9. Do students and teachers treat each other with respect?			
10. Is there evidence that the teacher is making appropriate use of student support services?			
11. Does the teacher tactfully handle issues with students and/or parents?			
12. Does the teacher discuss student problems in a sensitive and constructive way?			

FIGURE 8-4 (continued)

13. Does the teacher maintain a classroom climate conducive to learning?				
EVALUATION AND RECORD KEEPING				
1. Are there indicators that learning progress and achievement are being recorded?				
2. Are students kept aware of their progress toward specific objectives?				
3. Are meaningful records of progress available to students, parents, and other professionals?				
4. Are student records used as a base for developing instructional plans?				
PROFESSIONAL RELATIONS AND GROWTH				
1. Does the teacher recognize and deal positively with individuals of differing backgrounds?				
2. Does the teacher consistently demonstrate good work habits (e.g., punctuality, completion of required records, neatness, effective use of planning time, etc.)?				
3. Does the teacher work cooperatively with other staff members?				
4. Does the teacher demonstrate professional growth (e.g. self study, course work, conferences, committee work, etc.)?				

Date of observation conference _____ I have received a copy of this report of an observation of my performance and had an opportunity to discuss it

_____ _____   _____ _____
Observer's signature   Date   Teacher's signature   Date

COMMENTS (optional by staff member)

Reprinted with permission of Parsippany-Troy Hills Township Schools, Parsippany, New Jersey.

FIGURE 8-4 (continued)

	SCALE: Y = Yes S = To Some Extent N = No N.O. = Not Observed				
Y	**S**	**N**	**N.O.**	**ITEM**	**COMMENTS**
				1. Was knowledge and understanding of subject matter sufficient for the lesson observed?	
				2. Were instructional objectives readily apparent?	
				3 Was the planbook current and sufficiently detailed?	
				4. Did the quality/quantity of teacher questions motivate and challenge students?	
				5. Was the flow and pace of lesson activities geared to students' abilities?	
				6. Was allowance made for individual differences?	
				7. Was sufficiently diversified practice provided?	
				8. Were motivational/instructional techniques and student manipulative materials used effectively?	
				9. Were pupil progress indicators available?	
				10. Was the classroom atmosphere conducive to learning?	
				11. Was provision made for housekeeping, equipment maintenance, and safety management?	
				12. Was classroom discipline satisfactory?	
				13. Were summary and assignment clear?	
				14. Did the teacher display professional composure?	
				15. Did the teacher's voice and speech enhance the lesson delivery?	

Reprinted with permission of Perth Amboy Schools, Perth Amboy, New Jersey

FIGURE 8-5. Teacher proficiency form.

teacher. You can emphasize what you deem important so that the report is personal and timely. You are not restricted by items that seem minor or even irrelevant to the teacher and you at this time. You can pinpoint your comments and not clutter the report with extraneous remarks, thus adding strength to the report.

- The blank piece of paper allows supervisory acuteness to shine. Because you don't just mark checks on a form but use your own mind to choose issues and phrase your words, your report reflects your supervisory perceptions. Your skills in identifying issues, finding solutions for and with your teacher, and helping your teacher develop further have the opportunity to come forth on paper. You have an opportunity to personalize the message about yourself and make a positive statement, too, as you personalize the report about your teacher.

FOUR DISADVANTAGES

The blank piece of paper also has several clear disadvantages of which you should be aware. These are:

- The blank piece of paper demands much time. Consider how long it takes you to write a friendly letter to a friend or relative. You don't have to worry much about writing style or the mechanics of writing because of the informal setting. You don't have to worry much about logical flow of ideas because an informal letter is primarily a "written" conversation. Nevertheless, it takes you almost an hour to write a letter of just a few pages. It takes even more time to write a formal report that demands proper writing mechanics, a smooth flow of language, an internal coherence, and a logic that makes your points clear. Report-writing consumes time with a hungry appetite.

- The blank piece of paper allows omissions to slip by unnoticed. When caught up in trying to make specific and personal comments about a teacher, it is relatively easy for you to neglect matters about which the teacher and reader would like to know. Even if you have a guide for writing your report, it is easy to omit remarks, for example, about routine matters such as personal appearance or attendance. Yet others may think such information important.

- The blank piece of paper is often scary and often tough to fill. You may find the proverbial "blank piece of paper staring you in the face" imposing and forbidding. It is all the more difficult to fill up the paper when you are omitting items unknowingly. You may feel additional pressure to fill up the paper in order to show that you have something to say. After all, it is your job to say something about the teacher that is meaningful and substantial.

- The blank piece of paper makes supervisory weaknesses apparent, and shows them quickly and clearly. If you are not as sharp a human observer and helper as you might be, not as good an organizer of ideas as you might be, not as skillful a writer and user of language as you might be (especially in light of our society's renewed emphasis on writing skills), then the blank piece of paper can make your weaknesses apparent to your teacher and reader. The blank piece of paper can be scary and forbidding because your report can display your limitations rather than emphasize your strengths.

The Combined Checklist and Blank Piece of Paper

Most evaluation reports combine a checklist format with the opportunity for you to write about your teacher. In a way, you have the benefits of both—the opportunity for a fast, easy, and structured report via the checklist and the opportunity to personalize your report via the open space for your comments. Nevertheless, there are the disadvantages of (1) being influenced and even constrained by the items in the checklist and (2) being expected to comment on the items you may wish to deemphasize at this particular point. You need to keep in mind the advantages available to you and then persevere in making use of these so that your report will serve your teacher, your reader, and you well. To accomplish this you may need to modify the printed combined form you are currently using, or omit certain aspects of it, or write lengthy comments on certain items in order to avoid potential pitfalls. You must use your judgment regarding what will promote your efforts, and you can better do this by keeping in mind the characteristics of the two basic formats.

BASIC TYPES OF WRITTEN REPORTS

The report should be the written equivalent of your conference with the teacher. Just as there should be congruence between observing and conferring, so should there be congruence between conferring and reporting in writing. This means that just as you must make and maintain distinctions between observations, inferences, generalizations, evaluations, and recommendations in the conference, so must you continue to do so while preparing the written report. (See Chapter 3 for details on these distinctions.)

There are two basic types of written report, the observation report and the evaluation report. Unfortunately most schools do not make a strong distinction between the two, and the result is confusion for the supervisor as well as the teacher. Although many schools entitle their form "Observation Report," some supervisors conceive of the report as the opportunity to evaluate. These supervisors do not conceive of the report as one in which they report and emphasize their *observations* of one lesson. Rather, they consider the report the opportunity to *evaluate* their teachers based on their observations of one lesson. The difference is subtle but important, as are many of the distinctions made in supervision.

The Observation Report

The following are *obligatory features* of the complete observation report which you *should provide* in one way or another.

ADMINISTRATIVE (TECHNICAL/CLERICAL) INFORMATION

This includes:

1. Name of teacher
2. Employment status (tenure/nontenure and/or number of years experience)

3. Name of school
4. Date and time of preobservation conference (if held)
5. Date and time of observation
6. Date and time of postobservation conference
7. Grade level and subject taught
8. Name of supervisor
9. Space for teacher's signature (with date) acknowledging receipt of the report
10. Opportunity and space for teacher's comments

BRIEF OVERVIEW OF THE LESSON TAUGHT

In a few sentences you should describe the lesson that you observed. This description will serve to set the context for the data and comments that follow in the remainder of the report.

PURPOSE AND/OR FOCUS OF THE OBSERVATION

Here you should indicate why the observation took place and/or what was the focus of the observation. For example, you might write that the observation was part of the three mandatory observations required for every nontenured teacher and that, as agreed upon in the preobservation conference (or previous postobservation conference), you focused on the types of question asked by the teacher.

OBSERVATIONS (DATA)

Here you should write in descriptive, empirical terms what occurred during the lesson in consideration of the purpose previously indicated.

An example of an observation report that contains just these features appears in Figure 8-6. Note that the principal carefully stayed with an account of what occurred. (NOTE: A further explanation of Figure 8-6 appears later in this section.)

In contrast to the four obligatory features above, the following are features of an observation report that you *may or may not* wish to include. They are *discretionary features* whose inclusion depends on your assessment of the relationship between your teacher and the requirements or expectations set by your school system. Inclusion or exclusion of these items should be deliberate rather than due to an oversight. If there is trust between your teacher and you, if you have had a fruitful conference geared toward joint problem solving, if, for example, you want to give direction to an inexperienced teacher, you will feel comfortable including the discretionary features listed below. On the other hand, if you wish to be strictly empirical, if you wish to allow your teacher to choose his or her own direction as a sign of your trust, or if the teacher is particularly

FIGURE 8-6. Observation report.

Date ____October 16____   Subject or Grade Level _____10th grade English_____

Teacher's Name/School _____Pat Jones, Hamilton H.S. (nontenured)_____

Observed by ___C. Johnson, Principal__ Time __3rd period (35 min., short)__

Date and Time of Conference _____October 20   2:30 p.m._____

Reason for Observation _____first of three required for this year_____

COMMENTS:

During the lesson (10:15 to 10:50 a.m.) Pat and the students discussed a story by Brenda Brickford, "Home at Last." They talked about the story and the motives Nancy, the main character, had for running away from home and then returning on her own after six hours. The focus of the observation was the type of teacher questions and who spoke after whom:

    A. Teacher Questions
        1. Cognitive-Memory   = 41
        2. Convergent   = 6
        3. Divergent   = 1
        4. Evaluative   = 1
        5. Routine   = 8

    B. Who Speaks After Whom
        1. Teacher after boy   = 26
        2. Teacher after girl   = 15
        3. **Student** after boy   = 3
        4. Student after girl   = 22
        5. Other   = 0

Homework assignment: Students are to ask their parents if they ever ran away from home as children.

Teacher's Signature _____ Date _____

☐ Check if you wish to comment. Submit comments with three copies to be attached.

sensitive and reacts negatively to anything that goes beyond "observation," then you will want to exclude these discretionary features.

You may include some or all of the following discretionary features. They can be in separate sections and labeled individually, or they can appear under the single heading "Comments."

INTERPRETATIONS

Here you should comment on the importance, significance, or meaning of the data. You can offer explanations of what happened. Such explanations can be yours or those offered by the teacher or jointly by the two of you during the conference. You can also make some generalizations to condense information that occurred in the lesson. (Point out, for example, that all of the teacher's questions were for facts only.) You should avoid generalizations that can serve a predictive function. (For example, avoid stating that the teacher talks to boys more than to girls.)

QUESTIONS

You can raise questions based on the data designed to motivate the teacher to reconsider certain aspects of the lesson. The purpose of your questions is not criticism in any way but rather stimulation of the teacher's thinking. For example, in the observation report in Figure 8-6, if you were Principal C. Johnson you might ask, "How could you adjust the lesson on this same story in order to increase the number of divergent questions?" Or, "What is it about the boys that led you to treat them differently from the girls?" Posing a question is the easiest and safest of the discretionary features to include in your observation report. It can be most effective, too, because it keeps the matter open.

RECOMMENDATIONS (SUGGESTIONS)

Here you can offer new ideas to help the teacher develop further. You should phrase any recommendations in terms of action that your teacher should or could take. That is, since teachers are people who are active and oriented to doing things, you should write the recommendations using positive operational (that is, behavioral) verbs. For example, you might write, "After you ask a question, wait for at least four seconds for the student to respond."

If you do make some recommendations for growth, it is important to include as many of the following items as possible, especially regarding the time by which the recommendation should be implemented:

- the names of those who could help the teacher, such as other faculty members and supervisors
- indicators of development; that is, what actions or results will indicate that development exists?
- new skills that will help the teacher implement the new idea
- time lines by which the teacher can assess progress in the implementation of the recommendation

- your intended contributions and responsibilities for helping in the implementation
- the time when you will check, or follow up, with the teacher to see if the recommendation has been implemented

The recommendations can be ones that you suggest for the first time in the written report, those you have already offered during the postobservation conference, those offered during the postobservation conference by the teacher, or those which the teacher and you jointly proposed during the postobservation conference. It is preferable that the recommendations have the teacher's agreement before you write the report since this will give the teacher "ownership" and increase the likelihood of successful implementation. If they are the teacher's own recommendations or if the teacher already has agreed with the recommendations as discussed in the conference, you would be wise to indicate this. Such an indication will put the recommendations in a different light and lend a more positive tone to the entire observation report.

Some examples of recommendations along these lines are:

- I recommend that you use some of your free periods to observe Joe Glaston to see how he uses small group teaching. I'll check back with you within 2 weeks.
- As we agreed in our conference, it will be good for you to try to increase your use of divergent and other creative questions with all of your three reading groups.
- As you suggested and I agreed, you should begin working on including the use of manipulable materials with your slowest math students. Try it for 3 weeks and get back to me, please, with your reactions.
- It would be most helpful for you to rearrange your room in order to regroup the students. You should do this within a week.

EVALUATION (RATING)

This is the most sensitive feature of the observation report. The issue of including evaluation on the observation report centers on the answers to: "Should a supervisor evaluate each lesson observed?" "Should an observation report focus solely on development of professional competencies or should it contain a double approach to teacher supervision?" "Does the evaluation of the lesson, however succinctly reported, detract from the efforts toward teacher development embodied in the observation report?"

Even though your answers to the above questions lead you personally to omit the evaluation feature from the observation report, your district may require you to include it. You may have no choice. Nevertheless, you must keep in mind these questions and your answers because they will influence how you write your report. Indeed, many writers on staff development make strong claims about separating professional development and evaluation. The movement toward separation is strongest in the community colleges where the staff development officers and the evaluators are not the same people at all. There the two functions of development and evaluation are deliberately separated so that one will not interfere with the other.

The reality in most elementary and secondary schools, however, is that the staff developer/observer is the same person as the evaluator. Yet it is still possible to separate the two parts (observation/development and evaluation) on the same report. That is, even though you may be responsible (1) for helping your teacher develop and (2) for evaluating him, you don't have to do both things at the same time. Or, you could limit (and thus strengthen) your observation report to the development function, saving your evaluation for a separate document.

On the other hand, you might wish to argue for including the evaluation features in the observation report. Since teachers expect to be evaluated and since the board of education expects you to evaluate your teachers, you might as well do it when expected to. Moreover, you might as well do it frequently so that there is no great fuss about it. It isn't the evaluating (that is, using such ratings as outstanding, good, excellent, fair, poor, and unacceptable) that hinders professional development. It is the way in which evaluations are made that does so. If done rationally and sensitively, by connecting the evaluation to the data and the individual teacher, the evaluation process can become a part of professional development and even foster it.

All in all, it is preferable not to include evaluations on the observation reports because of their potential interference in the process of development. It is better, if at all possible, to keep the two functions apart. This does not in any way deny or remove the supervisor's responsibility for evaluating the teacher. Rather, it means that you ought not to confuse the functions or let their interaction impede progress.

There are good reasons for including the discretionary features and good reasons for excluding them. You may wish to *include* interpretations, questions, and/or recommendations because:

- you can help set a new direction with your recommendations and questions
- your teacher may expect or request your personal interpretations and recommendations
- you want or need to document officially that you have commented on what has transpired and that you have offered help via your recommendations
- you want to show that during the conference your teacher and you jointly explored the data and came up with the included remarks; that is, you want to indicate only what occurred (but this time in the conference) and as such you once again are only reporting what happened—the obligatory features are in essence a report on the teaching lesson and the discretionary features are a report on the postobservation conference
- you must do so; that is, it is a requirement of your school district, in accordance with a board of education policy, that a supervisor offer comments and recommendations

You may wish to *exclude* interpretations, questions, and/or recommendations because:

- you wish to keep your observation report purely as an observation, saving any comments for your conference with the teacher and for your evaluation report
- you prefer that the teacher and any other reader be faced with the bare facts so that they can form their own opinions without being influenced by you
- you believe that sometimes silence is louder than talk
- you must do so; that is, it is a requirement of your school district (this situation is very rare, however)

The key is not the inclusion or exclusion of the discretionary features. Rather, the key is the manner in which you deal with them in light of other factors present in the school and in your supervisory relationship with your teacher. There is a world of difference between a recommendation made by a supervisor before a conference is even held to discuss with the teacher what happened during the lesson and a recommendation jointly made by the supervisor and teacher during the conference. You must keep in mind the source and manner used for coming up with the interpretations, questions, and recommendations.

No matter what the reason for inclusion of the discretionary features—if they are included—you should clearly separate them from the obligatory features which report what you observed. By separating them and identifying them appropriately you send the clear message to your teacher and any other reader that you are fully aware of what you are writing in the report. The discretionary features can be presented separately with a subheading for each, or they can be presented under a common heading such as "Comments" or "Interpretations" or "Commentary."

This separation between observations and comments allows for disagreement in a healthy way. This approach is similar to the one used in daily newspapers which restricts commentary to the editorial page where such commentary is clearly labeled as the opinions of the editor. Indeed, we who purchase newspapers do not object to commentary at all but rather expect and desire it. We just want it labeled as such so that we know when we are reading the news report and when we are reading the editor's interpretation of the news. The same is true of the observation report.

WHEN TO WRITE THE OBSERVATION REPORT

Once you know what you prefer to include or must include in your observation report, you should consider when to write your report. There are three possibilities regarding the timing of the report: (1) you can write the entire report before conferring with your teacher; (2) you can write the entire report after conferring with your teacher; or (3) you can write part of the report before conferring with your teacher and then complete the report afterward. The choice depends, obviously, on what sections are contained in the report as well as how the conference is conducted.

Suppose you observe teacher Taylor on Thursday morning. If you confer with Taylor immediately after the lesson, basing your conference only on your notes, you will write the entire report after the conference. If you confer sometime later on Thursday or Friday, however, you have a choice to make. You can utilize the time you have had since Taylor taught the lesson to organize your notes and prepare a more formal report to show Taylor during the conference. Or, because the elapsed time is not really great, you can still rely strictly on your notes. The question then becomes, "How do I know which way to go—with notes or with a prepared, fuller report?"

To help answer this question, let's take a look at a second question: "If I'd like to write a fuller report before the conference, what should I write?" One answer is: Write up all the obligatory features cited earlier. That is, write a formal description of what you observed—just a description based on whatever system of observation you have used to gather data. Another answer is: Write up the obligatory features plus the discretionary features. That is, write a description of the lesson, including the data you have gathered, and add some interpretations, explanations, and recommendations. If you try the latter approach, however, you are in effect handing Taylor a document to sign. In effect you are then saying, "Here is my report; my mind is made up; I've figured out what it all means, but if you really must raise a point, I'll discuss it with you. I'd really prefer that you'd just sign the report since I don't want to have to revise it now; after all, I've already spent my allotted time writing it up and I'd rather not put in more time on this." Such a situation doesn't lead to effective, sound supervision in that it closes off discussion and distances you from your teacher.

Consequently, the first answer is the better one. If you feel that you must write something more complete or formal before the conference, you should only write a *description,* an objective account, of the lesson. You should not write up comments, interpretations, explanations, or recommendations before the conference. You should jot down some of your ideas, some comments, some recommendations, some possible explanations, in *note form* before the conference to serve only as personal reminders. These should *not* be presented to your teacher *before* the conference or *even at* the conference in writing. They are to guide you in conferring with the teacher. They are for you and not for your teacher.

Formal or even informal written comments given to the teacher before the conference is completed are unnecessary. They contradict the entire approach to conferences espoused in the earlier chapters on conferring. They restrain you and do not encourage your teacher and you to explore the data *jointly.*

The benefits of *joint exploration* of observation data are several and deserve repetition here:

- your teacher will see you in a positive light for being open to interpretation of what happened
- your teacher will feel trusted as competent and able to interpret the data
- your teacher will view you as a collaborator in helping him or her grow professionally

In summary, *the discretionary sections of an observation report, if you are going to include them, should be written only after the conference.* They should reflect your teacher's input and interaction with you.

Let us return now to the first question, "Should I stay with my notes or should I prepare a formal description of the lesson before the conference?" That is, "Should I prepare the obligatory features of an observation report before the conference or should I just come in with my notes?" Your answer will be based in part on your assessment of your relationship with your teacher, your own style and comfort, and the degree of flexibility you desire and can work with. If you want to be maximally flexible in order to draw out the teacher's sense of what happened *objectively* in the lesson, or if you want to decide on what to emphasize after hearing your teacher's perception of the lesson, you should stay with your notes and not write anything formal. If, however, you want to direct the conference along a particular line in order to emphasize a particular event or characteristic of the teacher's classroom behavior, you should write up your notes. If you want to structure the conference for whatever good reason—to lead an inexperienced teacher or to press a persistent point, for example,—you should prepare a formal, full descriptive account. When you do this, you are in effect saying, "This is what happened as I understand it. Let's talk based on this account."

Before making your decision, you should check with your school system. The choice may not be yours. For whatever the reason, some schools prescribe when the report should be written and when it should be presented to the teacher. However, you must check what the school *actually* requires and not accept what people *think* is required. Often people believe that there is a requirement set by the board of education or prescribed by the contract with the teachers' organization when in actuality there may only be an informal custom or habit that allows you to make your own decision.

If you prepare the obligatory features beforehand, you should give the report to your teacher at the beginning of the conference—or whenever required—to read for a few minutes. This will set the direction of the conference and provide the basis of your teacher's reactions. In essence your conference will be a long commentary on this part of the observation report. What you subsequently write, if you add to the obligatory features, will be based on your interaction with the teacher reacting to your prepared description.

In summary, you have three options:

1. You can write nothing before the conference in addition to your observation notes; that is, you prepare the entire observation report *after* the conference. This report will include the obligatory features, obviously, and may or may not include discretionary features.

2. You can write the obligatory features of the report before the conference and add discretionary features afterwards. You can modify the obligatory features after the conference in light of your interaction with the teacher.

3. You can write the obligatory features—which constitute all you intend to write in any case—before the conference; if you do this, your report is finished *before* the conference.

Option 1 offers you maximum flexibility while option 3 offers you the least flexibiity. Option 2 provides some middle ground. Whether you use option 1 or 2, however, you have a great opportunity to build on the conference and use the observation report as an opportunity to report in some measure on the conference itself. Either option 1 or 2 is recommended. Option 3 is not recommended because it flies in the face of sound supervision. It is too rigid. The disadvantages (1) of restricting the conference to the content of your prepared report, (2) of not being able to use the report as a device for building on and reporting on the conference, and (3) of conveying a negative message to the teacher regarding your openness far outweigh the advantages of saving time and giving direction to the teacher. Therefore, try to avoid option 3.

Keep in mind, also, that writing part of the report before the conference and part after it does not in reality take more time. It only splits the writing time into two sittings. In fact, the split effort pays off in terms of what is gained by working *with* the teacher in regard to interpretations and recommendations. In most cases, it is better to work *with* the teacher than to work *without* the teacher. Options 1 and 2 allow you to work *with* the teacher.

Figure 8-6, which appeared earlier, is an example of a report written in two parts. The principal wrote the obligatory features that constitute Figure 8-6 before a conference. The observation took place on a Thursday, but the conference occurred on a Monday. In order not to forget some of the details during the interval, the principal prepared this formal report to give the teacher at the start of the conference on Monday.

Figure 8-7 is the rest of the observation report, written *after* the conference. Notice that under the general heading "Comments," the principal writes some interpretations regarding future teaching and adds questions to direct the teacher's thinking. There are no recommendations by the principal since the teacher volunteered to work on changing the situation himself. Notice, also, that much of the report is written in the past tense since the principal uses this opportunity to report on the postobservation conference. The principal and teacher had talked about the "surprising" data and sought

Comments:

Our conference focused on the "surprising" number of cognitive-memory questions as compared with the divergent and evaluation questions. The data were "surprising," as you said, because the lesson plan called for an emphasis on discussing the author's technique for hooking the reader into siding with the main character. We agreed that the imbalance probably occurred because you weren't sure exactly how to elicit the evaluations from the students. So due to insecurity, you resorted to the old secure standby of checking to see who knew the details of the plot. We agreed that you could try to relate the story to the students' own feelings about escaping from their families. You volunteered to work out a technique for eliciting such evaluations with Jan Barrett and to practice it before I come in for a similar observation after Thanksgiving. I look forward to observing a different distribution of questions as you do to achieving it.

We didn't come up with a satisfactory explanation for the other important point arising from the data: you talked immediately after a boy spoke much more often than after a girl spoke. You were totally unaware of this. Could it be that the boys were tougher for you to deal with in class, and therefore, you thought it possible to control them by controlling the verbal interaction more tightly? Do you have some ideas on how you can change things around to balance your interaction with boys and girls better? Stop by my office next week so we can talk over your ideas together.

Commendations on your sincere efforts to develop further professionally.

Teacher's Signature _____ Date _____

FIGURE 8-7. Observation comments.

to explain them. The principal clearly indicates that the two of them agreed on several issues, thus strengthening the points he is making while enlisting the cooperation of the teacher.

The principal also points out that there will be a follow-up observation. As a result of the conference and this report, the teacher knows what to do in the six weeks before the forthcoming observation. The teacher is to work with another teacher and also talk to the principal. Finally, note that the commendation is not about the lesson but about the teacher's renewed efforts toward development. Although there is no explicit evaluation of the lesson, the principal has found an effective way to express support for the teacher who has agreed to seek ways to change. The teacher has direction, support, and the knowledge that change is necessary.

The Evaluation Report

There are two types of written evaluation reports, and both are obviously related to the observation report.

COMBINED OBSERVATION AND EVALUATION REPORT

This is the evaluation report that is an extension of the observation report and that becomes part of the same document as the observation report. Even though the title of the document in some school districts is "Observation Report," the document actually is an evaluation report. The title, to be correct, should be "Visitation Report," "Observation and Evaluation Report," or something else that is not limiting. As noted earlier, some school districts intend each observation to be an opportunity for the supervisor to evaluate the teacher. The title "Observation Report" on their forms may be used because it is a holdover from an earlier period when the report was used exclusively for observation or because the district wishes to emphasize that classroom observation is the basis of the report. Perhaps the misnomer appears because the district is simply not precise in its use of the title. In any case, there is every official or unofficial intention that an evaluation report be included with the observation report.

For this first type of evaluation report (that is, an evaluation report that is combined with an observation report) you should include all the obligatory and discretionary features of the observation report. That is, if you are going to evaluate your teacher based on an observation of a particular lesson, then you should include all the discretionary features—interpretations, questions, and recommendations—which will add support to the obligatory features in order to justify your evaluation. Of course, the evaluation may be done simply by checking an item within a scale (for example, outstanding, good, satisfactory, poor) or it may be done by way of your own choice of value terms to show your judgment (for example, excellent, good, beautiful, adequate, first-rate, A−, highly competent, a real asset to our faculty).

Figure 8-8 is an example of a combined observation and evaluation report. Note that in this format the data are presented alongside of the interpretations, questions, and recommendations so as to make it perfectly clear what the supervisor, Alex Morgan, is commenting on. Morgan also notes that one of the purposes of the visit was to observe the students Carl and Marvin, as requested by the teacher. Morgan uses a final paragraph to summarize, commend, evaluate, and set up a future activity with the teacher. Thus, the short paragraph of just three sentences serves several functions simultaneously. Take a careful look at Figure 8-8 because it is a good example of a concise document that combines a report on the observation with comments on the conference and the giving of an evaluation.

THE ANNUAL REPORT

The second type of evaluation report is typically the annual report, although it need not be so necessarily. In reports of this type, you write from a broad perspective not tied to an observation. Here, you write a report in which there is no doubt about the scope and the purpose. Your scope is not restricted to classroom activity whether you have made one or even five observations. On the contrary, you consider the wide range of the teacher's activities, including classroom teaching; relations with staff; participation in school affairs such as dances, concerts, and athletic games; work on faculty committees; and relations with students in such places as the classroom, the halls, and the cafeteria. In this second type of evaluation report you take into account the teacher's entire job while focusing on the essential part of it—classroom teaching.

Teacher_____Sandy Wallace_____ Date and Time of:

Grade Level/Subject _Gr. 1/Reading_ Preobservation Conference _Dec. 10 8:15_

Report by _____Alex Morgan_____ Observation _____8:55-10:20_____

Postobservation Conference ____1:30____

I. BRIEF LESSON DESCRIPTION:

I was present to observe the presentation of five independent seatwork activities that were to be done between 9:00 and 11:00 by every student. During my visit I observed directed lessons with three of the four reading groups.

II. PURPOSE(S) OF OBSERVATION:

As I stated in the preobservation conference, I wanted to observe the independent seatwork activities during the reading period. As usual, I also noted your use of time and your interaction with students. You asked me to observe the behavior of Carl and Marvin.

III. REPORT OF DATA OBSERVED	IV. INTERPRETATION/ CONSIDERATIONS/ RECOMMENDATIONS
You have four reading groups, having split the large top group into two. Each received 30 minutes of instruction today.	This is an indication of your concern for meeting the reading needs of your class. You need to resolve the problem of the additional instructional time and its effect on the remainder of your curriculum areas.
With the three groups you met, you followed accepted principles for directed reading. Your directions were clever and precise as you worked with each group.	This is a demonstration of your competency in the teaching of reading.
Marvin was out of his seat more than others, but did get most of his work done.	He probably is seeking your attention and wants more than he is getting. Checking on him between groups may put you in control of that situation. Perhaps rewarding half-day good behavior will be more effective.
Carl was unable to function and spent the time trying to write his name on the papers and do his handwriting.	Carl needs to be transferred to at least the transitional class as soon as possible. In the meantime, obtain some kindergarten materials that he can do independently.

FIGURE 8-8. Observation and postobservation conference report form.

You devoted 130 minutes to reading today. You, as teacher, were engaged in reading activities all that time. Students, however, were engaged in reading activities for about 60–90 minutes.	If "time on task" improves achievement, then it would seem that the more students either directly or independently work on reading, the greater the reading achievement. How great a problem is it to plan more reading activities?
	For example, Jane spent about 40 minutes cutting, pasting, and coloring. Although some students need these activities, Jane may not and could benefit from other activities. Probably others could, too.
The students at their seats became more inattentive and less productive when the uninterrupted worktime exceeded the 40-minute mark.	I am sure the days you met groups twice for 15 minutes are more productive. It might help to circulate among the students in the transition between reading groups. Some groups you might call up and prescribe just one activity.

You indicated a concern in the area of reading seatwork and stated you would talk to other teachers and confer with the Reading Specialist. I'll check back with you in about a month as to what progress you are making. As I said in the postobservation conference, on the basis of this observation, you demonstrate very adequate classroom management skills; lessons are prepared with objectives; and sufficient organization is used to make your teaching satisfactory.

FIGURE 8-8. (continued)

There is also no doubt as to the purpose of this report, especially if it is the annual report. You are to evaluate the teacher in general, and by definition this indicates that more than observational data is expected. This in no way implies that you are to omit or even shorten the section devoted to data from observations you have made in the classroom, halls, cafeteria, or faculty meetings. Nor does this imply omission of data gained through comments from students, parents, and other staff members, and through inspection of school records concerning attendance and student grades. On the contrary, your evaluations, recommendations, interpretations, and questions make sense only in the light of the data you present or have presented in earlier reports and now refer to. Without the data section there is no available support for your evaluations. Without the data your evaluations are vulnerable to severe criticism and to challenge. As with the observation report, you should separate the data section from the sections in which you present your interpretations, questions, recommendations, and evaluation. Figure 8-9 is an example of an annual report.

RECOMMENDATIONS ON WRITING STYLE AND APPROACH

So far, this chapter has offered comments about the formats of the written report and recommendations about what to include in observation as well as evaluation reports.

Teacher _____ Sandy Wallace _____   Date ___ June 10 ___

Evaluator _____ Alex Morgan _____

In keeping with the option allowed to us by school policy, the data gathered from my observations will not be repeated here since they are on the observation reports which you have already.

Other relevant data about you are: you participated in the school textbook committee; you were teacher delegate to the Parents Organization; when, infrequently, you were absent, you provided adequate plans for a substitute; you graciously performed all extracurricular tasks (chaperoning and class trips) assigned to you.

As is evident from a review of your observation reports, you progressed in your main goal for the year, which was to personalize your contacts with the students having difficulty in reading. You worked with them after school, both individually and in small groups. You are on the road to becoming an excellent teacher who is an asset to our school district both in and out of the classroom.

In preparation for our goal-setting conference in the near future, I would like you to think about the following two questions: What will be your objective for the next year regarding continued professional development? In what ways do you want me to help you next year?

In consideration of your progress this year, I recommend that you seek to become more active with other reading teachers in the county. By participating in regional activities such meetings and conferences devoted to using the computer in reading, and by bringing new ideas back to our school, you will be able to foster "cross-pollenization." I also recommend that next year in your classroom you try to utilize more small group cooperative activities while bearing in mind the need to pay more attention to classroom management.

You had a good year overall because of two main factors: one was your genuine interest in your students as individuals; the other was your ability to work with them as a group in the classroom. Your confidence in yourself seems to be growing. However, you sometimes fall short in your efforts to maintain an orderly classroom. With some improvement in classroom management, you will realize your potential.

I shall contact you soon to set a date for our annual conference in order to plan for next year. Again, I appreciate your classroom efforts and your schoolwide efforts this year. You did a commendable job in both areas. Keep up your search for ways to develop professionally.

FIGURE 8-9. Annual report.

Now let's turn to some recommendations about the actual writing of your reports. If you accept and follow these suggestions—if not all then at least a significant number—you will strengthen your written reports. This will ultimately lead to a better supervisory relationship between your teacher and you. There is an interdependency at work here. The more effective your written reports become, the more solid and sound your supervisory relationship with your teacher becomes. The further your supervisory relationship with your teacher develops along positive lines, the more you're able to write meaningful reports.

The following items concern writing style, approach, mind-set, process, and some other factors that are part of a helpful report. They are not presented in any particular order. Accept them as recommendations meant to help you with a serious and official responsibility.

1. *Provide Data and Insights to Help Teachers Grow.* The written report is critical to the supervisory process since it is generally the only part of the process for which there is a file. It is a permanent document that should reflect your efforts aimed at helping the teacher teach better. The report is your opportunity to end one cycle in the supervisory process and at the same time begin another. It makes sense to have the written report congruent with your efforts in observing and conferring because of the nonverbal effect on the teacher. It also makes sense to help the teacher teach better because your success is linked with the teacher's. This is especially true if the teacher is tenured because the odds are high that the tenured teacher will be with you next year. The current job market doesn't permit easy switching of positions and the likelihood of dismissing a tenured teacher is not great. In short, concentrate on teacher development.

2. *Provide Feedback to the Teacher on Vital Aspects of Teaching from Your Vantage Point.* What you write will convey a strong message to the teacher—and anyone else who reads the report—about your view of supervising and teaching. The report will nonverbally say, "Here's what I think is important." Capitalize on this aspect of the written report to inform the teacher about your views on teaching.

3. *Accept Your School's Current Written Report Form and Write a Sound Report Using It.* If you do not have it in your power to change unilaterally the form now used in your school, it does no good to bemoan the situation and to become paralyzed. There is always an escape hatch in every form which permits you to write what is necessary for sound supervision. It is called The Blank Piece of Paper. By adding a separate sheet to the report you can make up for just about anything lacking in the form. With a blank piece of paper before you, you need not restrict yourself to the items listed on the form. If the curent form needs change, keep a file on the form's deficiencies and advocate correction whenever you can.

4. *Use Appropriate Job Description for Each Teacher with Other School Policy Documents.* If your school has developed a written job description for each teacher or type of teacher, make specific reference to the items in that description. The job description constitutes the basis for observing, commenting on, and evaluating the teacher. If possible, when you write a year-end evaluation report attach a copy of the job description to your report. While writing your report, keep notes regarding your thoughts on the job description so that you can advocate any necessary changes in it when the time is appropriate. Refer also to the curriculum guide and other school policies established by the board of education that apply to your teacher.

5. *Include All Five Senses in the Observation Process.* It is a narrow conception of observation that includes only the senses of sight and hearing and excludes the senses of touch, smell, and taste. Whenever possible, use as many of the five senses as you can so as to expand the teacher's awareness of the various aspects of teaching.

6. *Keep Your Eye on the Classroom When You Write Your Observations.* It is easy and tempting to write many observations of your teachers based on events which occurred in the faculty room, the halls, and the lunchroom. It is more convenient to observe your teachers in these areas than in the classroom because no appointment is necessary and no extra planning is required. Yet the critical spot is the classroom where your teacher is engaged in the central responsibilities of teaching. It is absolutely essential to visit the classroom when teaching takes place. What is more, it is a compliment to the teacher that you consider it important to spend your time in the classroom. Your written report should reflect your concern for the classroom domain where the essential activities of teaching occur.

7. *Concentrate on the Teacher's Primary Responsibilities.* In your written report focus on the primary and crucial tasks of the teacher. Hardly anything is more disturbing to a teacher than a supervisor's emphasis on minor aspects of teaching. By concentrating on significant elements of a teacher's performance you demonstrate that you are ready and willing to help the teacher teach better.

8. *Refer to the Teacher's Specific Activities and Events During the Time Covered.* By writing specifically about the individual teacher and the individual lesson(s) observed you demonstrate that your report is unique. To be meaningful the report must be personalized so that your teacher does not get the impression that the same report is written about each teacher. By referring to specifics (for example, the film on blood disorders, the role play concerning nuclear war, and the bake sale) about that particular lesson or group of lessons, you demonstrate your attention to the teacher's individuality. Such reference also allows you to separate one lesson from the next and to keep a record of how the teacher teaches over a stretch of time.

9. *Refer to Previous Written Reports.* Especially in an evaluation report that deals with several observations or a long period of time, you can establish continuity if you refer to previous reports available to your teacher. A reference to what was observed or recommended during the previous month, semester, or year will serve as a reminder of your earlier supervisory efforts. For example, you might write in June 1986, "You have been able to alter your style of questioning since November 1985 when you asked about six questions per minute. At the last observation in May 1986, you asked about one and a half. I agree with you in attributing this change to the course on questioning that you took at the university during this past semester."

10. *Write the Report as Soon as Possible After the Observation and Conference.* If you write the observation data section of the observation report soon after your classroom visit, your memory will supplement your notes. The same holds true regarding your report about any conferences that you hold with your teacher. Temptation to postpone writing a report is always a problem, especially when the observation or conference session was less than satisfactory. This temptation must yield, however, to the greater goal of achieving objectivity, promptness, and good timing as important factors in helping your teacher teach better.

11. *Incorporate Teacher's Data, Comments, and Agreements.* By using the data and remarks of your teacher you convey the strong nonverbal message, "I listen to you."

This message is important from the modeling point of view as well as for clearly showing that the supervisory relationship is a cooperative one. No one has all the facts or a monopoly on interpretations and recommendations. Moreover, if you include or refer to a point on which you and the teacher have agreed, you indicate that the teacher has "ownership" in the supervisory process. You remind the teacher of what he said and let any other reader know that the teacher has already made this particular commitment about teaching. It will be much easier for you to expect change and to hold the teacher to an agreement if you explicitly include comments and agreements in your written report.

12. *Review Evaluating Criteria Before You Write.* Many schools have established a set of criteria for what they believe constitutes good or excellent teaching. Obviously, you do not personally have to agree 100 percent with these criteria, but you should know them well and recognize that as a supervisor you are bound by them just as the teacher is. Make sure the criteria are clear to you. For example, if your school uses such terms as Outstanding, Above Average, Average, Below Average, and Unacceptable, make sure that you know what distinguishes an Outstanding teacher from an Above Average or Average teacher, and a Below Average from an Unacceptable teacher. Without a clear understanding of the applicable criteria you cannot evaluate your teachers fairly. Thus, you would do well to confer with your teachers early in the year, before writing any reports, specifically in regard to this delicate issue of the criteria you are to apply to them. It is upsetting for teachers to be evaluated on a rating scale with criteria that have not been clearly defined.

13. *Indicate Both Positive and Negative Teacher Behavior.* In your evaluation report, in which evaluation is not only appropriate but expected, make sure to indicate to your teachers what aspects of their teaching are good. These are probably the aspects that served as the basis for hiring or granting them tenure. Explicitly encourage them to continue to manifest their positive qualities. Commend them for changes they have made and for efforts expended toward self-development. Everyone, age one day through one hundred years, welcomes and needs encouragement. At the same time, you must not shy away from explicitly indicating negative aspects of a teacher's behavior. (Note that you should direct negative as well as positive comments toward behavior and not personality.) Nobody is perfect; the perfect teacher has not yet appeared in any school classroom. Every teacher has room for further development. According to the Stanford study cited in Chapter 1, principals felt that they communicated dissatisfaction to teachers on the four teaching tasks involved in that study (teaching subject matter, character development, maintaining control, and record keeping) more frequently than teachers reported receiving.

14. *Justify Your Evaluations by Referring to the Data.* Give reasons for your positive as well as your negative evaluations so that your teacher can understand your point of view. An unsupported evaluation is not helpful to a teacher who is eager and willing to grow.

15. *Make Recommendations to Help the Teacher Develop.* If you include recommendations in your report, list those which you and your teacher have jointly agreed upon, if at all possible. In this way you will indicate that your teacher already has some stake in the suggested change of direction. If you are making recommendations not yet discussed with your teacher, make sure that they are tailored to the needs of the particular teacher. Ask your teacher to react to these suggestions because you can modify them if necessary in an appendix to your report or in the report itself before it is filed. In either case, the emphasis should be on what is appropriate for your individual teacher. *In general, it is advisable to include at least one recommendation in your report.* You can omit a recommendation (1) if you are writing only a purely descriptive report of a lesson observed or (2) if the teacher has made his own recommendation for a change to which you agree. If the latter is the case, you must so indicate, as suggested earlier. Recommendations demonstrate that you are trying to help your teacher develop. Also, recommendations serve as the bridge to your next observation, conference, or report. You can efficiently begin your next supervisory cycle by focusing on how the teacher responded to the recommendation.

16.   *Suggest Resource People Who Can Help the Teacher.* Sometimes the teacher needs the guidance of a person already proficient in a new skill or needs a specific model to emulate. Sometimes the teacher needs additional support and encouragement. For these reasons you should suggest the names of people, including yourself, who can and will be willing to help your teacher change.

17.   *Set Dates for Future Observing, Conferring, and Evaluating.* By setting intermediate- and long-range deadlines, you will give guidance to your teacher in terms of your expectations. The teacher will be able to plan accordingly and set a reasonable pace for learning new skills so as to implement the recommendations made.

18.   *Decide Who Your Audience Is.* You have essentially one of two alternatives regarding audience. You can write to the teacher or you can write to your own supervisor (your principal, superintendent, or board of education). Either is legitimate. If you wish to direct your remarks to the teacher, you can write using the second person "you" and easily refer to events and people known to the teacher. The tone of a report written to the teacher is generally more informal than that of one written to your own supervisor. If your own supervisor is considered to be the audience, you will have to write in the third person about the teacher and explain events that may be unknown outside of your private relationship with the teacher. *In general, it is preferable for you to think of your teacher as your audience.* A report written to your teacher on a personal level can help you develop your supervisory relationship in a way not possible with a formal, "whoever the audience may be" style.

19.   *Keep Up with Professional Literature.* It is easy to lose sight of professional obligations and fresh ideas about writing and supervising when you are involved daily with the plethora of details encountered in a supervisor's job. One way to keep your eye on the forest instead of the trees, so to speak, is to keep up with professional literature. Just as you expect your teachers to stay aware of new developments in their chosen teaching fields, so you too need to remain alive, alert, and aware professionally.

20.   *Be Sure Your Report Includes the Necessary Features.* If you have a form to complete, it is no major problem to ensure that you have included all of the required features. Without a printed form, however, it is easy to omit something. Checking over your report is an essential step. When you use a blank sheet of paper you need to check yourself in order to be sure that you have included the brief overview of the lesson, the purpose of the report, adequate observations, interpretations, questions, recommendations, and evaluations. In short, be sure that the features of the report are what they ought to be according to your school's and your own requirements.

21.   *Practice Writing and Consult with Colleagues.* Writing is a skill, and everyone—musician, athlete, teacher, or supervisor—involved with a skill needs to practice. What is more, no writer publishes first draft material. Writers ask friends, colleagues, or editors to give them feedback on draft copy. What you read in print is at least second draft material. More likely it is material resulting from a third or fourth revision. Before submitting a written observation report or an annual evaluation report that will remain on permanent file, revise it. Talk confidentially with your fellow supervisors about what you have written. If possible, show them a draft copy so that they can recommend improvements. You will not regret filing a polished report; you might well regret one that is hastily and poorly prepared.

22. *Write Recommendations in Direct, Simple Language, Using Positive Behavioral Verbs.* Since your recommendations are meant to help the teacher change, you should write them in a clear style that will aid the teacher in implementing them. For example, if you find that your teacher needs to improve in the area of questioning, you might write, "I suggested that to change your questioning pattern you can (1) simplify your questions, (2) ask one question at a time, (3) vary the types of questions by asking more convergent and divergent questions, and (4) ask Tom Longer to share with you the ideas he learned at the NEA Convention." Note that with these specific operational verbs there is an emphasis on what *to do* rather than on what not to do. These are "do" verbs and not "don't" verbs. It is certainly permissible and often necessary to include some "don't" items, but you must take care to have the "do" verbs clearly outnumber the "don't" verbs. *Emphasis should be on the positive.* All the "don't" verbs never add up to a "do." Telling your teacher what not to do does not indicate what you want the teacher to do. Development, in order to be meaningful, should be based on change occurring as new skills are learned and new activities are performed, as well as through the strengthening of old and positive skills and activities. Let the negatives disappear as they are replaced by the new positives. Concentration on the negatives is destructive rather than constructive; it does not lead easily to change nor does it foster good relations between your teacher and you. Concentration on specific positive behaviors your teacher can implement will lead to the desired change. (For more on using specific terms see the next recommendation.)

23. *Use Specific Language Often.* By using specific terms rather than general ones, the meaning of your observations, recommendations, and interpretations will be clearer to your teacher. With specific terms you will be able to personalize your report more easily. The key to writing in specific terms is word choice, as illustrated in Figure 8-10. In the left column are examples of words, terms, and phrases that you can use to offer your teacher specific feedback about what happened in the classroom. In the right column are nonspecific, subjective counterparts. Those in the right column are vague, ambiguous, inferential, or subjective. It is difficult to understand what constitutes, for example, "good pupil participation in the lesson" or the meaning of "teacher employed a few new methods." It would be possible to recognize change in your teacher's actions over time if your reports are written with expressions from the left column, but virtually impossible to do so with terms like those in the right column. Figure 8-10 plus a sheet with your own additions will be a helpful guide to you as you write your reports.

Summing Up

It is impossible to implement all twenty-three of the above recommendations in every written report. Nor is there any implication that as a supervisor you should even try to do so. Nevertheless, a sound, well-written report should include most of them. With these recommendations in mind, you might try to edit or rewrite some of your old reports. More important, however, begin to incorporate these ideas and the other suggestions offered throughout this book to make your supervisory tasks more meaningful and helpful.

Specific			Nonspecific, subjective	

15
10% of the
all but 2
only 3
	boys
	students
	girls
	children
		spoke
		asked questions
		answered
		    questions
		took part in
		    discussion
			adequate
			much
			ample
			active
			good
			broad
			poor
			a lot of
				pupil participation
				    in the lesson

6 test
3 homework
9 classwork
	entries in the
	    teacher's record book
	    since February
			some
			series of
			enough
			insufficient
			scattered
			comprehensive
				entries in the
				    teacher's record
				    book since
				    February

students did not interrupt each
    other
students look at the person
    being spoken to in the discussion
Anne disagreed with previous
    speaker
Ruth paraphrased Charles' opinion
    before asking him a question
			students showed
			girls frequently
			    evidenced
			boys occasionally
			    had
				enthusiastic
				    concern
				
				good rapport
				
				proper feelings

teacher began with a short lecture
    and then went on to answer student
    questions
teacher introduced the film, showed
    it, and led discussion on points
    students raised
			teacher varied his
			teacher used many
			
			teacher employed a
			    few
			
			teacher utilized
			    several appropriate
				techniques
				new methods
				
				strategies
				
				tactics

3 students were chewing gum
 	
all boys reported on time to gym
 	
for each test item there was a
    point value indicated
 	
homework developed out of the
    map exercise on the Sun Belt
			ignored
			
			emphasized
			
			followed
			
			overlooked
			
			reinforced
				school policy

FIGURE 8-10. Examples of specific terms for written reports.

INDEX